A YEAR'S TURNING

◆

WRITTEN AND ILLUSTRATED BY

MICHAEL VINEY

THE
BLACKSTAFF
PRESS

BELFAST

Quotations from 'Death of a Naturalist' by Seamus Heaney on page 10 from *Death of a Naturalist* (Faber and Faber, 1966); from 'Carrigskeewaun' by Michael Longley on page 52 from *Poems 1963–1983* (Salamander Press, 1984; Penguin Books, 1985); from 'Cows' by Eamon Grennan on page 100 from *As If It Matters* (Gallery Press, 1991); from 'Song for a Corncrake' by Richard Murphy on page 116 from *High Island* (Faber and Faber, 1974); from 'The Mayo Accent' by Paul Durcan on pages 121–2 from *Daddy, Daddy* (Blackstaff Press, 1990); from 'Otters' by Michael Longley on page 182 from *Gorse Fires* (Secker and Warburg, 1991); from 'Incident' by Eamon Grennan on page 196 from *What Light There Is* (Gallery Press, 1987); and from 'Between Hovers' by Michael Longley on pages 203–4 from *Gorse Fires* (Secker and Warburg, 1991).

First published in 1996 by
The Blackstaff Press Limited
3 Galway Park, Dundonald, Belfast BT16 0AN, Northern Ireland

© Text and illustrations, Michael Viney, 1996
All rights reserved

Typeset by Techniset, Newton-le-Willows, Merseyside

Printed in England by Biddles Limited

A CIP catalogue record for this book
is available from the British Library

ISBN 0-85640-562-0

CONTENTS

O may my heart's truth
Still be sung
On this high hill in a year's turning

DYLAN THOMAS, 'POEM IN OCTOBER'

PREFACE

In the south of County Mayo the coast road narrows between field-banks and dry-stone walls until, a mere tendril, it winds to a halt in the sands at the foot of Mweelrea Mountain. Thallabawn is one of the last townlands on this road, a stripe of hillside running down to a large and lonely strand.

One thorn-edged acre of Thallabawn has been the Viney homestead for almost twenty years. Ethna and I had turned forty; we were both successful in the media and had signed up our small daughter Michele for a good school, when gradually we became convinced of a need for much less in our lives — and much more. 'Much less' had to do with a notion then in the air of a self-reliant country life as the alternative to metropolitan complexity, consumption and frustration. This was before the general greening of the middle classes and 'organic' shelves in city supermarkets. 'Much more' had to do with freedom and beauty: freedom to experiment, to manage our own time, and every day to wake up in delight with where we were. The acre held our small holiday house, but also some of the best and warmest soil on the hillside: it dared us not to wait until we were too old.

For the first decade or so, through my Saturday column in the *Irish Times*, we found ourselves acting out 'other people's dreams'. So our mailbag assured us, and callers to the gate. There were others, all too familiar with rural realities, who wondered what we thought we were trying to prove. I did have a few personal themes, among them the need to make choices, and the satisfaction of learning, with Henry Thoreau, 'to want but little'. But mostly I was setting out to intrigue and entertain, thereby earning money for the electricity bills. It was the era of popular books about 'self-sufficient' lifestyles, typically with joky titles: *Bucketful of Nuts* ... *Milk My Ewes and Weep*. You could tell who had actually stayed the course by how carefully they wrote about their neighbours.

Then my column, 'Another Life', began to change. Partly this was to please a new editor, who felt readers might be tiring of so much talk about compost heaps and muck-shifting, partly because I was finding new meanings for beauty, new directions in what we were 'trying to prove'. These had to do with our deeper responses to nature, our growing appetite for the insights of ecology.

Thallabawn has taught us a relationship with nature, open equally to science and poetry, that is the moving spirit of this book. Its chronicle of a year has many switches of focus, shifts through time, changes of mood and manner: it is a mosaic of all the years, each month an essay in remembrance. 'January' reaches back into my origins for clues to present passions and absurdities. The record of our many clumsy endeavours is a counterpoint to the competence of the wild lives around us – and, indeed, of the human ones. This is not, to their relief, a book about our friends and neighbours, but a little of what we owe them can be read between the lines.

JANUARY

The sky in the west was darkening on cue, the waves already panicky and jostling where the channel meets the sea. There was a gleam of borrowed light on the far swells, but beyond them the horizon had vanished in a smoky pall. It seemed time to batten down the hatches. The hens complained at being ushered to bed so early but better that, I thought, than try to round them up as errant shuttlecocks in the violent gusts promised by dusk. I cut enough logs with the bush-saw for two days and then took the hammer and a tin of four-inch nails and went around the windbreak fences, making firm. They were creaking and shifting in the wind like the timbers of an old boat.

In the event, we'd known worse, as winter storms go, and we didn't lose the electricity until dawn. Then, venturing out between the hedges to visit the nest-boxes (three eggs, and they can't have slept very much), I had the illusion of moving in a personal capsule of calm while the whine and rush of wind continued all around. But within the house, the great press of air on the walls and windows webbed the rooms with unfamiliar draughts. On the second night I stuffed my ears with cotton wool, so that the squalls rumbled and shook in the depths of my pillow. Ethna slept on imperturbably.

What made the storm memorable was the way it piled up the breakers at the mouth of the channel and then drove the sea ahead, drowning the *duach* in a silvery green flood, subsuming both lakes and swirling on through the reeds to mingle with the streams from the hill. The ebbing tide left the fences strung blackly with seaweed, and here and there the drag of water toppled a whole line of stakes. We needed waders to cross the ford on the boreen. A coppery flood from the mountain tugged at our knees and rolled the rocks from under our feet; the rush of water was giddying, so that we felt for our footholds without looking down.

The whole landscape, for that matter, was still shuddering and excited after the gale. The fences and briars were flying white pennants of wool, and sinister flags of black plastic torn from silage covers. At the channel from the lake there were waves around the stepping stones – waves from the wrong direction, from the land – and out on the beach the sand seethed in long, wintry skeins, like the snow in films about Antarctic explorers. Grains rattled on my boots and hissed through the banners of wrack. We had to lean to walk, as if hauling an invisible sledge.

Trudging there, monitoring a tideline monotonously innocent of whatever it is I hope to find on these occasions, my mind skipped back forty years to winter days on Brighton beach, to the town's fishermen strung out in silhouette against the surf beside the pier. They walked the wet shingle at this same angle, heads lowered, bellies bulging their jerseys, hands clasped behind their buttocks. They paced back and forth in a slow trance, ignoring each other, as if summoned there to consider some enormous problem on humanity's behalf. But they were watching for money: for half-crowns, florins, shillings, sixpences. The coins, fumbled and rolling irrecoverably, sifted through the planks of the pier all summer, glinting briefly like fish in the waves. The sea rolled them landwards, burying them deep in the beach, and the winter gales, hammering at a shuttered promenade, dragged back the shingle to expose them. The fishermen descried them as of right, stalking, intent as herons, in the salt-mist beyond the hauled-up boats. No one else went near.

Half a lifetime has passed since my youth in that town. I have fetched up at a further shore, a deeper ocean, with no one to covet whatever it is that I watch for.

The strand, this particular arena, has played an odd part in our lives. It has obsessed us separately and together, like some echoing amphitheatre waiting for a pair of actors (for what use is one?).

In my first winter in Ireland, more than thirty years ago, I used to look across the bay from Connemara to this long, pale gleam of dunes below the mountain, so apparently remote and wild. I focused upon it all the yearning for what was unspoiled, all the young outsider's fantasy of life in a simple, secret place. I did not need to go there with any urgency, simply to have it there in the distance, to store it up in the mind.

This was at a time when I had no future, in any settled sense. On the pretext of a 'sabbatical' year – painting, writing a book, whatever it took to feel free – I had come from a Fleet Street (the real Fleet Street) then sunk in one of its periodic bouts of ennui. England seemed a sullen, fearful place in 1961, with little to admire along the road from Aldermaston. I did not wait for London to start swinging, or for any sanction of 'getting one's head together', but rode out for Connacht. My shiny new bicycle, with ten gears, spun through a landscape shorn and chastened by a hurricane.

At precisely this time, the young Ethna McManus was crossing Ireland the other way, ponytail bouncing in a skirl of decision just as sudden as my own. She closed the door of her chemist's shop under the crumbling round tower of Killala and opened another door by signing on for Economics and Politics in the milling front hall of University College Dublin. She was an activist, a community development worker, before those terms were current. She was tired of being indulged by officials and thanked for her ideas; the degree might make a difference. On weekends at home in Westport, she drove out to the strand in her little Morris Minor, there to wade the channel and to walk and think along the tide's edge. She would have seemed very small on that great apron of sand. I watch her today from our window: a brisk figure rounding the end of the dunes with a knapsack of seaweed, for the garden, on her back, and the dog Meg inscribing endless loops around her.

When we met, all those years ago in Dublin, we offered the strand to each other as a sort of guarantee of who and what we were. It is not a place to spread a rug and sit down idly; it is simply too big, and refuses any sort of prettiness. Soon after we married, we found a huge vertebra from the sperm whale that was washed up here fifty years ago; we dug it out of the sand and took it home to Dublin to stand among the daffodils in the garden. Now that we live here, we have another of these verte-brae propped inside the gate, where the farm dogs come and piss on it.

Between the convulsions of memorable storms, the strand seems to shuffle its grains into new contours every day. The wind scours it so fiercely that stones and shells are left perched on little stalks of sand, like a host of petrified mushrooms. Among the stones are plaques of polished, grey-green slate, em-bossed with intricate hieroglyphs in white: runic characters affixed by tube worms at the bottom of the sea. They look as if they have been squeezed out in icing sugar by a pastry chef, but they are hollow and calcareous and homes for the worms. The stones arrive ashore clutched in the rubbery claws of seaweed holdfasts; the weed rots and the stones remain, their white curli-cues as crisp and enduring as the moulding on a Wedgwood tea-pot. Over several winters I have armoured the living room chimney breast with these decorative undersea doodlings, set-ting the slates into mortar as a mosaic. Once, carrying half a rucksack of them, I met a neighbour at the ford, and confided what was weighing me down. He rubbed at the proffered slate with his thumb and breathed my name softly several times in a baffled incantation. Finally: 'It passes the time, I suppose.' We all pass the time, in his sense, between the cradle and the grave.

A long run of westerlies hustles flotsam across the Atlantic: plastic milk crates from New Brunswick, plastic light-sticks from Florida (fluorescent undersea lures for fish and squid). And often, a scattering of plastic buoys, lost by the huge foreign trawlers in the deeps just over the horizon. Hard as billiard balls, bright as party balloons, the buoys are irresistible. We take them home, to brighten up the garden path in winter (the milk crates, too, to fill with geraniums).

On the shore are other floats of unfamiliar design, sausage-shaped affairs in fluorescent pinks and acid greens. Their gaiety is tropical – Caribbean, as I like to think. In any event, the swags of goose-necked barnacles anchored to their cordage speak of many months at sea. The Portuguese and Spaniards find these barnacles good to eat: they chew on the rubbery-looking stalk for 'an exquisitely strong taste of the sea'. That's Alan Davidson, whose seafood Penguin has an honoured place on our kitchen dresser. The barnacle flavour is, he insists, a 'real revelation'. But though we have followed him gratefully into recipes for conger eel and Ballan wrasse, the salty gristle of *Pollicipes cornucopia* is a treat we have foregone.

Waste not, want not: it rang through both our childhoods. Ethna in her lost Cavan valley, just over the mountain from the Protestants, I in my wartime backstreet next to the gasometers, were dinned with the basic instinct that makes such ardent beachcombers of us now.

Every few winters there comes a notable storm, one that sends the needle swinging downwards on the barometer and lifts the hand of God from the top of the sea. In these sudden plummetings of atmospheric pressure and the mighty risings and churnings that ensue, the ocean can deliver a strange harvest. To go down to the shore next morning may be to find, as one blinks away the wind-tears, a strand littered with washed-up fish, hundreds of them lying limp under a thin dusting of sand. Among them are conger eels a yard long or more, and drifts of little cuckoo wrasse like pink goldfish. In between, and all sizes, are the familiar whitefish of the fishmonger's slab – ling, whiting, hake, pollack. There are oddities and surprises, too: the coal-black forkbeards, with button eyes, or a warty lumpsucker torn loose from its grip on an undersea rock. They are all rock species, living deep in the reefs among the islands. What kills them? Scientists I have asked talk of massive overturnings of water between the cold and warm layers of the sea. In the sudden change of temperature, the fish die of something like shock.

They are perfectly fresh – why leave them to the gulls? We go down with plastic bags and the wheelbarrow, and ferry away as many as the freezer has room for, not disdaining congers or even the wrasse. When the prime fish are gone, we experiment with fish cakes and bouillabaisse and feed the dog free for weeks.

My father would have approved; might also smile to see me picking up bits of cord from the tideline and coiling them for my pocket. I remember the galvanised chest in the yard in Brighton, where his carpenter's tools were kept, and all the little rolls of string and wire, each neatly finished with a knot.

Harry Viney came from a Hampshire village, where he was apprenticed at twelve to the carpenter; my mother, Lily Carter, from a village in Oxfordshire. Both were from the older order of rural England, one remove from peasantry; Flora Thompson described their world in *Lark Rise to Candleford*. The First World War snatched them from a countryside of thatch and woodstacks and earth privies, entwined their lives and made townies of them. After the war (in which Harry joined the marines and saw Murmansk and Yokohama), they ran chips-with-everything cafés, first in the middle of London, then in Brighton, where Londoners took their kids for the day. The Second World War put a halt to the railway trippers and laced the beach with barbed wire and land mines. The café was closed, and Harry withdrew to the edge of town and the skills he began with: carpenter's tools and housepainter's brush. He was a whizz at graining front doors. He also mended our shoes (knife pulled expertly through leather, brads glinting in his lips). He made me trousers from old jackets of his own, confidently marking out the cloth with a disc of tailor's chalk. He fed us well from the allotment, and grew tobacco there. He knew, remarkably, how to cure it with molasses, how to whip a long plug of it with cord, sailor-style, and shave it with a penknife for his pipe.

In the England of 'Dig for Victory', of 'Make Do and Mend', he was clearly the right stuff. The general fever of improvisation blurred lines of comparative income: with a show of ingenuity and skill, one could be quite hard-up without anyone noticing. But he also enjoyed reclaiming old crafts; he had a need for self-reliance. It was a value I did not always respect.

In his sixties, widowed, forced off his housepainter's ladder by dizziness and rheumatism, he went through a spell of feeling useless. I was a teenage apprentice reporter, indentured at sixteen to the local paper; only my older brother, Tony, was earning a proper wage. I came home to find my father chopping drift-wood into kindling and tying it into bundles. He had found an old perambulator and picked up the driftwood from the beaches on the Undercliff Walk. Now he proposed to load the pram with his bundles and sell them from door to door. From the shaky pedestal of my scholarship education, my imminently up-ward mobility, I beseeched him not to do this, and eventually, he submitted. I have more or less stopped hating myself for this, and all the other ways in which I condescended to my father in his old age. Sometimes, sowing carrots or cabbages, I notice the way my finger and thumb work slowly together to let the seeds fall, one by one; how I save those left over by trapping them in a crease of my palm and trickling them back into the packet. It is Henry William Viney who seals the packet, scoring each tiny fold, a whole concertina of folds, with a chipped and grimy thumbnail.

What would he have thought of our mid-life decampment from the city? I heard his voice once, or some echo of it, in a question flung up to me as I stood high on a trailer of turf on the mountain bog road. I was catching the sods tossed up from the stack and building a *croibhín*, or capping on the load. It was a dismal day, at the end of a gloomy summer. The islands had vanished in another grey pall of rain. 'Will you tell us, Michael' – my neighbour's tone was amiable, rhetorical – 'what a man of your education is doing up there, with water running down his neck?'

The acre in midwinter has the melancholy of a rail-side allotment examined through the steamed-up window of a train waiting overlong at a signal: a glimpse of horticulture at its lowest ebb, husbandry as wasteland. Soil dug over last autumn has been hammered smooth and grey, like skin in a cold sweat. Leaves are grey, too, curled and desiccated by their burden of salt. The tool shed leans a little more. But the fuchsia windbreaks have held up well, and in their lee stand tattered squads of leeks and sprouts and winter cabbages.

The acre is bounded on all sides by a hedge-bank built of rocks and sods, and planted, originally, with hawthorn quicks. I have seen hawthorn hedges as they should be, regularly trimmed and laid into tightly woven walls (the 'Presbyterian hedges' of the North), but that is not what we came to. Every bush on this hillside is shaped by the salty winds – not, as you might think, in straining away from the gales, but from constant withering of the windward shoots. By the time we inherited our hedge its bushes leaned in from the bank like ballet dancers in mid-fall. I tried 'laying' them in winter, sawing the old, mossy boughs half-through and heaving them back against the bank. Most, indeed, survived this treatment and put out new growth. The reward is in shelter, in cascading blossom in May; above all in the birds – robin, dunnock, wren, stonechat, thrush – that make the hedge their home.

The gales find weak spots in the windbreak fences when the last generation of nails has rusted through: the gaps leave the hens free to wander through the garden, but they prefer to peck for grubs in the battered timbers of their stockade.

Hens are *Gallus gallus*, a species of junglefowl of the family Phasianidae, but sometimes they need reminding of their origins. After four thousand years on the road to the modern egg battery, it is a marvel that their wilder instincts have survived at all.

When we brought this lot home from the hatchery, at point of lay, they huddled in the doorway of the ark, gazing out at the puddles like refugees in a Nissen hut, listless and sceptical. If this was freedom, they were not at all sure they wanted it. In the poultry station there was at least a steamy warmth and close-pressed company; here, all was healthy and well-ventilated and chillingly cold. The pullets found themselves on straw, which they had never seen, and were offered a wooden perching rack they didn't know to use. All ten of them spent their first night jammed together like wrens in one of the nest-boxes, while a rising gale roared about their heads. In the weeks that followed, storm after storm buffeted the ark, held down by ropes to concrete blocks. 'The poor hens!' murmured Ethna in the night.

But the nature of *Gallus gallus* will reassert itself, given any sort of chance. Even a hatchery hybrid, raised to point of lay in a cage of steel mesh, quickly learns that her big, strong feet and sharp claws were meant for scratching up the soil for seeds and insects. A chicken with a piece of the Earth to wander will scoop out a hole in some sheltered corner and settle into it, scratching the cool soil into her feathers and up under her wings to groom away her parasites. The sheltered and sunnier corners of the hen run are pitted with the hollows of these dust-baths, untidy testimony to the happiness of hens.

The fox got the last batch. It happened at Christmas, always a perilous time for routine. There were visitors and afternoon glasses of wine; each of us thought the other had slipped out to close the ark. Next morning there were bodies all round the hen run and more little mounds of feathers up at the mountain fence. We blamed ourselves, not the fox. Even the excessiveness of it, while awful and provoking, seems easier to take when one knows that 'surplus killing' is not just the vice of foxes, but of most carnivores: mink and mongooses, even lions go in for it (and dogs, of course, among sheep). Birds that do not fly away as they should keep the fox's murderous instincts firing until everything around lies still.

And we had, of course, conspired at it in other ways. In

winter, foxes commute between the forestry on the mountain and the tideline of the shore, and on their way they check the security of hens in arks and geese in sheds. Their approach brings them over the mountain wall and down the grassy gullies of the streams. One of the streams dips under the road, debouches into The Hollow at a corner of our acre and plunges on through the thicket of alders and willows beside the hen run. Quixotically, we threw a fence around the thicket and made it a refuge for 'wildlife', by which we meant hedgehogs and songbirds, badgers and stoats. But wildlife is foxes, too.

In our first Mayo winter, we were walking the shore together on St Stephen's Day and came upon a fox writhing in a gin-trap. It had been gnawing at its one trapped paw and tufts of fur lay all around. I found a club of driftwood and 'put it out of its misery' with a wild, blind swing: which is to say that I funked letting it go. Today I am better prepared to be myself, to choose the other side from the one set out in Seamus Heaney's lines:

> 'Prevention of cruelty' talk cuts ice in town
> Where they consider death unnatural,
> But on well-run farms pests have to be kept down.

It is not just in January that we can walk for miles along the shore, crossing long strands and cobbled beaches and the low, grassy cliffs in between, all without meeting a soul. This holds true for most of the year. The experience of solitude is part of what we came for; we never tire of it, separately or – as it were – together. The solitary experience of nature, the observations that come when walking quietly and alone, have become central to the chronicle of 'Another Life' and to my own, particular brand of romantic misanthropy. I may have overdone it, at least to the point of misleading the fantasy life of some of my readers. 'But I thought you were halfway up the mountain! I didn't expect all these houses!' Thus, on occasion, their reproaches at the gate.

There aren't that many houses really, but rather more than

there used to be, and they are getting smarter and bigger all the time. From the bend where the road winds round the hill to disclose our ocean panorama, to its unexpected burrowing in the sand at the foot of the mountain, is about four miles. Strung out along this narrow road and its branching boreens are some thirty houses, half a dozen of them within Christmas-candle distance. Nowhere on this side of the hill, however, is there any gathering place, any village feeling: all that takes place miles away round the hill at Killadoon. And even there, the fields space out the post-office shop from the Beach Hotel and both from the crossroads church with its little row of sodium street lamps.

We don't go to mass, draw the dole, play twenty-five for Christmas turkeys, or drink in pubs late at night. A lot of the time, when we are writing, we go to bed at nine and get up at five to sit at our separate word-processor screens like monks at matins. This ritual matches our mind-cycles – we are both bright as robins at that hour - and it is one that comes even more easily in the dark of winter mornings.

All this seals us off, though not by any special intent, from the social routines of our neighbours. We are all spaced out on our hillside stripes, with a good view of each other's comings and goings and porch-lights and chimney fires. We see each other working, with dogs and sheep or on the land, and wave to each other across the ditches or when a tractor passes. But since we live to such a different rhythm, weeks can go by without us actually meeting or talking with our friends among the figures in the landscape.

Nor, nowadays, do I write about them much.

In the early days, when everything was new, I used to relate in my column how Fergus did this or Martin said that, all to give a colour to events and all, I hoped, tactfully done (usually, indeed, to make a point against myself). But the same Ferguses and Martins (names which do not, to my knowledge, belong to this townland) soon began to make their unhappiness clear. It was not, perhaps, what I actually wrote that worried them, but the jokes that could be spun at their expense from a casual phrase or adjective of mine. This became a pub sport, with its own little lurches into cruelty, and my careful vaguenesses about identity seemed no defence against it: they all knew at once who I meant. My neighbours decided they had no wish to figure in my unpredictable weekly chronicle of rural life, or as Fergus put it firmly at his gable: 'You are not going to make a *Tailor and Ansty* out of this house.' Regretfully, I took his point.

'Good fences make good neighbours,' says the man in Robert Frost's poem, but neighbours in these parts seem rather to get by on a mutual lack of reproach. Only at the land's first boundary, with the Atlantic, is there much of what the town-dweller means by a fence: an upstanding, shining palisade stretched evenly above the grass. It is shining because it is new, the storm-driven tides having bitten, yet again, inside the old line of posts, and it is straight because fencing is easier where the grass is a carpet over sand – machair land, as the Scots call it. But even here, very often, fences have a hand-me-down look, with each stake along the sheep-wire a separate gift from the sea.

As you walk up from the shore the fencing changes. The boreen runs between high sod ditches that make shelter, as well as boundaries, and then, as the land becomes rockier, the ditches give way to dry-stone walls. Ditches and walls are topped by a frieze of two-foot sheep netting or a couple of strands of barbed wire. Because so much of this wire is, so to speak, symbolic, deceiving the agile Blackface sheep by its mere continuity against the sky, it is renewed as seldom as possible. It holds together by the habit of its molecules, even when these are changed to rust.

The boreen is sheltered for part of the way by a high creggan of rock, and there, sun-warmed in a thicket of stunted hazels, the first and solitary wildflower of the year shone out today: *Taraxacum officinale*. I have a soft spot for the dandelion, weed or not.

The first flowers of my life were the weeds of a town back yard: tiny, scarlet stars of pimpernel, blue birds' eyes of speedwell, the rosy lips of dead-nettle, all precariously rooted in the flint-walled alley behind the café. And the dandelion, with its big golden crowns, became, for a special reason, the flower of my street-urchin days.

In my mother's dowry of skills was the art of wine-making, absorbed among the rhubarb and parsnips of Oxfordshire. She could have bought these in Brighton, and sometimes did, but it went against her culture: wine should be a sharing from a country harvest. Dandelions, for her favourite flower wine, were picked by tradition on St George's Day, 23 April. On that date or thereabouts, I made trips with a bucket to the town's oldest churchyard, at the top of the hill, and gathered dandelions – just the flower-tops – among the old white tombs. I remember the smell of the wine fermenting, the strange, acrid scent stealing out from the earthenware crock that seethed in the darkness of the cupboard under the stairs. *Pissenlit*, piss-a-bed ... the dandelion's folk-names were well suggested at this stage of the brew. But by Christmas, racked and sparkling, the wine spoke only of nectar and springtime.

Dandelion is not one of the wines in our own country cellar, because I wouldn't know where to go to pick enough of them. In hill country, the yellow 'dandelions' along the roads are much more likely to be flowers of the hawkbit family. But dandelions do seize their chance among the vegetable beds of my well-dug acre, so, having admired their magnificent blooms at the start of the year, I sometimes panic and sneak up on the seed-heads with a lighted taper, to torch them before they can fly.

Those lacy globes are so exquisitely engineered, all of a piece with a plant that is full of invisible wheels and cogs and calculations. One set responds to changes in light, stretching the florets to the sun and tracking its course across the sky, or closing the head as soon as rain threatens; opening it, also, at sunrise and closing it at evening. Another set of pulleys keeps the plant the proper shape. Each year, the dandelion produces new leaves at the top of its rosette, and every now and then the taproot contracts to pull the rosette downwards. This keeps the new leaves spread at ground level, smothering any competing plants and conducting every raindrop straight to the centre of the rosette, and thus to the root. Being a man, my imagination runs more readily, perhaps, to machinery than to any sort of plant sentience or spirit, but the more we learn about plants (their 'defensive strategies', their 'communication'), the more elaborate and sensitive the revelation of their lives becomes.

Even the naming of plants can be deeply mysterious. 'Dandelion' is a corruption of the French *dent de lion*, which in turn echoed its old Latin name, *Dens leonis*. In most of the languages of Europe the flower's name means the same thing – the lion's tooth. Yet what was it that suggested the image: the jagged shape of the leaf, the form of the individual florets in the head, the interior whiteness of the dark taproot? A whole continent of different peoples come to settle on a single, graphic metaphor – perhaps, I suppose, through the spread of the Romans. In Ireland, which Caesar never bothered with, plant names leaned more to the literal and utilitarian: *caisearbhán* is the stalk of bitterness.

We tend to think that all the familiar things in nature have always had names, but living in a countryside of working farmers brings home the prior function of utility, what things are 'good for'. Most flowers got their names at a time when all the plants were being tested for their usefulness: as food, as medicine, as instruments of magic, or whatever. It was the herbalists, concerned with healing, who probably spread the notion of the 'lion's tooth' – a metaphor, perhaps, for the dandelion's speedy, powerful action. But at doing what, exactly?

The scientific name *Taraxacum* comes from Greek words for 'disorder' and 'remedy'; and *officinalis* in any plant name speaks for a long history as an official pharmaceutical herb. The *British Pharmacopeia*, one of Ethna's bibles behind the counter of her chemist's shop, used to recommend the harvesting of dandelion roots between September and February: one can imagine golden fields of it, hedged in from anxious neighbours. As to its purpose, the names of *pissenlit* or piss-a-bed could not be plainer. Part of the respect for dandelion wine in my mother's countryside, and for dandelion beer among the workers in the British steel and pottery industries, was for its value as a herbal tonic. It 'flushes you out'!

Where do I get all this stuff – botany, folklore, history, etymology? From books, obviously: often a dozen or more wedged under my chin as I retire to write the weekly column. The more of them there are, the more improbable their combination, the more subtle the flavour of the 'well-rounded piece' I am aiming at. What began as a job of work, a way to live as we do, has become a vocation of perpetual curiosity. At one level, it is a mere ransacking of indexes to other people's work, but it has also taught me, rather later in life than I would like, to go out and observe things for myself and through several sets of mental spectacles. I sometimes think that one square yard of our acre, looked at closely enough in all seasons and interpreted with all that science and poetry and art could bring to bear, would support a rapt lifetime of discovery. My friend Tim Robinson, in his great work *Stones of Aran*, puts forward the notion of a single, impossible step in a landscape, one that encompasses all possible modes of awareness, of a surpassing 'density of content and richness of connectivity'. So, once again, I am only trotting after someone else.

The first snow of the New Year makes an etching of the mountain, discovering in white on black the fine grain of its rock, each fissure and scree-fall defined in a finicky monochrome. These crisp, obsessional definitions are scratched on a landscape which, elsewhere, blurs the moors into dove-dark clouds and loses the horizon for ever between the greys of sea and sky.

   Even without snow the mountain in winter is a forbiddingly empty place. A scurry of sheep or the panicky dash of a hare only emphasise the bleakness of bog and rock and the vacant rush of wind. No twitter of lark or pipit, and thus no merlin to chase them; the peregrine gone after waders on the shore, the kestrel hovering over lowland worms and mice. Ravens alone hold the high ground, commuting to the dunes to check if anything has died since morning. To a raven I must seem an insignificant comma in the landscape, stooped over a spade or rummaging in the soil. Sometimes, in midwinter stillness, I call the bird back (or make it look round, at least) by a sonorous *kronk!* of my own.

Digging is repetitive; so is weeding: what is going through my mind as I labour on alone, hour by hour? Nothing too exalted; little, certainly, of creative ferment or of thinking important thoughts. Mostly, the mind fills up with the immediate physical process, with pauses to rescue an earthworm or exchange a glance with a robin. There is pleasure in the rasp of the spade, a sand castle satisfaction in turning the soil over and stacking it back neatly as it was. There is delight, always, in being where I am, doing what I'm doing, instead of standing at a bus stop or drinking more coffee in Bewley's. I lean on my spade to look up at the mountain, or down at the breakers on the strand, and never, ever, feel bored. You'd think after so many years I'd stop being surprised, being relieved, to find this out.

A changed view of time is one of the really momentous recognitions of the other, self-directed life. From waiting for Friday, for Christmas, for the holidays, you are suddenly free to live in the present: what shall I do today? But sneaking in with that excitement comes another revelation. It alighted on me suddenly one day when I was pushing the bicycle up the bog road.

I was fifty or so. For most of my life I had been postponing happiness to some other time and place, some other job. If I was not happy waiting for Godot, part of the frustration was all the time a journalist wastes, just hanging around for other people, or for the world to turn. Now, by some rashness and sleight-of-hand, I had wangled my way into the future: this was it. I had better be happy today, or else. If I was not, there was no one left to blame.

The flux, the flow, the drifting balance of our days needs a particular kind of patience. Newspaper work was actually a good preparation for it, demanding a readiness to take what comes, to stop doing this and do that, instead. Our life is like that now, but with the illusion of empowerment. I step out the door in the morning intending to do one thing, and come back having done four others. (Ethna, born organiser, is better at bullying life into shape.)

'Simplicity, simplicity, simplicity!' urged Thoreau, but only as we get older are we taking this to heart. The 'simple' life of our early country years was a complicated grappling with entirely new skills: goat-keeping, bee-keeping, duck-raising, wine-making, spillet-fishing, horse-breaking, fence-straining, shed-building. 'What do you do all day?' asked people from the city. 'It passes the time, I suppose,' said the locals. I don't know which seemed more uncomprehending.

Our little roads run narrowly between stone walls and rocky ditches; tractors and cars squeeze past with an inch to spare. By the end of a wet and stormy January, the grassy verges are rutted and minced into mud and where stones have slipped from the walls they stay fallen, their mosses and lichens flourishing in the graveyard dampness of the air. The roads themselves are broken; the thin, black skin of the boreens burst open by hidden springs or ploughed by floods. Not even the sun could make anything of this but bleak disorder, a disarray echoed in many wayside details: streams choked with silt and rocks, Coke tins and ferti-liser bags; ditch-gaps and fences trailing loose wire and dead branches.

Sheep rise nervously at my approach, or, mistaking my silhouette, jostle along the fence to be fed. Not all of them move. A ewe in the briars lies utterly still, bound to the ditch by those thorny hawsers. What is left of her heartbeat and the lift of her breath takes up small room beneath the fleece. 'Are you dead?' I enquire, stooping over her. Deep in the glazed and open stare, an amber rheostat flickers. My knife cuts the briars as

crisply as celery. Unbound and disentranced, she totters away
down the boreen, trailing the severed stems.

You notice the briars all the way to the sea. They are what
remains uneaten along the bare ditches, where even the rushes –
every stem in every clump of rushes – display their cropped
white tips a few inches from the ground. The high briars whip
about in the wind, black and spiny. They snatch at your sleeve;
they would take your eye out. But all the lower briars are furred
with wool, so often have they dragged through the fleece of
sheep reaching for a last leaf.

FEBRUARY

The ridge above us has no name of its own, even though it humps its back almost to the thousand-foot contour. It is there to help anchor the mountain and we call it by townland names: Corrymhaile on the far side, Six Noggins on this. It is a dull, windy limb of a hill, its contours innocent of anything but effort: a serious trudge up one of the stripes to the mountain fence, dodging around rocks and rushes and the ribs of lazy-beds; a steady plod beyond the wall, over soggy moss and sedge, and a final, staircase climb to a height where the bog splits open in multiple lacerations of rain and wind. Unless you have a few sheep (or too many), you have no business going up there. But at that height over the sea there is, of course, the view. What is it that sends us panting up the Earth's protuberances – hills, cliffs, towers, follies – for mere command of distance? Biologists might put it down to some vestigial peering after predators or prey, all of a piece with the stoat on the wall or a bear on its hind legs. A year or two past, an elderly millionaire with his own chauffeured helicopter would sometimes touch down on the ridge on clear February mornings and spend a few minutes smoking a cheroot and meditating on mountains and islands.

I have envied moneyed people only this freedom to choose their surroundings, or to invent them. As a young theatre critic in Brighton, and an aspiring social chameleon, I found myself quite often propped against elegant walls, drinking other people's gin. In a town of Regency terraces, antique dealers and much high camp, the homes of successful people in the arts were often exceedingly beautiful. At that time, a conscious pleasure in colour, pattern, texture – not finished 'art', so much, as its raw ingredients – was a daily essential for me, rather as rock music would be to many young men today. In my early teens I watched, from the tops of buses, men dressing the windows of old-fashioned department stores, draping great swatches of vivid fabric at nine-and-eleven a yard. I could do that, I thought, almost yearningly, knowing this was not an aspiration for a grammar-school boy. Later, in the joss-stick years, I papered my bedroom in black and gold, hung it with white-painted picture frames lined with scarlet felt, and pinned up Braque and Picasso.

This was not an identity my father could feel easy with. At our closest, rubbing his widower's back, his milky skin, with Thermolene, I was still as estranged from his life and times as the son in some play about New York emigrants. As Dad aged, it was my brother and his wife who coped with the downside of the young-aesthete-about-town: the hangovers and broodings, the swishings in and out. They came to visit us a few years after the move to Thallabawn – a time, still, of pioneering discomfort – and Tony helped me plant the sprouting broccoli for spring. He looked at me across the ridge of seedlings. 'There were many ways I thought you might end up,' he said, 'but never here, doing this.'

The first touch of sun these mornings, spilling out of Killary like gold from a crucible, lights up the unfenced commonage along the shore: first, the rough creggans and ivied cliffs beyond the lake, then the great flat lawn of machair behind the dunes. It is all very wild and primal looking, especially if the swans are flying. As the sun gets up over Mweelrea and rakes the amphitheatre of the hillside, it discovers bright green lozenges of land where boulders have been swept aside and the land reseeded, but also fields where nothing much has changed in a hundred years. Their fences observe modern, Land Commission parallels, but within them are grassed-over walls and ridges that follow a different geometry. In the pasture above us, too rocky to mow and split by the gully of the mountain stream, there are ridges, lazybeds, so substantial that I cross them by leaping from one to another, and also miniature ridges tucked into folds of the land to use the last square yard. Here and there, on flat boulders, are collections of small stones, fixed in a matrix of windblown dust and grass, and webbed over with grey lichens.

I find these little pyramids and bracelets of stones most affecting, since they were left there (by children?) no later, I am sure, than the 1840s, before the Famine and before the clearances that turned these hills into a sheep ranch, with Scottish laird and Scottish 'hornies' and Presbyterian shepherds. Until the sheep took over, there were three hundred people in fifty cabins where half a dozen families live now; the land must have been black with cultivation from the mountain bog to the sea.

> The hawthorn hedge and harrowed field
> Point out the village still
> And I'll go back and claim my own
> Says Rory of the Hill.
> The blackheads and the kyloes
> Our homes and valleys fill
> But from Thallabawn we'll rout them all
> Says Rory of the Hill.

The kyloes were West Highland cattle, with shaggy hides and spreading horns: the sort that Landseer painted. The laird, Captain Boswell-Houston, kept a couple of hundred of them at the fringes of his leasehold mountains: Mweelrea and the Sheeffrys. But his Blackface flocks were huge. Several thousand ewes were washed and sheared at Doolough itself, below the lodge the captain built there. It was his flocks, one could say, that began the degradation of these hills, although two acres to a ewe must have seemed adequate enough. Today, the descendants of his shepherds ('the various Macs from Ross and Inverness-shire', as Mrs Boswell-Houston described them) have melded into native Irishness on the small farms around, and now lead their own flocks past the clipboard of the headage inspector.

To face sun and the mountain, as seems natural in winter, is to find each of the ewes in a separate nimbus of light. As they straddle to piss, uncertain of a stranger's intentions, a cloud of bright steam rises among the rushes. The Blackface started out in Kurdistan eleven thousand years ago and their imagination still twitches with wolves. I watch flocks swirling about the fields, bullied by dogs which, sooner or later, manage to do something right for the little figure with the stick. 'Come up! . . . Go back!' Hearing one's commands echo about the hill on a winter's day must be a very satisfying rite of manhood.

There can be something unnervingly surreal about the odd 'pet' days of February. First, the stillness of the landscape: all that's moving is the neighbours' turf-smoke, and beyond it, a slow unzipping of foam at the very edge of the sea. Then, the oddly Greek look of the sea itself, a calm and silky aquamarine; Inishturk as Corinth adrift in a golden haze. Go inland – through the mountains, say, to Doolough and Delphi (a real place, a grove of trees between the lakes) – and the illusion deepens of having stepped into some highly varnished Victorian oil painting, so exact are the reflections of rocks and ferns. I feel myself becoming immobile, enamelled, like a figure discovered in the bottom left-hand corner, helping the scale of the hills.

What, after all, do you do with a day like this? What it deserves is the kind of delirium which used to overtake Michele's Connemara pony, set free in his field after weeks in the stable: a wild buck-lepping, a rolling on grass with his hoofs in the air, then a flying gallop, his white mane like a wing. There is, I am sure, some human equivalent one could devise. Instead, urged on by robins, I seek salvation in work.

> How wondrous, how mysterious!
> I carry fuel, I draw water.

Peter Matthiessen quotes the Zen couplet in *The Snow Leopard* (on his way, as it happens, to stalk the wild blue sheep of Tibet). And there is at least a hint of the transcendental in a total surrender, on my knees, or even prostrate, to pursuit of the roots of *Agropyron repens*, otherwise couch grass, scutch or twitch. These roots, which increase with great rapidity in the loose soil of vegetable beds, are as substantial as good thick parcel-string and their pointed ends can pierce a potato clean through. Their very strength is encouraging, even seductive: great lengths can be pulled clear of the soil complete with every node, branch and bud. But other stretches, followed with the fingers deeper and deeper until my whole forearm is buried, ultimately resist, like a big fish on a line. I pull a little harder, and harder still, and for a moment the world stands poised between profound opposites; then . . . snap. Every unretrieved morsel of root will begin to spread again.

On tillage farms, in the days before herbicides, labourers found couch grass a great strain on the sense of a day's work well done. 'You cultivate the field,' wrote John Stewart Collis in *The Worm Forgives the Plough*, 'drag it, chain-harrow it, pulling up enough couch to build a rick – which you then burn in bundles and lines. But you can get more up – and then more. I refuse to use space in writing about it . . .' Collis's years as agricultural labourer brought him what he wanted, 'a complete participation in the ordinary work of the world', but no hint of the infinite was to be found, obviously, in a losing battle with another man's couch grass.

The scent of the soil, the sun on my neck, can make me impatient to sow something. I start the first seedlings of the year in the greenhouse: trays of cabbage and cauliflower, and red cabbages that need to wrap themselves, round and round, in many months of growth. As I stoop above modules of compost, dibbing a hole into each with the tip of a finger and dropping in two seeds, the day's quietude condenses around me. I sense some other activity in progress in a far corner, a small but persistent heaving and shifting in the soil.

In a little pit I could cover with my hand lies a bundle of

feathers: a dead wren. It has crept in through a hole, after spiders (the wren is *Troglodytes troglodytes*, the cave dweller) and then panicked and perished in its glass prison. It is being buried by a beetle, *Necrophorus humator*, the black 'sexton' beetle, as an underground larder for its young-to-be. I can see it beavering away at the bottom of the pit, raking out crumbs of soil from beneath the wren with strong and spiny legs: a long job. I make myself watch, trying to admire the actuality as much as I applaud the idea.

I think of this as the month of whales and dolphins – of attending their corpses, that is, along the shore between here and Roonagh Quay, five miles north. I used to consider our own strand some special graveyard for cetaceans, gathering in their bones from a particular meander of ocean: an endless procession of funerals heaving eastwards, single file, under the slow press of storms. If there are elephants' graveyards, there ought to be others for whales. But over the years, I have met sad humps of cetaceans all the way to the black rocks of Emlagh and round the corner into Clew Bay.

It was near Emlagh, in February, that we also met dolphins alive for the first time. The whole circle of mountains from Connemara round to Achill was white with snow; even the islands shone. We walked in an incandescent mist beside the breakers, savouring the salt and the unfamiliar coldness. And here, suddenly, were half a dozen dolphins, leaping out of the breakers beyond the third wave like marlin in a Hemingway film. The shining snow, gleaming dolphins, tumbling terraces of foam: they are with me now, even as I crouch above some reeking corpse on the shore, counting teeth.

I knew so little, then. Today, meeting dolphins arching through the sea (but never again that wild, winter play), I look first for the snouts of our resident group of bottle-noses, which patrol the kelp forest between Slyne Head and Achill Island; neighbours of a sort. Or I might glimpse the white scallops of the common dolphin or the scars on the grey flanks of Risso's,

hunting wrasse around Carraig. But in that first winter I knew
so little as to call the dolphins 'porpoises', the blunt-nosed
minors of their tribe. Worse, that winter, I found my first whale
on Thallabawn strand, a long-finned pilot with a toothy grin,
and described it in print as a killer whale.

I was chancing my arm, inexcusably gauche. And I might
have got away with it but for the presence in University College
Galway of the zoologist James Fairley, whose *Irish Whales and
Whaling* was the book I should have had on my shelf. He drove
out through the mountains, stood in disgust before the very
ordinary corpse of a pilot whale and went home to pen an acer-
bic letter to the editor of the *Irish Times*. I sulked about this for a
good while; no gentleman would sneak in on a fellow like that.
But then, a few years later, something happened to unite us in
the brotherhood of science.

As February began in 1983, the tide delivered another small
whale to that same northern curve of the strand. The carcass
was torn open to the ribs and missing most of its skin, but had,
at the front end, some unusual features. Instead of the blunt or
bulging forehead of most whales, this animal's brow merged
gradually into jaws like a beak.

There are whales which filter out plankton and krill from the
sea through 'whalebone' curtains in the mouth – the baleen
whales – and others, with teeth, that feed exclusively on fish
and squid. The enormous sperm whale, for example, lunges
after giant squid with sixty teeth shining like goose-eggs. But
there are also small, beaked whales, like outsized dolphins, and
of these the Ziphiidae family are the most mysterious. They
spend their lives in the remote, cathedral depths and rarely im-
pinge on the world above. Rather bafflingly, most of them
make do with just one or two pairs of teeth, perhaps for fighting, and it is the precise position and shape of these that sorts one
Ziphiidae species from another.

I had already measured the length of my beast, mincing un-
steadily in wellingtons in the gusts of the dying gale: fifteen feet
or thereabouts. I studied the size and shape of the dorsal fin,

checked the conformation of the tail and noted (but not
measured) the penis. Now, kneeling in the stinging rush of sand,
I heaved up the head and prised the jaws open.

Two small conical tusks jutted forward at the tip of the lower
jaw like the last, defiant molars of a peasant centenarian. I consulted an oil-stained page in the British Museum's field-guide.
Were the teeth round in section (Cuvier's whale, unusual
enough) or slightly oval, as if pressed between finger and thumb
(True's whale, found only three times in British waters)? 'Like
flattened bananas,' agreed James when he came, post-haste, to
chop off the tip of the jaw with his little red hatchet. My heart
swelled up. Mr Frederick William True, an American mammal-
ogist, had discovered the species on a beach in Carolina in 1913,
calling it *Mesoplodon mirus*, meaning 'wonderful'. Three strand-
ings in Britain and three or four in Ireland were pretty well all
that was known of it. And now mine: wonderful, indeed.

As the weeks of authentication went by, the whale sank
steadily into the sand, trampled and pecked by rapacious gulls,
until only the bloodied blowhole floated there, like a pink water
lily. Its bones, everyone agreed, belonged in a museum – but
whose? The National Museum of Ireland had nothing left in
petty cash. The British Museum feared its van might be am-
bushed and burned by a Fenian rabble. Ultimately a plain,
rented van set out from the Ulster Museum in Belfast, a lone
technician at the wheel.

He was a burly, ebullient man who had started life as a sheet-
metal worker in east Belfast: a Communist, too, who prowled
our books on economics. The window showed him the distant
dunes, the blowing sand, an ominous, navy-blue horizon. He
collected his butcher's knives and borrowed a shovel.

Nobody helped him: not the farmers or their sons; not me. As
the pit deepened, we stood around it, carefully upwind, as at an
exhumation. Nobody joked. We watched him hacking into
blubber, into dark red muscle. Sand clung to his greasy knives
and blunted them; he stopped at intervals to sharpen one on
steel, like my father carving the roast at Sunday dinner. Once, a

knife flew from his hand and landed at a farmer's feet. The man took a shovel and used it to proffer the knife, apologetically.

The vertebrae and ribs, revealed, were surprisingly delicate. They were severed into three large sections and ferried through the dunes, with head and tail, in a tractor's transport box. When the technician had bundled the pieces up in plastic and heaved them into the van, a farmer let him wash, and change his clothes, and gave him tea. The technician was Terry Bruton, currently Curator of Mammals in the Ulster Museum: so some things work out as they should.

For a year or two afterwards, people would ring up from various parts of the coast to tell me of stranded whales or dolphins; some of them sounded hopeful that 'my' museum might buy the corpse. And in the winter of 1987, up towards Emlagh, I found another True's beaked whale, sixth ever in Ireland, ninth ever in the world. Rarity can be very much a matter of who's around to see. I sawed off the tip of the jaw with the teeth and sent it to the Natural History Museum in Dublin, who thanked me nicely. But nobody came for the rest.

Of the many human pleasures that seem to get even better after a few glasses of wine, the most ecstatically innocent may be looking at the stars on a clear night in midwinter. To emerge from the house with friends, after a few bottles of vintage gooseberry or blackcurrant wine, is sometimes to be quite overwhelmed by the exquisite infinity of the universe – or at least of that corner of it stretched between the distant sweep of Slyne Head lighthouse and the dark bulk of Mweelrea, close at hand. City friends, especially, have been known to cry out at this sudden revelation of the night sky, like blind people magically restored to sight. And this, in a sense, is what has happened, since the enveloping encounter with a star-filled sky, its infinite recessions, its million points of light, needs clear air and total rural darkness. I still reckon it a privilege, and an enormous aesthetic delight, to experience the night sky as my ancestors did.

I don't know much about the stars, if this means pointing out

the constellations. In our enraptured processions to the gate, it is
up to someone else to guide us to Orion, or the misty precincts
of the Pleiades. Once, on a February evening in one of our early
winters (and quite sober) I noticed a brilliant point of light on
the ocean horizon. In the binoculars it swirled strangely, red
and white, much as a boat on fire might look. The planet Venus,
descending, was thus reported to the guards.

Cities dull the night sky with extraneous light for scores of
miles around, so that astronomers are exiled to the mountain-
tops. Even in remote Irish countryside, light is now a token
shield against the world's evil: solitary houses shine out with
porch-lights, yard-lights, sometimes a full floodlighting of
stalag intensity. Perpetual light becomes a habit, and the loss in
perception, in feeling for the natural world, is too subtle to be
recognised.

The adaptation to darkness increases the eye's sensitivity ten-
thousandfold, something that happened quite naturally in our
great-grandparents as twilight deepened into dusk; lighting the
lamp came later. 'The old people' knew the great modulations
in what we now call, simply, night: the chiaroscuro of clouds;
the moon in its phases. In the countryside, fear of the dark was a
cultivated thing, essential to the storytelling that filled the
evenings with speculation, terror and wonder. Ethna remembers, in her Cavan childhood, creeping out to the balcony above
the kitchen to eavesdrop on late-night ghost stories among
neighbours gathered at the fire. Fear of the dark is with her
still.

I have my own horrors, but not this one, and sometimes go
walking alone in the dark for the novelty of it: also in the hope
of meeting something – but something wild and nocturnal, not
a ghost. I envy the Englishwoman, Chris Ferris, whose astonishing night vision lets her fraternise with amiable badgers and
foxes in the woods. In this bare landscape, everything sees me
coming half a mile ahead, and swerves to cover of the nearest
ditch or clump of rushes.

What I enjoy is the sensual adventure, the nuances of extra

awareness unfolding minute by minute. On a walk to the sea, the soundtrack has totally changed – or rather, I am listening to it attentively for once. A fuchsia hedge creaks in the wind; streams clatter over gravel; an animated rustling is plastic snagged on the wire. I kick a stone ahead of me and it rattles on for ever, catching the ear of the dog in the last barn on the boreen. Its frenzied barking shames me as I tiptoe, in wellingtons, past the house in the black sycamores.

Even by day, if the wind is right, the sound of breakers at the *srutha*, where the channel of the mountain river runs into the sea, asserts itself far up the hillside. At night, as I ford the channel's shallows beside long-defunct stepping-stones, it advances to meet me in a roar of – well, 'white sound' would be quite appropriate.

Without a moon to give them form, breaking waves by night have a sinister anarchy, the white foam flinging itself ashore as if separately alive. I have grown uneasy walking here, even safely above the tideline: on one side the breakers, hurling themselves down so aggressively, out of nowhere; on the other, a landscape grown suddenly wild and uncertain. Even the strand, so firm underfoot, is promising nothing past the next ten yards. I retreat around the dunes, to the known cries of curlews and the comfortable quacking of duck.

When a gale arrives in the night, the house reads it for us like a compass. A squall explodes against this window or that and, startled awake, we are told its bearing from sea or mountain: a little north of west, perhaps, past the tip of Inishturk; or a little east of south, across the shoulder of the mountain. Another gust gathers speed, seizes the house and shakes it, hoses it down with a spasm of rain, a blitz of hailstones.

The house as we found it in the early 1970s was a rural labourer's cottage, exactly half the size of the Land Commission farmhouse: half the kitchen, and two small bedrooms off, instead of four. In this county council doll's house, two adults raised five children, with no sink, bathroom, or running water:

the most fertile part of the acre, still, is a corner in the lee of the furthest hedge.

To make this a 'summer house', we built an extension on the sea side, doubling the area. We hadn't much to spend: what we got was a flat, felted roof and a door opening straight into the wind. Fortunately, we gave a gale nothing to get its fingertips under, and for fifteen years the roof remained totally watertight. During these years, however, the enormous suction that storm-force winds exert upon a flat roof set up an ominous creaking at wind speeds past fifty miles an hour, and the crack in the plaster at the junction of walls and ceilings would open and close while we watched. As winters went by, and the roof survived gusts of seventy, eighty, even close on one hundred miles an hour, I learned the sort of fatalism that is almost equanimity. (Ethna came equipped with equanimity, or self-discipline, or whatever it is makes Irish women strong.)

These great winds come from the sea. They lean on us power-fully, howling to appalling crescendos and bending the window-panes, but they have, as it were, no malice in them. A gale from Mweelrea, on the other hand, has been squeezed and pum-melled on its way through the mountain passes, cannoning from wall to wall, and it breaks free finally in lurching and furious gusts. One of these, a few Februarys ago, slammed into the gable of the old house and began lifting slates one by one, like crows flying up from a stubble-field.

We had lost odd slates before. The whole roof was a crusted patchwork of blue Bangors, repaired piecemeal over the years. Black gobs of Rito, the farmer's friend, trowelled on with freez-ing fingers at full stretch from a shaky ladder – I had been through that. But this was past Rito. This was rusted nails and rotten laths, the wind chewing away: one rafter, two rafters, three, in a steady baring of bones.

Like any house on this side of the hill, we had all the trappings of a jury-rig: canvas, ropes, empty fertiliser bags; even, right underfoot, a sand-and-gravel 'street' from which to fill them. Above all, we had a good neighbour, Paddy, with courage, great strength and agility. It was he who went up with the canvas, a writhing, whipping thing, and wrestled it flat, knees astride the roof ridge like a rodeo rider. Ethna filled sandbags, I heaved them up to Paddy, and hauled on ropes and tied them, lying in puddles on the flat roof for fear of being blown away. When it was finished, we came in and drank a lot of whiskey and listened to the canvas thudding away on the slates.

That gale persisted through two more days and nights and then, after a lull, the wind went west and rose to storm force again. The canvas was still there – thank God it was still there! – and its thudding was getting on my nerves. Someone had sent me a proof copy of Bill McKibben's *The End of Nature*, in which he argues that nature has been irredeemably altered by man's actions, that we can no longer trust the fall of leaves or the turn of the weather as being natural phenomena. 'The uncertainty itself,' he wrote, 'is the first cataclysm.' I found his conclusions terrible and darkly depressing. On the second morning of the storm, I went out to take it up directly with the wind.

Ethna drove me a few miles up the coast and let me out behind a wall, as close to the shore as it was safe for a light little car to go. At the top of the beach I was thrown to my knees and made to crawl: only down in the gravelly lee of the waves could I stay moderately upright. I advanced erratically through the flying blobs of spume, one eyebrow jutting seawards above my collar. I thought of those Brighton fishermen, pacing the storm beach with ponderous frowns. In Sussex we made fun of the countryman's phrase, 'T'ain't natural', and here was Bill McKibben saying it another way.

Think of what it means to doubt the 'naturalness' of weather. We have never been sure what it would do, but we could be fairly sure of what it would *not* do, on average and over a period. Given a windy winter like this one, we could count on 'fickle' nature not to do it too often or too catastrophically. But supposing we lost that assurance: supposing, after sixteen storms since Christmas, we had no good reason for trusting that there would not be sixty more?

At the end of the beach the boreen had been freshly breached by the waves: all along this coast, the old 'green' roads that linked the currach coves and seaweed beaches are being washed away. At the cliffs a quirk of wind-flow let me walk the grassy path with only occasional need to throw an anchoring arm across the wall. Behind it, a line of derelict cars had been finally dismembered by the winds, their three rusting chassis now almost as organic and formless as rocks. Such reduction of man-made things at this jagged frontier seemed proper. What was surreal was having to ask of the wind, and the driven, tumbling sea: do you still belong to nature?

It cannot help that the people who might make decisions about global warming are themselves so totally insulated from natural things and especially from weather. One sees them on television, being ushered beneath umbrellas from one heated capsule to the next. What can they possibly know of life amid wind and rain?

Where the cliffs step down to the dunes, a fence made of bleached driftwood now hung over space where sand had been: the wind played upon the dangling spars as if they were notes on a keyboard. A neighbour joined me; we leaned together. He spoke of the 'wynd', as many on this coast still do. The old word evoked a long past of struggle and storm: the past of Admiral Beaufort and his Force 11, at which ferocity no ship could carry any canvas.

The 'wynd' we can cope with: it is part of what brought us to Thallabawn, part of our sense of space and freedom. We are used to it soughing through the hedges and around the house. Even in gales and storms we have never resented it, the way people dread the fret of mistral, föhn or sirocco. With new twin roofs, peaked side by side, we can live with even the windiest of winters – so long as we know that this is nature's chaos, not humankind's.

Life at ground level (really at ground level, I mean, at the first few inches of interface between soil and air) has to be a harsh affair this month. Even on a coast where frost is rare, the soil is so often awash in icy water, every burrow silted up, the clearings between grass-tufts pounded by rain-drops. Life goes about, one imagines, with head tucked well down into its fur or its chitinous coat-collar. Thus caught off guard, perhaps, one of the acre's inhabitants turned up dead on the doorstep the other morning, being batted from paw to paw by Number Three cat.

A prostrate pygmy shrew is the most pathetic of miniatures: scarcely more than two inches of velvety body, tipped with a snout so slender and delicate as to seem made only for sniffing the air. But the tiny teeth within have tips of ruby-red and are designed for chomping woodlice, beetles or spiders ('shrews,' says James Fairley, who has studied them in affectionate depth, 'are incredibly noisy eaters'). Rushing along its little tunnels in the undergrowth and twittering to itself like a creature from *Alice in Wonderland*, the shrew is murderously obsessed with food. At this point in winter it must eat well over its own weight just to keep warm, and a couple of hours without food means virtually certain death.

Why bother? I wondered, stroking its whiskers with a fingertip: why not curl up to sleep for the winter? Other insectivores have the sense to hibernate – the hedgehog snug beneath a pile of twigs, bats clustered in their caves. But the shrew is too tiny among mammals to store enough life for itself: it is fated to be an 'annual', living two summers at most. Then, with its teeth blunted by all that insect armour, it is driven from its territory by some aggressive and uppity first-summer shrew.

The study of nature's calendar – the dates of first bud-bursts and flowerings, emergence of bumblebees and butterflies, arrivals and departures of migratory birds, first cuckoo calls – is called phenology (without an 'r': phrenology is about bumps on the head). It was never exactly a science, more a secret understanding between nature and her more passionate observers. But the impact of climate on these dates, charting the advance of spring, the retreat of summer, across the countries of Europe, has seemed a fit subject for science.

Woodland flowers, for example, which must get their blooming done before the canopy of leaves closes over, respond in a very regular way to the lengthening of daylight and rise in temperature. The march of spring can be mapped in terms of their first opening, with contours based on 'isophenes' – lines that join the points at which the average first flowering of celandine, primrose, wood anemone, falls on particular days. Thus, botanists have calculated that spring moves north across flat ground at roughly two miles an hour – 'strolling pace, in fact', as Richard Mabey puts it in his book, *The Flowering of Britain*, 'which means that you can indulge in the pleasant fantasy of following it on foot, the guest behind the unrolling carpet'.

In Britain, too, there is a map that shows the average contours of 'first frog spawning', beginning in Cornwall in early February but not reaching England's cold North Sea coast until late March, and the high mountains in the Lake District until April. In Ireland, the carpet of silvery frogspawn unrolls in a similar way, beginning in west Cork around 13 February and ending, many weeks later, in peaty pools on the peaks of the Sperrins and Mournes.

What draws the hibernating frogs out of the mud to breed is not, it now seems, any consistent effects of temperature or light, but the smell of food – the scent given off by algae growing strongly in ponds and lakes. The urgency this scent impels was vividly caught in a letter to me in mid-February 1989 from a woman who lives near a small lake at the foot of the Knockmealdown Mountains in County Waterford:

Everywhere you look you can see frogs, singly and in pairs, urgently making their way to the lake. The streams boil with their efforts to meet a partner and fight their passage to the main spawning spot among the reeds. The driveway is a sea of jumping bodies, some nimble and light, some mated couples lumbering along as the female manoeuvres not only her own weight but that of her partner. At the lake, already, an area the size of our kitchen is a mass of black, speckled jelly, writhing with couples adding more. At lunchtime nearly the whole lake

was alive with croaking frogs, their heads just above water, the
white throats pulsating . . .

Pond algae is the main food of tadpoles, but grown frogs eat
slugs and snails. It was this intelligence that prompted me to dig
out a pond beside the vegetable garden, stock it with water-
plants and tip into it, as a final priming, a bucketful of frogspawn from a pool on the hill. I need scarcely have bothered,
because, on the pond's first anniversary and long before the bap-
tismal froglets were old enough to breed, two pioneering
mounds of glistening spawn appeared. In a few years, the February frog assemblies in the pond have grown to a headcount of
well over one hundred animals. As early as the ninth of the
month they throng the water like pilgrims bathing in the
Ganges, and their churring pervades the acre in a soft but insistent echo of distant motorbikes or chain-saws.

Any sudden approach to the pond produces a convulsion of
alarm, a quicksilver boiling as the frogs dive for cover beneath
bog-bean leaves and lily-pads. Initially, enraptured with their
presence, I would sneak up on knees and elbows and peep
cautiously, at frog level, over the pond's rim of rocks. This gave
me an intimate view of the tangled knots of frogs, each with its
female swollen with eggs and pickaback male locked on, with
Velcro-tipped fingers, in his interminable embrace. As the insti-
gator of the scene, I have felt awed at its orgiastic nature. In
Februarys since, the panic in the pond that attends my every passage of the garden path, with wheelbarrow, has come to be quite
irritating. 'Do stop that!' I hear myself snapping.

Irish frogs are characterised by one American research team as
'explosive breeders with a greater annual reproductive output
than mainland conspecifics', and the potential of froglets from
this one little pond is certainly huge. Early in March, the glistening mat of black-dotted jelly, composed of some sixty or
seventy separate clumps of spawn, will dissolve into a thousand
times that many tadpoles; their wriggling whips the water into
froth. Most of them die in the first few days of life, eaten by the

great diving beetles and many lesser kinds. The beetles' larvae and the nymphs of dragonflies, like a swarm of vicious prawns, stab the tadpoles and suck out their insides, leaving the skins to drift like empty grapes.

Those that survive the spring to the midsummer metamorphosis – no more than five in a hundred – will climb out as froglets into a world of sharp beaks, teeth and claws. The herons, which even now are busy at the bog pools, gorging on the mating frogs, are only the most obvious of their assailants. Ducks and kestrels, crows and owls – even thrushes and blackbirds set a hazard to the young frogs' escape. After them come hedgehogs, mink, otters, rats, foxes, stoats and fieldmice, any of which will seize a frog in a flurry of little screams. Half the new frogs that escape the pond will be dead by next year, a defenceless takeaway food. Yet all these birds and animals managed perfectly well without frogs for thousands of years, until they were brought in for human food some time in the late Middle Ages. This, at least, is the scientists' best guess.

In studying 'nature', we mostly forget to include our own species, yet we are not entirely divorced from the phenological calendar.

> In the Spring a livelier iris changes on the burnish'd dove;
> In the Spring a young man's fancy lightly turns to thoughts of love.

But Tennyson was not writing in February, a month in which changing day-length and – perhaps – rising temperature are more likely to stir up some sort of Seasonal Affective Disorder (well yes, love can be that, too!). For me, the first crocuses in the park were often a cue for profound discontent, an ache to change jobs or flee abroad. Trinidad, Jordan, South Africa, Dahomey were among the destinations I 'nearly' set out for in my twenties, often on some quixotic impulse that had little to do with sunshine.

At Thallabawn, February can sometimes bring a touch of cabin fever. I think of Mrs Boswell-Houston, the sheep-laird's lady at Doolough Pass, who suffered so sorely when the mountain's winter shadows closed in on her valley, or when waterspouts, whipped up by the wind, hissed across the lake for days on end. She and the captain would sometimes arrange to be rowed in a currach right to the mouth of Killary harbour, just to see the sun go down, and the first two months of the year would often find them both gone from the lodge – and from Ireland.

But we can always see the sun go down, and even after all these years will call each other to a window to see some special colour washed over the sky or the sea. Atlantic weather in winter is a non-stop stage production and we have the best seat in the house. Clouds pile up into chorus lines, squalls leap in from the wings, curtains sweep across in hailstorms or lift from the islands in magical clearances and transformation scenes. It is all arriving, all new at each moment. Even the sunset promises change. These evenings, it has reached the northern cliffs of Inishbofin; soon it will edge into open sea on its journey back to spring.

MARCH

I feel sorry for the ewes across the hedge. One bitter hail-squall after another sweeps in from the islands, beats down the foam on the breakers, and hisses up from the dunes to blot out my window in a riotous tattoo. Wild geese in a hail-storm point their beaks to the sky, to save their skulls from being hammered. Sheep gallop to the nearest rushy hollow, turn their backs and put their heads down. The hailstones whack into their fleeces and hang there like rhinestones.

The ewes are down from the high ground for lambing next month ('yeaning', as it's called here, a word so special to the place that I use it always with a hesitant awkwardness). There have been lambs on the east coast since January, but the western Blackface crop is still timed for spring and sown by the rams in November. This old cycle gives the ewes a chance of reaching their time with a dry fleece, and udders full of milk from the first new grass.

How warming and traditional that sounds! But it leaves out of account what has been happening to the hills: a devastation owing everything to the modern economist's distant view of life on the land (well, not everything: there is greed in the equation, too, indigenous and timeless). Hill-farmers at this raw edge of Europe were, indeed, having a hard life, and extra headage payments for their sheep seemed an equitable way of easing it. But nobody thought what might happen when you double the number of sheep on the most fragile land surface in Europe.

In the quiet days after Christmas, a friend who lives on the other side of the mountains suggested a walk at the head of his valley – 'And it's wellingtons, I'm afraid – there's something I want to show you.' I had a good idea of what to expect. Almost any road through these hills now will show you the wear and tear of overgrazed mountain peatland: sometimes whole hill-sides have the black and glistening look of melting bitumen, sagging in folds and ready to flow. But some of the worst sights are hidden away in lost triangles of moorland, far off the usual track.

The road we took ran up into the Sheeffry Hills through a glen of white granite boulders, a 'secret' place of the sort tourists love to discover. The boreen keeps company with a rapid mountain river and then stops, on its brink, at a neat little clachan of houses. The one beside the river has a subtly tilting kitchen floor and a bed in a wall-niche by the fire (how a city bureaucrat might savour this folk-park interior and the oil-cloth-covered table on which his headage forms are filled, the signatures endorsing, as he would feel, his own existence).

Ruination begins on the far bank. The bog rises gently at this point, a slope of a mile or two to the steep northern scarp of the Sheeffrys. I came this way some winters ago, looking for a cliff of alpine plants that Robert Lloyd Praeger wrote about. It was a rough and splashy tramp up the hill, the sheep scattering away over sedges and moorgrass. Now we tramped a desert of black slime, pricked by a miserable stubble of sedge. Here and there we hesitated, apprehensive of the glaze of icy water, but below it the substance of the bog was oddly firm; it had merely been skinned of anything that grew. Bog plants have adapted to a very meagre nourishment, sucked mainly out of rain, and to a slow recycling of minerals as dead plants are broken down. Only in Arctic tundra is there so delicate a balance in the long cycle of regrowth, and the process of overgrazing can hover for years, perhaps decades, between the chance of recovery and a steady, irreversible dissolution.

There were few sheep about at this level – what would they

eat? Even up at the north scarp, where wethers were nudging the snowline a little higher every day, their numbers seemed quite inadequate to the devastation below. But then, I have never looked at any one piece of mountain and thought there were too many sheep on it. It is only when rocks stick up from the bog like white skulls on an old battlefield, or when trout redds in the streams are smothered by deep black silt, that disaster becomes undeniable.

A fence can make the story plainer. On a plateau above the Sheeffry 'blackland' (a term that, like 'dust bowl', invents itself almost unaided) is an enclave of bog tightly fenced for private forestry. The planting was never completed, so that a large piece of the moor has been protected for years: only at the very edge, where sheep stick their heads through the wire, have the plants been shaved to the ground. Inside, there is heather: knee-high bushes of it, twined with pale ribbons of moorgrass. As we walked a pipit rose up. There was a fox scat on a hummock, and an otter's trail, like a tunnel, through the tall vegetation on a river-bank. My friend, who knows his wildlife and once shot grouse on this hill, found for me also the 'form' of a hare – a deep, warm hollow in the moorgrass that had taken on, precisely, the shape of its absent owner. The image haunts and touches me, like something out of Zen: the shape of the absent hare, and the blackland, bare of any grass to hold it.

On this side of the hill we have been rather more fortunate. Perhaps it is simply a matter of numbers; also, I am sure, the way the sheep sidle over the ridge, out of sight, to shelter from the worst of the ocean weather. Even so, there are black bruises spreading on the hill by March, and every big flood in the mountain river sends a current of brown silt churning through the waves and sweeping in a great arc out to sea.

My friend feels, I know, a sick sort of anger at what has happened to the bog at the head of his valley. It is, in one way, none of his business; the forces that caused it are quite outside his control, as are its remedies. But helplessness has its own slow ache. For years I have been trying to condition my spirit to cope with whatever comes of the discovery of gold in the hill above our home.

The first omens arrived one wintry day in March 1985, with the bizarre sight of a man panning for minerals in the stream that gives us our water – I mean really panning, with a big two-handled dish, swirling the fine gravel to its lip and poking at it with a gloved finger. I joined him where he squatted above the ice-rimmed boulders, and he confided that our stream was 'quite good on the heavies' – the oxides of gold, copper, zinc and lead. He was a professional prospector. He trowelled a sample into a bag and wrote the map reference on it and drove off in his station wagon to the next stream along the hill.

This may, as it happened, have been coincidence, for the really big discovery of gold began amid the creggans of bedrock in the boggy floor of Doolough Pass, on the other side of the mountain. In March 1988, with the first 'Gold Versus Environment' heading in the *Mayo News*, I hiked across the shoulder of Mweelrea and perched on a ledge like a Comanche scout, inspecting the strangers far off on the bog below.

One of them I came to know a little, when both might have wished it was more. He was the exploration geologist who found the gold, an uncrushably cheerful, bearded young man with a wind-tan and very white teeth. We had each spent time in Greenland, in the High Arctic wilderness; we loved the hills. We should have been off together, exploring rocks and drinking pints in Charley Gaffney's. He was a scientist with no interest at all in the mining of gold – just in finding it and tracing the shape of the orebody underground. He took me out along the creggans and showed me bright flecks in the quartz. He talked of tuff-folds and fault-lines and pods. There was much I longed to learn from him. But it was no good: I could not forgive him. He had opened Pandora's Box.

By the autumn of 1990 the company had drilled thirty-six holes. They marched steadily westwards across the valley, up through the conifers of Doogan's Wood and out onto the ridge above the sea. They were following, said the company, 'a

westerly plunging, tightly folded volcanic horizon which holds
extensive gold mineralisation up to a depth of 160 metres'. The
line on the map swooped down to the rocks at Bunlough Point
and headed for the ancient Ordovician folds of Inishturk.

For week after week that autumn, the drill-rig stuck up in
silhouette from our profile of the hillside, and whenever the
wind dropped, or went north, the distant whine would drive
me, with my word processor, to the other side of the house.
On one of these painful days, the geologist dropped in for coffee, but also to tell us of a phenomenal assay from one rib of rock
on our side of the ridge: nine ounces of gold to the ton! He was
radiantly talkative, while we moved about with mugs and milk
and took biscuits out of a tin, quite frozen with dismay.

In the end (because I still don't want to think about it, or talk
about it much), the whole thing went away. The county council
bravely decided that it would rather have tourists in these hills
than dumper trucks, tailings ponds and poisoned streams. The
company will come back, of course (that company or another),
when the trend in the world price of gold is right and the politi-
cians are more malleable.

For a full year more, I could not bring myself to climb to the
ridge and wander across to Doogan's Wood, always a favourite
walk until *they* came. I was afraid I should come across
surveyors' posts, with their painted, painstaking numbers still
in place. But at last I pushed myself up the fields of lazy-beds,
and swung a leg over at the same place in the mountain fence.
It was all as it used to be: as soggy and unaccommodating, a little
barer. And from the shoulder of the ridge, where the sheep lie,
the air was wild and silent again, all the way to the mountain,
and the mountain behind that.

We go abroad on the land together, Bombus and I, dodging
around each other on our separate affairs. Her deep, full-engined
buzz is startling after the empty air of winter and for a moment
we almost collide. If she's enormous she's *terrestris*, of the earth,
otherwise I squint after her, trying to catch the exact sequence of

her football-jersey stripes. A white tail, so probably *lucorum*, often the earliest bumblebee queen to stir from hibernation in the hedge-bank.

If I were a proper naturalist, raptly obsessed instead of merely 'interested', I should long ago have found some worthy ecological project to do with bumblebees. Here I am, after all, on one of Europe's remoter coastlines, of distinctive climatic character, with an acre of prime bumblebee terrain at my door (sheltered, densely vegetated, unsprayed and unpolluted, topographically varied, bounded with highly desirable mossy banks for nesting in, and so on).

What would there be to study? Species of Bombus, size of colonies, distribution and spacing, fluctuation over a ten-year period – that might be the basic framework, rather dull stuff. Then zero in, perhaps, on some unanswered question about foraging behaviour or flower preference. I do not see myself catching bees to stick numbered discs on their backs (half an hour in the fridge will quieten them), or killing them to analyse the nectar in their honeystomachs, the pollen in their pockets. What I really fancy is the sort of inspired observation and deduction that Charles Bethune Moffat went in for.

Moffat worked in the Dublin office of the *Daily Express* in the early 1900s, but our kindredness of spirit may be less than that suggests. In my newspaper years I was forever discovering the discreet achievements of men who slipped in and out of the office at odd hours and who listened much more than they talked: sub-editors, in particular, would actually have written novels or works of history in the time they saved from the pub. Moffat, apparently, would turn in to work having spent the night with owls, or the dawn with early songsters in the Phoenix Park (he was remembered, almost inevitably, as 'bird-like', from a habit of poking his head round the door). His research was not, of course, of much interest to the *Daily Express*, but gave weight to his research papers in the *Irish Naturalists' Journal*. Its editor, Praeger, called him 'the most accomplished naturalist that Ireland has produced, capable of ranking beside

Gilbert White himself', which is as high as praise comes.

Moffat spent a lot of time watching bumblebees, and he became fascinated with one particular exception to the rule that bees gather nectar from only one kind of flower on any one foraging trip. The carder bumblebees he watched in a wood in County Wexford would gather honey from the blue flower-spikes of bugle, and then dash off to embrace a pretty vetch called heath pea before returning to a plant of bugle. After twelve summers of checking this behaviour, he found 'four stupefied specimens' of carder on bugle flowers and concluded that its nectar was too potent for the bees unless they used the heath pea honey as a mixer. But Moffat's genius was to work out the possible mutual benefit, for bugle and bee, of such an erratic foraging pattern.

Bugle (*Ajuga reptans*) spreads by creeping with great vigour, a single plant extending itself to carpet the ground in all directions. A carder bee could spend a long time on the flower-spikes without ever leaving the parent plant. But if, now and then, it is forced to go off for a drink of heath pea or some other recuperative honey, it is likely to find itself near a new bugle plant. Thus, by making the bee move around, the bugle achieves a healthier cross-fertilisation for its own species. I don't know if Moffat was right about this, I just envy his application in spotting the odd behaviour and thinking the answer through.

In March there seems little choice of food for the emergent queens, apart from pussy willow catkins or a few untidy mounds of aubrietia. Certainly the bees show little interest in the flowers that give me such particular pleasure – flowers that, as a boy, I cycled many miles to pick in spring. The pleasure is all the keener because, on the face of it, few habitats could be more different than Thallabawn's windswept, rushy hillside and the gentle woods of the Sussex Weald. Yet here I am, sowing early potatoes in a field bounded by hedge-banks full of celandines, primroses and violets.

Primroses are usually reckoned as woodland plants, blooming early (*prima rosa*, the first rose) to catch the light before the trees break into leaf. But they need moisture just as much: look how the wrinkles in a primrose leaf guide every last drop inwards, to the roots. Woodland suits primroses because moisture evaporates more slowly in the shade. But on field-banks in rainy Mayo, as on those in Cornwall or Wales, the balance of moisture and drainage, light and shade, seems to suit the primrose every bit as happily. Nothing makes me feel more of a millionaire than the casual abundance of these wild flowers beside me: originals beyond price.

An acre is not much land to own, but you can live on it if you have to, or want to, and if the soil allows. On this hillside before the Famine, the people were eating, on average, more than six pounds of potatoes a day, or about one ton a year each. An acre manured with seaweed will grow six tons at least, so there is room to grow other things besides.

Six tons is about what we harvested, with neighbourly help, in the autumn of our move from Dublin – not with any thought of living on them, but as a way, supposedly, of bringing a field of rough pasture into cultivation. We clamped them in several long heaps, each thatched with rushes under a heaping of soil. An Irish countryman would not need that description: we pitted them. But such was my innocence that the first 'rushes' I cut with a sickle, having been directed to a field beside the saltmarsh, were real and actual bulrushes, growing in the water, and not the dark green clumps of *Juncus* I had walked through to reach them. I learned better, just as I learned how to loop a rope and pile it with rushes and pull the noose tight, to hoist up a whole bristling haystack onto my shoulders and walk off with it, stooped like a Chinese peasant. Such manual labour on my own behalf, filling days I had no need to answer for, felt deliciously liberating.

The potatoes themselves underpinned this euphoria. They were huge and floury and baked beautifully, or made boxty in a pan on the range in the Cavan way. They were reassurance, meal by meal, of the rock-bottom security the acre had brought to our lives. If our folly in abandoning the city should ever catch up with us, our little patch of earth would see us through. We ate close to one ton of the six in that lean winter, and sold the rest to neighbours when their potatoes ran out in spring. It became a point of pride with me to keep our own good potatoes from one crop right round to the next, and to have the first of the earlies sown by St Patrick's Day.

The soil at this time is hammered smooth by hail and rain, but under the pale skin of silt is a fast-draining, sandy loam that breaks apart cleanly and takes a trench without collapsing: an obliging soil that any gardener would appreciate. But it is a hungry soil, too. It seizes on my barrowloads of compost or sea-weed and strips them right down to their fibres, and whatever nourishment remains at summer's end is soon washed down through the soil and leached away. Sometimes I cover the beds in autumn with a thick rug of straw, but this, as it decays, breeds more slugs than any number of frogs could cope with. When we had ducks, they shovelled up slugs with enthusiasm, but they also ate frogs (untidily, the little webbed feet hanging from their beaks, awaiting the final gulp).

Our half-dozen Aylesburys roosted in a shed in The Hollow, where the stream runs, but they arrived below the kitchen window each morning to wave placards and chant for food. In summer, unfortunately, they hid away at evening in nests they made in lush undergrowth along the stream. Their eggs were stolen by hedgehogs, their nestlings killed by the stoat and they themselves were picked off by otters which travelled up from the shore for the purpose. It seemed, in the end, too callous to keep ducks as relays of charming jesters, when we were never there at the right time to cry 'Watch out!'

The storms have uncovered a shiny terrace of black peat below the sandbank at the edge of the strand. Some young university palaeobotanists were there the other day, drilling through the peat in a laborious, muscle-powered way. They were excited when the core came out like layer cake, alternating peat and sand, peat and sand. But we couldn't tempt them up for coffee, biscuits, and diverting speculation about the climate cycles of our prehistoric past.

The past crops up everywhere along this shore. At Carrowniskey there are pine stumps like smooth black molars sticking out of the sand below high water. These must also be rooted in Bronze Age peat and perhaps, below that again, there is a sandy beach of the Stone Age. Even the strand we have now feels prehistoric at the worn end of winter, when the sun finds the rough edges of a world being made and unmade.

I was walking along beside the warren, where scallops of turf hang down like old carpet, when a big rabbit came hurtling onto the sand with a stoat wrapped round its neck. It collapsed and lay still and the stoat carried on butting and biting deeper, a viciously animated stole of chestnut fur (like the fox fur my mother owned, a thirties creation complete with glass eyes in the head and a clasp to fasten nose to tail, the little feet dangling: so there's a horrid, Roald Dahl image if you want one). Part of the shock was the fact that this had happened before, in my first winter in Ireland, on a frosty bog road across the bay in Connemara. On that occasion the rabbit fell right at my feet. The stoat let go and backed off a few feet and circled me on the road, intently possessive. The rabbit was half-dead with fear and refused to move when I nudged it with my toe, so the question was which of us was to kill and eat it. I was living on mussels and potatoes at that time and liked the idea of rabbit stew, with cloves and onions. I swung the rabbit from one hand and chopped hard at the back of its neck with the other, which seemed to work. The stoat followed me some of the way home, running along the top of the ditch, and then gave up: but still I kept looking back.

This later stoat was so busy with the job of killing, so bloodily persevering (being female and small, it was taking her longer) that only the touch of my shadow made her take flight. The black tip of her tail floated high as she bounded for cover. I should have left the rabbit to her; one backwards peep of hers would have earned it. But minutes passed and she did not reappear. Halfway home with the rabbit I was suddenly disgusted with my petty sense of ritual in picking up something for nothing.

In the first years of our trials in self-sufficiency, the healthy rabbits teeming in the dunes seemed an obvious challenge. I had bought a shotgun as part of the essential countryman's kit, only to discover that I hated the noise it made. Hours of screwing myself up to pull the trigger, in target practice alone on the shore, made the bangs no more tolerable and my aim no better. A shotgun, moreover, is not what is used to kill rabbits, unless you like the taste of lead and have money to waste on cartridges.

Snaring them seemed much more in keeping with the 'simple' life as we saw it then. After I had made the usual mistakes, readers of 'Another Life' wrote long letters of advice, enclosing diagrams and even sample snares. A number of professional men seemed pleased to relive the skills of a rural childhood. The snares are not, of course, set in the entrance to the burrows, where all beginners put them, but out on the runs, where rabbits in full bouncing stride mark the ground with their hops. The snare's height off the ground, four fingers, is crucial, as is its shape and aperture. I would mark each one with a seagull's feather, the easier to find it again.

Through one notable autumn I caught a few rabbits on most days and became quite adept at skinning them (the softness and warmth of their fur). We bought alum, for curing, and the shed doors filled up with skins pinned out to dry. We had Christmas mittens and slippers in mind. But as gales and rain set in, the discipline of going out at dawn to visit my snares at the shore became too penitential and its results too uncertain. I also found too many rabbits alive and suffering in the snares, and this helped me face the truth I had been keeping out of mind: that snaring actually relies on the animal's terror to tighten the noose to strangulation – a savage means of killing anything. There is, perhaps, one sadder fate for rabbits, and by spring I was to meet its first victims, wandering blindly on the shore with puffed-up faces. Now, years on, there are sometimes rabbits and sometimes not, as the virus comes and goes, but never again that pathetic litter of matted, rain-soaked skins and picked-over skeletons.

> This is raven's territory, skulls, bones,
> The marrow of these boulders supervised
> From the upper air . . .

Michael Longley wrote this in the cottage beside the far lake, looking out to his adopted landscape. He is right about the ravens: from summit to sea, this is their land. They are in residence now on a cliff beyond the lake, the nest wedged in a gash in the black rock. They had the sky to themselves for their courtship flights, rising and falling against the silhouette of the mountain. Raven manoeuvres have been analysed in detail – 'during a half-roll, the raven folds one wing back at the wrist, rolls rapidly onto its back, bends the other wrist and reverses direction to extend both wings' – but this is like studying Nureyev frame by frame: what holds me rapt is the whole glorious *pas de deux* of exuberant rolls and dives. The beauty of their flight is, I suppose, like the squalor of their feeding habits, mediated by utility. They breed this early in the year to catch animal carrion at its most abundant: if not sick rabbits, then weakened sheep. Sometimes we meet ravens on the *duach*, reluctant to rise from some putrid portcullis of ribs, and try not to see the vulture in their heavy little hops.

Ravens keep their distance, in every sense, from their lesser relatives among the crows. If they pick rows, it has to be with peregrines, princes among falcons and often their close neighbours in the mountains or on the island cliffs. By contrast, rooks seem cheerfully plebeian, never more so than in their noisy tree-top colony of nests in March.

When the sun rises over the ridge these mornings, it picks out the white foam of the breakers, the white fleeces of early lambs in Bridie's meadow, the whiteness of her two-storey gable in its grove of bare sycamores halfway between my window and the

sea. In this first flare of sunlight, the shadows of the trees are
etched upon the gable with a vividness special to the moment;
so also, the rooks in their nests are never again so glossily animated and dramatically black.

Watching from my higher perch on the hill, I peer down to
the little rookery as into a tribal village, the circle of untidy nests
wreathed in turf-smoke from the chimney. Birds don't mind
smoke: indeed, rooks perch on chimneys sometimes, wings
voluptuously spread and feathers fluffed out. If Bridie's fire does
waft some comfort to the birds, it is the only obvious amenity in
an exceptionally exposed and windy rookery. That so many of
last year's nests survived the big storms of February speaks for
the birds' choice of branches and their skill at basketwork. They
are supposed, for good engineering reasons, to prefer snapping
off fresh twigs to picking up old, brittle ones, but I have never
seen them at it. At the height of this year's nest-building, on the
other hand, a rook was battling into the sea winds with two-
foot-long sticks stolen from the long-vacated magpie nest in
the spruce tree at our gate.

We do not envy Bridie her rookery. There are about fifty
nests in the sycamores: not a great many as rookeries go, but
quite enough to envelop her house in spring in a constant, wearing clamour of dissension and complaint. Echoes of it drift up
the hill to us, mixed with the rumble of surf. At other seasons
the rooks roost in the trees, with separate phalanxes of jackdaws
and starlings spread at either side. Books talk of their 'morning
and evening flights' as a familiar ritual, but this says nothing of
the mystery of a dawn so dark that one sees the birds only as
softly rustling shadows, and nothing of the grand, wheeling
frieze they make against an ocean shimmering with afterglow.
There are also times – perhaps as pressure falls, ahead of a storm –
when the rooks engage in reckless aerobatics, hurling themselves
around the sky and darkening our windows in sudden black
waterfalls of wings.

Vineys' Acre, at a quick swoop from the rookery, has consid-
erably enriched their lives. Our experiments with summer

grain, our careless ways with layers' pellets, the guaranteed orgy as rain betrays our potatoes in autumn: these have all improved their chances of 'adventitious feeding'. The free snacks may, indeed, have helped a few more rooks to survive in a rough winter, but the size of their colony is fixed by the wider hillside and its supply of invertebrate food. The ravens nest early to coincide with carrion; the rooks, to feed their young when pastures are soft, moist and glistening with earthworms.

Two heifers were stripping a holly tree. Their soft, pink noses glistened moistly, tilted up to the sun, and their long, pink tongues were hesitant as they curled around a mouthful of prickles. They would try the clump of glossy leaves two or three ways, seeking the least painful fit, and then bite through the twig with an audible *snip!*

I was fascinated and aghast. My fingers tingled with the agony I have known in scooping up leaf mould with holly prickles in it. These trees developed sharp points on their lower leaves precisely to discourage the browsing of herbivores. (No they didn't: that is teleology, or the sin of imputing purpose retrospectively. Holly trees which developed prickly leaves – gradually and by chance – were more likely to be left to fruit and reproduce themselves: thus they came, by natural selection, to dominate the species. I try to be a good neo-Darwinian, but still have trouble with ideology: what good was a prickle before it actually pricked?)

The holly tree stood at the edge of a fragment of old woodland, hollies mixed with sessile oaks, birch and hazel. There is another dark grove like this below the ravens' cliff, and one might suppose that protection from sea winds was the key to its survival. But what best preserves the ferny heart of it is its isolation between cliff and lake. At each end, where cattle graze, the hazels and hawthorns have dwindled to skeletal remnants, rising like gibbets from a litter of brittle boughs.

In March, when so much of the landscape is so drab, the interiors of the western woods can have an unexpected richness:

even the State's conifer plantations hide a gallery of diverting forms and textures. Up beyond Six Noggins, a high plateau of peatland stretches back to the edge of Doolough Pass, where a planting of sitka spruce presents a solid barrier to the rambler off the hill. To infiltrate this wall of interwoven branches at a random point, blundering down through hummocks of moorgrass, sliding into deep, dark drains, face and hands incessantly pricked and scourged, is a hazardous and foolish piece of trespass. But with a skein of mountain drizzle drifting down, there can be something magically sensuous in the close and scented embrace of these young conifers. In a secret niche within the forest, co-ordinates quite unknown, you sink to your knees in soft cushions of intricate mosses – emerald feathers, plumes and rosettes – and crusting the trunks and branches pressing in from all sides are elaborate lichens like Christmas stars and snowflakes. All this, lit from above in an exact and silvery light, excites, as the Victorians might have said, a most exquisite impression.

There was an art in building the high sod ditch of the West. The base is broadly set on rocks cleared from the land, but the top should be so narrow and its grass so readily plucked at the curl of a tongue that the cow on neither side feels moved to climb. One of my ditches may even go too far in this respect, since to balance on its knife edge and swing a sledgehammer in an accurate arc needs all one's concentration and poise. But the soft sod takes a new stake beautifully, *thock . . . thock . . .* and the sound echoes industriously along the hillside.

I do better at this than at building walls, for there is nothing in the shape of Thallabawn rocks to help keep a wall together. Other places have limestone, conveniently reaved into regular slabs or cuboids, or granite, with its gritty tooth to hold rocks where you put them. But our rocks are of sandstone, smoothed beneath a glacier, and their shape is no help to construction. 'Dogs' heads!' agreed my neighbour cheerfully. Thus it is not frost – either weather or poet – that 'spills the upper boulders in the sun' but the very temperament of the stone.

On our narrow roads and boreens, built for horse and cart, we have also to count the gigantism of today's transportation: great flat-topped trucks stacked with hundreds of hay-bales, or sheep in four storeys of cages; ten-ton lorries groaning with gravel or concrete blocks. Now that every boreen has a skin of potholed tarmacadam there is nowhere the brawny trucker will not go, even when the road is visibly wincing beneath him. All over the West the little culverts and bridges are crumbling, hand-built arches squeezed in upon their keystones, parapets cracking and shifting, upper boulders sliding in the rain . . .

It is the time of year for breaking spades, two handles in a week. The first did not surprise me; I had been leaving it out in the rain. The second gave way in prising up a bramble root and the diagonal break showed the crooked grain of the shaft. My fault, Paddy's father would have said, for not checking and picking a better handle from the Co-op rack. In the early years, before he discovered how fallible I was, Michael would use me as an example in chiding the young Paddy: 'Look at that man, how he cares for his tools. He doesn't leave the *sleán* up at the bog or the sledge out on the ditch.' Now he would find me burning broken handles out of their tools as often as anyone.

On the subject of spades, I can easily become passionate and even boring, like any convert with a revelation to share. But if one implement speaks for the difference between Irish and English experience of the soil, it is the average spade in use in Sussex (or any garden-centre suburb of these islands) and the one wielded anywhere in Connacht. In the old racist cartoons it was common to find the short, lumpish, ugly Irishman and the willowy dandy from England: in the matter of spades, however, the picture is quite reversed. The short, heavy, lumpy spade with a straight blade as broad as it is long is the backbreaking kind with which I grew up. It is the sort I brought to Mayo from Dublin, and took to the bog for scrawing turf. There, mercifully, I was introduced to the spade as descended from the loy: a plain handle four feet long, a long, slim blade hollowed like a spoon, widening to the tip and bent, as the trade says, with 'a strong cranked lift'. Light and streamlined, offering instantly to cut, chop, lever, thrust, scoop and flick, it will let you skim off weeds at a stroke and dig without bending your back.

But this is the spade as product of history: almost of evolution and natural selection. Our tiny hillside fields are, in Estyn Evans's words, 'a measure of spadework, just as the wide, prairie wheatlands mirror the multiple plough or the mounded garden plots of an African village are the mark of women's work with the mattock and digging stick'. Through the nineteenth century and the first half of the twentieth, Irish spademills routinely manufactured hundreds of different designs to fit every refinement of use or regional taste. The further west in Ireland, the longer and narrower the blade became. Mine is the Leenane, still made by Darby's and named for the village at the head of the fiord beside me. The steep hillsides above Leenane are quilted with grassed-over lazy-beds which a century and a half of trickling rain have not been enough to erase. The currach is Ireland: also the spade.

A hare beneath my window had the perfection of a young mammal entering its first spring – every wisp of brown fur immaculately separate and sparkling, the breeze stirring the hairs like a close, affectionate breath. Hares do not see well straight ahead, and I hung behind the glass in what seemed to be the one blind spot of those amber, taxidermist's eyes.

The peculiar bevels and bulges which sculpt the head of a hare sweep up to support the twin, twitching columns of its ears. Only at close proximity do you enter the force-field of the animal's ceaseless, neurotic anxiety, the constant radar scan of its fear. Its ears are never still, but swivel their dark tips in infinitesimal and separate adjustments, catching sound like a sail catches wind, every sigh and rustle in that untrustworthy vector of the world directly to the rear.

And next to sound, scent. The hare was eating short, young grass, curling its lip to drag the strands back to be chopped and ground. The split in the upper lip is moist, like a dog's nose, the better to sample data delivered in hints, in airborne parts per million. Yet, in the end, what triggered its absurd sideways spring into flight was nothing more subtle than the exit of a blackbird from the big veronica bush. But what an exit – a rocket at ground zero!

Arrivals: wheatears (Anglo-Saxon 'white arse') on the rocks in the next field; grey wagtails with yellow tummies under the bridge; shelducks, for the green weed at the stepping-stones in the channel; larks on the *duach*. I lie on my back in a hollow rimmed by shivering marram grass, and let the sun lull me and my head fill with lark-music.

APRIL

The clouds have condensed into such purposeful shapes: furry boomerangs and flying saucers whirl around the mountain. They are Arctic clouds, demanding tundra beneath them, and snowy owls. Instead, an uncertain lark ascends and east winds comb the dead grass into silvery waves. East winds in March are welcome, drying the land and putting a skin of parchment on the bog. In April they come trailing hunger and death. Distant figures stoop through the fields with bundles under their coats, and every kitchen has lambs warming up on the plate-rack over the range, pink, pointy tongues trembling in a miasma of medicinal *poitín*. I cross a wall in a hurry and startle a ewe licking the yolk, the bright yellow birth fluid, from the fleece of her lamb. She steps boldly towards me, head up, and I back off, apologising.

It is no weather for sowing anything, and the seedlings from the greenhouse must wait on in cold frames. I find a boiler suit to keep my kidneys warm and take a hoe to the weeds. Most hoeing in the year is wasted effort, the weeds right themselves the moment my back is turned; but this is a wind to curl their roots and crisp their leaves. The hoe is a clever Swiss device with a blade that rocks back and forth, cutting on the push as well as the pull. I spend an hour swishing and clicking over the soil, contented as Thoreau hoeing his bean field. He turned up arrowheads and remembered the Indians. I have turned up little donkey shoes and, once, a tarnished brass buckle from a harness: that seems to have exhausted the archaeology of my acre.

Thoreau worked out that his bean rows, placed end to end, would stretch seven miles. In the springs when I had manure brought up with a tractor from the farm below, it took one hundred and twenty trips with the wheelbarrow to shift the huge pile dumped in front of the house. Adding up rows, or wheelbarrow trips, is a lot of what one does on these occasions. 'I came to love my rows, my beans, though so many more than I wanted,' wrote Thoreau. 'They attached me to the earth and so I got strength like Antaeus.' With the same sort of Antaean infatuation, I grew long ridges of root crops, onions and leeks, and hedge upon hedge of peas. This avalanche of plenty (since sensibly attenuated) doomed Ethna to weeks on her knees between the pea-rows, and endless work at the kitchen sink, hacking away amid wet leaves, mud and slugs.

The early years were not, indeed, much of a bargain for a feminist, and the irony was not lost on either of us. In city life, with two incomes and a daily housekeeper, we would arrive home to find the house gleaming, a fire set in the grate, a casserole in the oven, our small daughter safely gathered in from school. If there were arguments about who should do the shopping, or who had the better right to be tired, these would dissolve in a couple of glasses of wine and the gossip from our separate careers.

Now we had brought our lives together, really together, all day every day, in a half-finished house with gaping ceilings, its few habitable rooms whirling with turf-smoke and grit. The chores were messy and laborious, and multiplied by the ducks, geese, goats or whatever came next in the long line of our affairs with animals. Ethna found herself back in the world of her Cavan grandmother, notwithstanding her insistence on washing machine and freezer. I stepped out the door each morning to a bright new world of pioneering – things to build, plants to grow, earth to move – while her role, inevitably, was largely one of service and supply, and of salvaging some comfort from the deepening litter of improvisation.

She had brought all this upon herself by her energetic habits.

Her instincts are to solve problems, make things happen, spread happiness. I would probably have fantasised indefinitely about an 'alternative' life in the West. It was Ethna, on those long drives back to Dublin, who made its achievement seem straight-forwardly a matter of logistics. We needed a currach? She knew the man to build it. A cultivator? We'd get catalogues – if I were serious. I shall never know how much of my seriousness was borrowed from this sort of momentum. To show what could be done seemed halfway into doing it, of having *decided* to do it.

As planning and stockpiling took hold, we found ourselves leading the second, shadow-life of defectors. It bred a certain light-headedness in me, as I rehearsed all the things I would do when my time became my own. There lay ahead, I felt sure, a great outpouring of creativity. I amassed tubes of oil paint like Gauguin on his way to Tahiti. I bought chisels and gouges for the carving of bog-deal, and various, arcane grits for the polishing of pebbles in a barrel. We were going to be poor for a while; perhaps a long while.

This was actually the least of our worries: although we enjoy material things, we are actually quite good at doing without them. Perhaps I should say the least of *my* worries, since, on the principle that each of us should do what we're best at, Ethna is family manager and looks after the money. She makes the arrangements and writes the cheques. This has gone down rather oddly in the small-farm culture around us, where my luxurious freedom from business dealings and book-keeping must seem deeply suspect. It is years, indeed, since anyone with something to sell has knocked on the door and tried to insist on talking to 'Himself'.

The bog road is a pale zigzag scar below the mountain, an M laid on its side. The upper zag dips to the white rocks of the mountain river, the water of which, for most of the year, has an almost sterile clarity and is raw and cold in the mouth. Only when the contract machines are working above the road, spooning out the fibrous guts of the bog into long parallel lines of chocolate piping, does the rain usher a brown porridge of peat into rivulets, into cascades, into the river – ultimately, into the sea.

In the late 1970s the first tractor-powered sausage-machine was still a temperamental prototype in somebody's back yard and April, after the potatoes were sown, was still a time of orderly and peaceful transhumance to the bog. I misapply the word knowingly: transhumance was (and still is, in Spain and other places) the seasonal movement of livestock to rough up-land grazing: 'booleying' was the Irish word for it and I could take you to stone remains of booley-houses up on the hill where people waited out the short summer nights, beside their cattle, under a thatch of heather.

But if the commencement of turf-cutting was not trans-humance (unless you count the donkeys), there was, in the drift of carts, bicycles, cars and tractors past our gate towards the bog road, a definite sense of exodus, of people changing their habitat. 'If I were at home now,' said Paddy, on my first day of tutelage beside him, 'there'd be a cow across a ditch, or a ewe in a drain or a stake broken, and I'd be called. But when you're on the bog you can't be got and that's that.' On a good spring day, with flooding sunshine and a breeze off the sea, there was the making of some rhapsodic Victorian sermon in the spectacle of dedi-cated energy, the rhythmic dipping and twisting of so many white-shirted figures, the space in the mural for well-composed groups of wives, children, dogs.

Our own bank was the highest on the hill at that time, at the far side of the river, which meant that I could make as many mistakes as I liked and no one would see. My nearest neighbour on the bog, a dark and wiry man, economical of movement as of words, worked as if each dry day might be the last. By June he might have seven trailerloads cut, dry and home, and then go on to cut three or four more; a Lenin hero. What awed and dis-mayed me was his rhythm. He cut so smoothly and rapidly that, almost before one sod had landed, another was flying from his *sleán*. Not once did he look to see where they were falling, yet each thumped down into its allotted space. The top of his bank, by evening, was lined with sods six deep, set out as closely and evenly on the heather-stubble as chocolates on a tray. This capacity of his obsessed me. The secret of his rhythm was clearly not to look and sometimes I would persevere, not looking, for a dozen minutes on end: thrust, swing, thrust, swing, thrust ... the momentum was intoxicating. The results, however, were disastrous, an agglomeration of black wodges to be prised apart. All rhythm gone, I would revert to watching each sod as it flew, cursing as it broke on landing, or smacked into its neighbour. There was a knack, and I did not have it.

Yet somehow I'd get the bank cut, and the two of us would spread and foot and refoot between the summer rains. Sometimes a neighbour would bring her children across to help us and they would move up the bank with small, brisk hands, bobbing and chattering like a flock of starlings. Their productivity made nonsense of our own ponderous stoopings. But the real, Siberian labour lay in carrying out the turf to the road, one fertiliser bagful after another, ton after ton. The way was painfully uneven, over hummocks of peat and boggy bits and then the river bed of loose white rocks. I had learned a small, manual trick of inestimable worth: a pebble twisted into a corner of the bag will give your fist something to lock against; otherwise, its weight will surely drag the slippery plastic, little by little, through your clenched fingers, until the whole lot falls from your back, humiliatingly, just as you are crossing the river. Ethna, who matched me bag for bag but on a smaller, neater scale, seemed able to avoid these crises of the lazy man's load.

Twenty sods (say) to a bag, each sod handled eight times between the *sleán* and the flame: another computation, another mantra for the journeys back and forth. 'If you don't get your turf off the mountain before Bonfire Night, you won't get it off at all.' There came a wet autumn after a wet summer after a wet spring when I found myself up there alone, stacking sods into a rick to get them off the ground. A gloomy morning, grey to bronze to black, the cloud right down on the mountain. A skift of rain sweeps in and I crouch under the rick. It's then that I

notice another lone figure working on the bog, an old bachelor
who rides his donkey like a peasant of La Mancha, sitting back
on its haunches with his boots splayed out. Now, with the
donkey parked at his kesh, he ignores the rain. He has donned a
hessian sack slit down one side to make a steep hood and cape all
in one: it makes a dark and oddly disturbing silhouette. His farm
has half a dozen dry cattle and one moist meadow he mows with
a scythe, all kingcups in spring and then pink stars of ragged
robin. I wonder if he is up here because he has nothing else to
do. Once, coming to work with me on the bog, Ethna was
greeted indulgently by someone beside the road: 'Ye have the
time to spend now!' The words were amiably meant, but they
rankled: 'As if it weren't just as much hard work for us!' Yes,
but we could, at a pinch, choose not to do it. And when time
grew too precious, after all, we stopped doing it.

> It's a warm wind, the west wind, full of birds' cries;
> I never hear the west wind but tears are in my eyes
> For it comes from the west lands, the old brown hills,
> And April's in the west wind, and daffodils.

If I borrow Masefield from my Sussex adolescence, it's because I
need that special tug of sentiment, belonging to long, solitary
cycle rides beyond the scarp of the South Downs. No Irish poet
seems to offer anything quite so potent – this in the land of
warm west winds. In Connacht, it is true, the seasons merge
with each other and borrow from each other, so that only the
calendar keeps track, say, of autumn's reluctant passage into
winter. But spring, in most years, does actually arrive from one
day to the next: an isotherm of human uplift confirming the
sway of willow-buds above the stream and the bobbing of
wheatears on the rocks. Within a week there is new grass strip-
ing the hill in the subtle furrows of the lazy-beds and sprouting
thick as a rug on the ungrazed banks of the acre. Our maze of
fuchsia hedges moves at once to close the paths, stroking my

shoulders with soft pink shoots. In the clearings where I grow
the vegetables, yeasty, fungal smells seep up from worm-tunnels
and the blackcurrant thickets give out startling wafts of perfume
(like passing the hairdresser's door in the village).

The blackcurrant's leaves are of the same crisp green as the
hawthorn's and unfurl in the same way, like paper fans. All
winter, the boundary hawthorn is a tangle of old black bones;
then suddenly this mist of singing colour creeps over all. The
lambs and their mothers in the field beyond become half-sensed
swirls and dashes of white fleece, a retinal flicker to go with the
constant, fretful bleating between the ewes and their young. A
few days of working in such close attendance on the crèche is
enough to get me edgy and muttering over my spade.

April brings the garden's 'hungry gap', its surge of growth be-
lying what we can actually gather and bring in to eat. The
Brussels sprouts have long gone, like the last of the winter
savoys; spring cabbages, if the slugs have spared them, will not
heart until May. For greenstuff we are left with gritty leeks and
shoots of various sorts: white and purple flower-buds of sprouting broccoli, and – this our special pride – blanched shoots of
seakale, springing powerfully in the dark beneath their upturned
buckets.

Crambe maritima is a wild plant, a perennial that grows, in the
words of John Gerard, herbalist to James I of England, on 'the
bayches and brimmes of the sea, where there is no earth to be
seene, but sande and rowling pebble-stones'. For centuries it
fed the shore-dwellers of my native Sussex: as the shoots
appeared in late winter on the windy shingle-bars beside the
Channel, they heaped stones and sand over the plants to make
them grow without their later, blue-green bitterness. In Ireland
the same harvest eventually made a rarity of 'strand cabbage'
and today it survives only on a few remote beaches: a low but
robust and sculptural plant with coarsely curly leaves and big
brooches of white flowers.

The idea of seakale appealed to me powerfully: a native

vegetable, squirrelled away into the spacious, walled gardens of Irish Big Houses and then almost lost to popular taste – this despite lyrical descriptions of its succulence and flavour. I had never seen it or eaten it, and despaired of tracking down the thongs, or root-cuttings, from which it might be grown. An exploratory, most unethical hint in my column brought parcels of soggy newspaper from discriminating gardeners nationwide, and in them were wrapped enough lengths of root to start a whole seakale plantation. Two further winters had to pass before the first harvest – but then, such affirmation, such lemony, buttery bliss! Delicious things are often insubstantial, but seakale comes in juicy, gluttonous chunks. We enjoy serving it to friends and watching them discover a new pleasure.

As a plant of northern coasts, seakale is a vegetable special to these islands, one of the few we did not borrow from the Greeks or Romans. There is also a native wild asparagus, a creeping, wispy plant now being trampled to extinction in its last niches in Irish sand dunes. But what follows seakale in our frugal spring diet (and in similarly liberal amounts) is the cultivated vegetable of posh restaurant menus and packet soup. If any of our doings were to speak for the state of enchantment in which we arrived at this shore, it would be The Great Asparagus Plan.

When the acre was cleared of that first, inordinate crop of potatoes, the expanse of bare soil was daunting. What was need-ed, I thought, was a permanent crop to fill half of it: something up-market and readily saleable, not subject to gluts but, at a pinch, worth freezing. Something that would go on for years without blights or pests – that would, so to speak, look after it-self. Something, perhaps, that liked salt in the air. Asparagus seemed just unlikely enough to be the answer. Ethna unearthed what seemed a significant fact from one of her tea-chests of sta-tistics: only eleven acres of asparagus were grown in all of Ire-land.

She also had a chat with the Agricultural Institute, where a wise woman advised sowing seed, not buying costly asparagus crowns. We would have to wait four years before cutting a single spear, but at least the plants that survived that long would be inured to life in Thallabawn. On a calculation which seems, now, to have been somewhat adrift, I ordered a kilo of seed from Britain.

One kilo was a great deal to be meted out into the ground between thumb and forefinger. A 'first instalment' (also, as it turned out, the last) produced perhaps two thousand seedlings, quickly devastated by slugs or smothered by weeds, this despite days on our knees, squinting after plants no bigger than bodkins. Enough survived, eventually, to furnish the fifty or so plants that feed us now. The shoots in spring are fiercely phallic, and later, when we have cut our share, they erupt into an impressive, feathery thicket, eight feet tall. I have tried to imagine the surreal appearance of half an acre of these ferns, and how I would ever have kept them upright in a storm.

Sometimes in spring, frowning over the wall-planner on which I keep track of sowings and transplantings, I have fantasised about a garden planted closely with edible perennials which, like seakale and asparagus, would grow year after year all by themselves. An acre should be ample for this ingenious Eden. Season by season, it would offer shoots and tubers, leaves and bulbs, berries and nuts, all flourishing naturally and gracefully together and quite crowding out the weeds: thickets of cardoons and Good King Henry, canebrakes of Jerusalem artichokes, clumps of salsify, ramsons, tree-onions! The ecologist in me lights up at the idea; the peasant wants his cabbage and potatoes.

What my neighbours mean by 'fern' is bracken, which in spring lifts a host of clenched fists from last year's rusty litter. Its roots are like telephone cables, black-skinned with tough white cores, and they ramify at a ruthless pace, so that one plant can choke a whole field. 'Horses which eat a few mouthfuls,' warned Anthony Huxley in *Plant and Planet*, 'have their Vitamin B destroyed and rapidly die.' When Michele's pony grazed the field next door, this sent me out in a panic, with the scythe, to

mow down bracken fiddleheads on the ditch before Báinín
could eat any more. In later springs he was left to take his
chances.

The archetype of ferny precision and grace is surely the common male fern, unfolding in a crown of fronds, each plant dis-
tinct and statuesque. There is one that I watch for beside a little
bridge on the road to the post office. The lifting and unwinding
of its crozier heads is part of spring's arrival (like the sudden,
lemony flash of wagtails under the bridge).

Early last century, the beautiful forms and soft colours of the
ferns enchanted the Victorian middle classes, who raided the
countryside by train to trowel up ferns for their conservatories.
Great cartloads were carried to the cities, for sale. Wales lost
much of its royal fern, *Osmunda regalis*, and Ireland a lot of its
Killarney fern, which grows in crevices near waterfalls.
Remembering this, I have tried to restrain my own thefts from
the wild: a single clump of *Osmunda* from a boggy stream to cast
reflections on the frogs' pond; one mossy twig with a frilly
polypody fern, kept living and growing for years in a damp
pot on the dinner table. At the foot of Mweelrea, water gushes
off the mountain through a deep ravine, where oak and aspen,
birch and holly lean above the spray. Branches crack and fall to
make bridges and here, rooting in moss on the bark, polypody
ferns weave aerial gardens. They enjoy, in all essentials, the conditions of a temperate rainforest.

The pond in April is a scene of leisurely predation, as great diving beetles the size of your thumb nuzzle at the tadpoles
thronged around the edge. Some aquatic insects I must have in-
stalled myself, in lumps of plant-life carried from the lake to
carpet the bare plastic. Later, as the pond began to breathe for
itself, the great beetles, *Dytiscus*, sought it out, as did the frogs
and dragonflies.

Something else, too, glimmering yellow in the depths beneath the water-lily pads. I had not seen a newt since childhood.
They have a gravitas, a suggestion of a past and thus a purpose,

of the sort frogs seem to lack: you can, on your knees, look a
newt in the eye. The creature is not, of course, yellow, except
for the belly of the male in spring. He then has another
singularity, sometimes cited, apparently, in scientific debate on
'decision-making strategies' in animals. The fertilising of the
female's eggs must be carried out on the bed of the pond. But
the male must keep coming up to the surface to breathe and the
female may have gone by the time he gets down again. Thus, at
some point, he must choose between breathing and ejaculating
(the dilemma, I suspect, has tormenting reality only in the minds
of young male biologists).

There is another, much richer, mystery about newts.

In many parts of Ireland it has the name 'mankeeper': this was
so, for example, in the Cavan valley of Ethna's childhood. I
wanted to know why, and slipped the question into my
column. The answers, trickling in by letter over several weeks,
led me into a maze of folklore and linguistic subtlety, a wholly
other culture of relationships with nature. 'Mankeeper', yes, but
also mancreeper, manleaper, manlepper, darklooker (this from
earc luachra, the 'creature of the rushes'). The names were fitted
interchangeably to either newt or common lizard (the one an
amphibian, the other quite averse to water), most rural people
taking them to be the same animal.

But there was also a significant geographical range. 'Mankeeper' belonged to the Scots-Irish culture of Ulster and it could
be traced even further to its home ground across the Mull of
Kintyre. In Dumfries and Roxburgh, for example, as recorded
in 1824, the newt as 'mankeeper' was credited with keeping a
watch for adders and warning man of their presence (a role
surely more appropriate to lizards in the adder's heathy terrain).
In Ulster, too, the 'mankeeper' could be a meritorious lizard.
One was incorporated into the crest of the O'Hanlon family
after Redmond O'Hanlon, on the run from the redcoats, was
woken by a lizard from an untimely nap on the slopes of Slieve
Gullion (it bit him on the neck just in time, et cetera).

So much for the mankeeper as a force for good, a token of

luck. A more potent and widespread rural belief is the sinister tale in which 'mankeeper' sometimes becomes 'manleaper' (or, further south, 'manlepper') and in which the protagonist is unmistakeably a newt.

A Cavan neighbour of Ethna's, the writer Tom MacIntyre, preserved the classic form of the tale in his short story 'The Man-keeper'. A man falls asleep near a stream and a newt jumps down his throat. Ensconced in his belly, it eats his food, hatches a brood of young, and slowly wastes him with starvation. When at last his affliction is diagnosed, he is persuaded to eat a big meal, and to lie on the stream-bank with his mouth open. In most ver-sions, the meal is of salty bacon, to make the newts thirsty. Tom MacIntyre prefers corned beef, but the outcome is the same: 'In a few minutes, he experienced a repeat of the stirrings, first the backwards and the forwards, then making headway, up into the mouth, out to the tip of the tongue, sliding back, no move at all, forward again, and plop again into the water. It was a pro-cession after that, a dozen in all.'

Stories like this crowd the national folklore archive in University College Dublin, a million or more pages, many handwritten and in Irish, bound into ledgers with polished leather spines. Whole careers have been built on collecting and deconstructing them, sometimes with Freud or Jung at hand. One senses, in Tom MacIntyre's treatment, the second, mythic language in which these stories speak and in which they travelled between the tribes of Europe.

There is more about the newt, if you can bear it.

In the watery midlands near Athlone, Jim Delaney, a folklore collector of solemn repute (we drank his whiskey together and talked of fairies), knew a man in the 1980s called Patsy who had 'the cure of the burn'. That is, you would take your burn to him and he would lick it and that would be that. To gain the power of the cure, he had licked the mankeeper's belly, being dared to do so by some neighbours when they were hanging around on a bridge. To tune in to what's at work here, a brand of sympa-thetic magic, it would help to think of salamanders, the fireproof lizards of mythology, and the bright yellow flame of the male newt's belly, flickering beneath the cool water.

We, too, have believed in magic – in something we learned to call The Flow. We borrowed the term from Patrick Rivers's book, *Living on a Little Land*, and he took it from a friend who had lived in a commune. Chief among the commune's worries was a recurring lack of money, yet again and again, just when the kitty was all but empty, something would turn up: an offer of work, a gift, a debt cancelled, a chance of barter. Long before we knew what to call it, we came to recognise, even to trust in, the inexplicable serendipity that would pay for the winter's hay for the pony or an extra load of turf. I might sell a painting to someone who walked in off the road or get a cheque of 'silly money' for a couple of thousand words in a far-off glossy magazine. Once (just once), there was a bank error that turned out in our favour.

Anybody might be pleased about such things. The Flow demands a broader act of faith: to live *as if* this is the way it will turn out. Ethna took to it quite readily, finding in it, I think, a reasonable reward for all her good management, a bonus for effort. But how did I, a natural worrier who had never added a cubit to his stature, ever come to feel that tomorrow might be trusted to look after itself? The extremely low income on which we lived in the first ten years or so at Thallabawn was a matter of deliberate choice – even recklessness, since it had no margin for insurance payments or pension plans. For a number of years, the computer of the Revenue Commissioners pursued us in red ink, frankly incredulous of our changed circumstances. ('Wherever a man goes,' wrote Thoreau, 'men will pursue and paw him with their dirty institutions.') It ought to have terrified me, but oddly did not. When you own the house you live in, and have enough land on which to grow food, what can they do to you, really?

The sun in genial humour peeping through the open door, gives to the long-imprisoned inmates assurance of kindlier

conditions without; and the bee-man, watching for signs of
survival, delights to see first one, and then another, and
presently many of his little pets appear upon the alighting
board . . . They move about the entrance; examine the doors
and porch; meet and salute each other; and rising fly for a
moment in front of the hive. A gladsome hour this for the
bee-man also; an infectious happiness.

Thus the Reverend Joseph Digges, rector of Mohill, celebrating
a rite of spring amid the willows of County Leitrim. His *Practical
Bee Guide*, in the edition of 1932 , is covered in a piece of bright
floral cotton, stitched by Mai McManus, Ethna's mother, as the
book began to fall apart from use. Mai was a great manager of
bees, as of poultry. How, given the chance, could her daughter
not pick up the smoker, as it were, and follow on?

We brought the first two hives from Dublin, full of bees and
heavy with honey, lids tied down with well-knotted cord,
sticky tape over the porches. They were to travel by train, but
we missed it, and had to set off through the night with the hives
in a trailer behind the car. We drove at thirty miles per hour
across Ireland, tensing at every bump, and pursued by a thinning
straggle of bees whose dilatory homecoming had made us late in
the first place. We arrived at Thallabawn at 3.30 a.m., settled the
hives on blocks beside the stream, and left them fizzing gently in
the dark.

Honey, like asparagus, was meant to be part of our economy.
We came well-equipped, as we did for everything: bee-veil,
copper smoker and hive-tool, sheets of wax in tissue paper, little
panel pins for nailing frames together; the big shiny drum for
spinning the honey out of the combs. I loved the smell of bees-
wax, and of the clean new cedarwood sections, so beautifully
dovetailed, for all the hives to come.

I admired the bees tremendously, and revelled in their skills
and social organisation. We moved their hives rather often, it
seemed (to escape a flood, or the goats, or the aggravating smell
of the pony), and each time the bees had to take a new fix and
realign their navigation systems. I knew about, even if I never

saw, the famous 'waggle' dance by which they tell each other how to find the most marvellous little pollen shop that's just opened down the boreen. I savoured the mystical twists of folklore, such as making sure to tell the bees when somebody is dying or getting married.

But all this admiration and interest led me no further. Summoned, in an emergency, to step forward and hold something, I was too heavily glazed with apprehension and stoicism to be open to any sort of trust. Puffing smoke at the bees to frighten them into filling themselves with honey ('Quick! A forest fire!') seemed to me a dubious basis for a relationship. But in these deliberate, slow-moving rituals at the hives, I never was, in fact, stung. There were moments, indeed, in helping Ethna to capture a swarm and coax it into new quarters, when I came quite close to hoping that my fear had gone away, that I could achieve a proper rapport with the glistening mass of insects. But this was because, at swarming-time, as well I knew, they are too raptly obsessed with concern for their queen to think of stinging at all.

Swarming-time came each June or July, when a hive, overcrowded with workers, allowed a second queen to develop and depart, supported by a work force sufficient to found a new colony. This was our chance to fill another hive, and Ethna was alert for the quickening tempo of coming and going which suggested that a swarm might be afoot. Just as often, we were taken by surprise. A deep, thrumming sound from The Hollow, more vibration than sound, would draw our attention, and then the air above the deep shadow of the stream would be clouded with a thousand dancing points of light. I hand the commentary over to Mr Digges:

A vast multitude it is, rushing hither and thither, with a great noise of humming, until the queen has joined them from the hive and has alighted upon some neighbouring tree. Then they gather round her – in very numbers assuring her timid heart, unaccustomed to rough exposure – and form a cluster with the faithful mother, so still that any passing traveller may hardly notice them. Now let the watchful owner hive them without delay, and set them to work in a new home, or they will rise and, following their scouts sent out before to find a dwelling, will settle in some distant tree or chimney, or will invade the ruined tower upon the neighbouring hill, and so be lost to useful purposes.

Once, trying to follow a 'risen' swarm, Ethna ended up high on the hill, where she met a farmer neighbour and explained what she was doing. He seemed taken aback. 'Do you not have them tamed?' he asked.

At the height of this multiplication, we had five hives. On a fine day in May we could open the door, and smell the honey-flow and find the bees flicking away over the hedge to five distant sources of nectar. But there was rarely much honey to spare. For all the wildflowers of the hillside, and those we added to the garden, it was not, after all, a kindly landscape for bees. The wind blew too strongly on too many days, and the air in the shelter of The Hollow grew too humid in winter. We lost our first colonies to disease, and, replacing them locally, found ourselves host to black bees of uncertain temper. They seemed annoyed by my choice of programmes on the transistor I took down the garden and would seek me out and sting me on the scalp. More importantly, they took to stinging Ethna, and she developed an allergy that only numbing doses of antihistamine could handle. Regretfully, she hung up her smoker and closed the book on Mr Digges and thus, alas, upon one remembrance of her mother.

MAY

Just over the hill, where the road swings north, there is a lofty view across the sea to Clare Island; even, on a clear day, to the Bills Rocks eight miles beyond. When the Atlantic swell is heavy I sometimes pause at the bend, one foot on the ditch, to savour the great collisions of wave and rock. The slow, gleaming pulses that engulf the distant Bills are all the more awesome to me for knowing the true height of those rocks and the way the waves boom and slap in the echoing shadows between them. Once, in an adventure with an ornithological friend, I spent a night on the Bills, netting storm petrels at their burrows a hundred feet above the water. A big swell could have held us there for days.

Inshore of Clare Island the sea is scarcely creased by a wave, but as the swell nears the shore at Barnabaun Point it grounds upon a hidden reef and heaps up over it, spilling into sudden, tumbling chevrons of foam. Between these two eruptions, near and far, the whole inner commotion of the sea is betrayed.

I try to imagine the hidden landscape of our corner of the Atlantic: its sandy slopes and plains, its bluffs and gullies and groves of waving kelp. An old admiralty chart we keep on the wall shows the soundings made with lead and line in 1848 and from this scattering of fathoms I can trace the contours of the sea bed as it rises to the glacial sill of Killary harbour. I furnish these depths with images from television, or from my own braver years with mask and snorkel. But for other, larger, illuminations about the undersea I turn to a trilogy of books that Rachel

Carson wrote. Her name belongs famously to *Silent Spring*, her 1960s book about the perils of insecticides: concern for the environment almost began with it. But before that she was a marine biologist with the United States Fish and Wildlife Service, and a poetic, passionate teacher about the sea. She lived above a rocky shore in Maine, a whole ocean's width from Thallabawn, but her crabs and sea urchins were cousins to our own and her tides were governed from much the same province of the moon. In my favourite glimpse of Ms Carson (never, I think, casually Rachel) she is clambering over weedy boulders at dead of night, with torch and bucket, returning a borrowed starfish to its exact pool among the rocks.

Her books taught me to feel the stirring of springtime in the sea, a revolution which sends winter-chilled water at the surface sliding heavily down, and lifts up warmer, deeper water, full of nourishing sea bed minerals, to replace it: a magical fertilisation worked by the laws of physics. As the sun's angle steepens, a thousand different shapes of microscopic plant are touched to sudden, fierce abundance, a seasonal 'greening' of the sea to match the greening of the soil ashore. Hoeing away at the first new weeds of May, uprooting a hundred two-leaved miniatures at a stroke, I think of all the tiny, glassy animals swimming out there among the islands, amphipods, copepods and the rest, gobbling at the brilliant mist of phytoplankton. As spring passes into summer, they are eaten up in turn by creatures big enough for us to imagine, and name.

When we changed lives all those summers ago, we had large and foolish hopes of the sea as a provider. It seemed logical that, living beside the ocean and seeking self-reliance, we should have some way of catching a lot of fish. Ethna, it must be said, enlisted in the fantasy of the currach at the earliest stage. I have tried to reconstruct our impossible innocence, our elementary neglect of realities; it was not like us.

I suppose it was simply the idea of the currach that seduced, the thought that we now had the right – at least a plausible excuse – to possess such a magical icon. Having a currach is hugely different from not having a currach, vastly more than the matter of its cost. The 'canoe' would join us to the landscape, fit us into the seaboard culture. How we would actually use it, launch and retrieve it, were details to be worked out later. Here at length it rested, black and gleaming on the grass beside the house. Two sets of oars were tucked beneath it, raw as toothpicks.

There are, as we should have considered, almost as many shapes and styles of currach as there are Irish fishing communities. What we had in our intoxicated minds was the light, primitive canoe of sheltered bays, portable on two sets of shoulders (as in certain old picture postcards from Kerry). What we got, from an islandman living 'ashore', was a beautifully crafted currach in the modern Inishturk tradition − deep, wide and robust and lined with an inner shell of lath. It took three strong men to carry it, and my share of the weight was beyond all expectation: my knees wobbled, eyes bulged in the shadow beneath the hull.

Then, where to keep it? The islands have harbours on their lee shores where currachs can ride to a mooring all summer. Ours is a 'weather' shore, facing west. A berth in the dunes would sift sand into the hull, adding further pounds to its weight, and on most days there would be too much surf for launching. A currach needs a cove for going out and coming in, and the best we could find was a half-sheltered corner of rock a long hike away along the shore. There we left it finally, well tied down, and there I went to sit beside it in summer, and to tar it in winter, twice.

It did go to sea a few times, with neighbours beside me at the oars. But we had misread their priorities for fine days. Hay, silage, turf, shearing: this was what you did when the sun shone. The few who really cared about fishing had currachs of their own, and settled habits which did not include a woman in the bow. When one of these men lost his currach, smashed to matchwood in a winter storm, he bought ours.

In my early teens in Brighton I was given a canoe (the sort with pointed ends) by someone moving house. It was a big, old-fashioned craft of wood and canvas, painted white and grossly heavy. Its journey to the beach on an old pram chassis was so erratic and noisy that people turned to stare. Then, I had to drag it a long way over the stones and launch it unaided and try to get into it with the paddle before the next wave turned it over. I was not yet a very good swimmer, or particularly brave. There were beaches without many people, which seemed too lonely and rough, and beaches with families where little children crowded the shallows. I needed a friend of my own age – we could have taken turns – but I seem not to have had one, or never one who could come to the beach when I wanted to go. The canoe remained for years on the roof of the shed below my window, where, in due course, it offered metaphor to poems of adolescent melancholy. In the story of the currach, my black canoe, there may be some further intimation about things abandoned, upside down.

Before the sun rises from the ridge above Six Noggins, it reaches through gaps in the mountains to light up the islands, one by one. Then, the very rim of the shore takes fire and the long strand slowly incandesces from purple to hot pink to creamy gold. Admiring all this from the carrot patch one morning, where I was weeding and contemplating by turns, the impulse suddenly took hold: I would go for a dip before breakfast.

Tucked away in the prospectus of our new existence was an image of myself as early-morning swimmer. In Dublin it would not have occurred to me to join the hearty walruses hauled out at the Forty Foot. Here at the Atlantic, however, where one could swim as solitary as a grey seal, my youthful affair with the sea might be taken up again. Our first few years did not encourage it. Fine days came one at a time; there was no spell of warmth to let the impulse germinate. But now, at half-past six on a quiet May morning, the will was there, if flickering somewhat in the cool breeze from the mountain. Rather than risk irresolution by walking to the strand, I took the bicycle from the shed and rattled off down the boreen, shocking awake the drowsing black cattle and sending the spring lambs running through the fields. The sun at this moment cleared the ridge like an arc lamp and my shadow leaped ahead between blackthorn blossom and yellow flags. At the farm beside the strand the breeze was soughing in the sycamores. I braked for second thoughts, then rattled on again.

The strand itself is enough to inspire stage fright in a swimmer: all that sand to cross to reach the sea. To stand at the water's edge, a tiny figure, and strip off there, was to become part Roman gladiator, part dreamer in one's undervest. But in this intimate golden light, hills rising silent behind me, the edge of the sea was the most private place in the world. There was no swell, and thus no breakers; just the regular lift and froth of quiet waves. It was not an occasion for a wild whoop and a charge, nor for loitering and wincing, but for steady, stoical advance. There is a branch of yoga which holds that the seat of a person's strength and spirit lies just above their stomach; the Atlantic in May reaches in with icy fingers to discover it. After no great time I retreated, and ran around to dry in a wind that was suddenly warm and lively.

'Tell them about the spillet,' says Ethna, 'or they'll think we're never at the sea together.' Indeed, I was coming to that.

The spillet was a present from Gustin, who did his best, God knows, to make honest fisherfolk of us. His house on Inishbofin looks down on an empty harbour of dazzling white sand, still haunted by the history of herring; all gone, long before his time. But the tradition is there, still, in Gustin's sea-sense, in his awesome range of skills. It amuses him occasionally, in between his electricals or lathe-work or boat-building, to reach back into the old life and make something useful as a gift for us.

The spillet started out as a long-line for the currach, one hundred yards of it with a plaice-hook on a swivel at every fathom. It was to be baited, coiled in a wooden tray, and slipped out over the stern. When the canoe departed our dreams, it made sense to try the line from the shore, in the manner of poor people who catch their fish discreetly and by night.

At low tide the prow of an old wreck projects from the strand at an angle, like the gnomon of a sundial or a distant figure leaning on the wind. When we started with the spillet, there were rows of black ribs curving up behind the prow, dowelled with wooden pegs and flying little banners of seaweed, but big storms and scavenging tractors have just about torn the wreck apart. Looking down from the hill, it has been our measure of where the tide is, and when the prow has finally vanished, with its carved marks of lading in Roman numerals, we shall be left with mere printed figures in the tide-tables.

Imagine, then, the strand at evening, the sea withdrawn beyond the wreck to a distant, aimless churning. Two tiny figures, vaguely burdened, splash through the channel at the end of the boreen and head out half a mile across the sand. With wreck as compass, they trudge the shortest line, crunching through cowries and scallop-shards, to where the channel, curving like a racetrack, seethes into the waves. It was always my theory that fish would be drawn to this mingling of waters for drowned worms or whatever else the river brought down, but really the little estuary was more of a destination, some hopeful place to aim for on the anonymous edge of the sea.

The bag across my shoulder held two small dinghy anchors, each tied to a rope and a buoy. In Ethna's bucket was the coiled line, its fifty sharp hooks tucked into holes at the rim. In what became a practised routine, we stretched the line out on the sand a few yards from the tide's edge and baited the hooks with strips of mackerel. Seagulls gathered above us, screaming, sometimes diving at the baited hooks. Ethna would run and wave her arms, a fishwife shouting back at the birds.

At first, before the gulls worked out what we were up to, we simply left the baited line to be covered by the rising tide. But then the birds would dive for the mackerel, hook themselves and drown, each sad wreath of feathers lifting the line from the sea bed as the tide rose. To sink the hooks beyond the reach of the birds, I had to wade out beyond the third wave and plunge each anchor down into the sand with the line stretched taut between them. Then we could retire with easy minds and let the sea creep up, erasing our last hundred paces.

Twelve hours pass between one low tide and the next – time enough for the glass to drop and a weather front to move in. We would set the line on a golden evening, then wake at dawn to fretful wind and rain. Like miners or mill-workers, we had to clatter down the boreen anyway, and trudge out across the grey sand with our sacks to be there at the appointed time. Sometimes, when atmospheric pressure was playing tricks with sea level, I had to strip off and swim to reach the buoys and heave the anchors up in something of a panic as the tide began to turn. And then, since there are no short cuts in dealing with a spillet, we might be on our knees for an hour, rain trickling down our necks, sand blowing over the fish and blunting the knives.

Rather, choose one of the good mornings, the buoys shining bright orange on a sea of pale blue silk. Great weight on the line and then, hauling on it gently, the curl and splash of ray wings at one hook after another. We nursed them in like kites and beached them softly: a dozen, perhaps two dozen, strung out along the sand. Here and there a dogfish, tying knots with a rasp of sandpaper skin. As a bonus, a turbot; even, once, a cod.

Thornback and dogfish were our staple catch. So different to look at, yet both of them sharks of a sort, 'elasmobranchs' with cartilage for bones. The ray is darkly marbled, like linoleum. Its tail is a jagged whip, a scourge, and more thorns stud its leathery skin. Intelligent, crocodile eyes on the upper side, hooded in twin cowls. Beneath, in white skin pressed to the sand, an epicene mouth with chitinous lips and the grip of a teething baby. The rays we caught might be two feet across; those we lost took the hook with them, unguessably huge. You kill with a stab between the eyes, carve out the wings – the 'rosy wedges' of Jane Grigson's fishmonger's slab – and leave the rest for the gulls. Our record was forty-five pounds of wings, a serious contribution to the freezer.

It was, of course, butchery (the mutilated rays like a litter of

bloody violins). We steeled ourselves to it as we steeled ourselves
to treacherous weather and rough seas, the line broken, hooks in
a nightmare tangle or buried in a drift of seaweed. It needed a
pitch of commitment week by week, a life ruled by tide-tables.
A row of bad summers was enough to feed the habit of excuses
(the bucket with the line still hangs ready in the shed, hooks
rusting). But we did, indeed, go to the sea together: a bonding,
even an adventure.

At the far end of the strand, where the otters run up to the lakes,
a bald outcrop of rock projects from the dunes: a rounded,
weathered bluff that invites you to stand on the top and gaze
out to sea. Up to a few weeks ago, the cracks in this rock were
lined with snails, scores and scores of the garden snail, *Helix
aspersa*, looking unlike themselves because the sandblasting of
the shells had abraded their mottled pattern. Instead of brownish
and glossy, they were bluish and matt: to restore them, you lick
them, like pebbles. In this totally exposed position beside the
ocean they were hibernating, indifferent to the assault of storms
and the hiss and rattle of the sand-grains on their shells.

But early this month came a mild, soft day, muffling even the
song of the larks in the low cloud over the dunes. When Ethna
came back from her daily walk, she was spangled with moisture,
like the fleece of a sheep. 'The snails are on the march!' she
announced. 'They're copulating everywhere – you have to see
it!' Down on the strand I found her footprints and followed
them into the dunes, where mossy paths of sheep and otters
wind among the marram grass.

The first snails I met were the colourful, banded sort, *Cepaea
nemoralis*. They travelled singly, with slow purpose, past buds of
yellow coltsfoot thrusting up like phallic totems from the sand.
Then I came to a pair of garden snails, circling each other in
courtship on a carpet of silvery mucus. And then to another pair,
entwined in unimaginable passion. These snails are hermaphro-
dite, with both penis and vagina, but still they need to couple
reciprocally, first discharging chalky 'love darts' to stimulate

each other's ardour. As I neared the outcrop, the mating snails were more and more frequent, until I had to pick my steps to avoid crushing them. The ground below the rock was a scene of unbridled conjugation, to the point of occasional threesomes, while, on the face of the bluff itself, dozens more snails were hastening downwards, their eyes out on stalks.

For all that we call it the garden snail, *Helix aspersa* really prefers a sunny, open place and sandy or limy soil. That is why, in the west of Ireland, you find it more commonly on the islands, or along the shore, than in the boggy and acid terrain of the interior. In the dunes, the snails build their shells from the lime in the sand, which in turn consists of fragments of seashells – sea molluscs, just as snails are land molluscs. This recycling of the very substance of their kind (a high point, surely, of Gaian economy) is echoed at an even further remove amid the limestone rocks of the Burren, in County Clare. Here, seventy kinds of snail make use of calcium laid down in the shells of their marine ancestors 340 million years ago.

The snail is born with its shell, emerging from one of a clutch of little pearly eggs laid in some moist crevice, and enlarges it by adding lime to the leading edge. The spiral is arrested, and finished with a lip, when the snail feels itself to be fully grown. Whatever the variations of pattern and colour between the species, the shell nearly always coils the same way, to the right. Biologists get a little flutter of the heart when they find a left-handed, or sinistral specimen of a normally dextral species. In the 1920s a Professor Boycott and a Captain Diver made an expedition to Bundoran, in County Donegal, to hunt for sinistral specimens of *C. nemoralis*. They hoped for a pair to breed from – to see, I suppose, how many of the offspring would inherit the left-hand turn.

What encouraged them was that so many of the left-handed *C. nemoralis* specimens in British and Irish museums had come from Bundoran, where 'old peasant women' collected empty shells by the thousand to make necklaces to sell to visitors for twopence. Professor Boycott and Captain Diver (who, my imagination insists, were an angular pair in hairy tweed jackets) inspected prodigious numbers of shells, which were sifted from the marram-stalks by winter storms and bowled together in heaps in the blow-outs. They went through eight thousand of them and the six thousand and twenty-first was a left-hander: the only one. Then they found a sinistral *C. nemoralis* alive at the roadside near Ballyshannon, but whether they crossed it with a right-handed partner and what the outcome was, I cannot tell you.

It has been good growing weather, humid and luminous, the sun breaking through to light a hill, an island, a patch of sea, or to mark out sudden lines of seedlings in the vegetable beds. For once I have no complaints about germination. Whole lines of peas have appeared on cue, yard after yard of immaculate shoots. The first dark rosettes of potatoes are pinned three abreast to their ridges; carrots, kohlrabi, Swiss chard, beetroot, salsify – row after row of seedlings gratify my appetite for order. May is not often so constant or so kind.

When I look at a climatological map of Ireland I am fascinated to see how precisely its curving isotherms of temperature, its contours of rainfall, are wrapped around our hillside. In a 'normal' year (as judged by that statistical chimera, the median) our grass starts growing on 1 March, just as it does on the sunny coast of Wexford. Our rainfall is no greater, in general, than in the leafy lanes below the Wicklows. The line on the map may, indeed, be unfair to us by the thickness of a nib, since it counts our townland in with the higher and rainier slopes of the hills. I can vouch that Mweelrea's showers cease, give or take a drop or two, at the gable of the old schoolhouse where the road turns up to the bog. And that's to say nothing of the extraordinary way in which huge clouds, trailing showers across the sea towards us, are pulled to one side and sucked up the Killary, as if the fiord exerted some powerful inward draught. When the sun is freshly risen over Mweelrea, these full-rigged galleons of clouds nourish the most vivid rainbows over the islands: an ominous sign, of course – one to be matched to the echo of surf from the channel's mouth, or the curlew calling three times as she flies up to the bog.

No one whose livelihood and wellbeing is not wrapped up in weather can appreciate the undercurrents which infect country life in a really bad year (or rather, the second bad year, for the first, however dismal and extreme, drifts by in a constant expectation of change).

There were two years like that in the middle 1980s. They are recalled for me now when the first peacock butterflies come out of hibernation and dash dramatically about between the hedges. Peacocks and tortoiseshells were extinguished from the acre by the chilling, sodden glooms of '85 and '86, and it was years before I could reinstate them, hatching them out of chrysalises gathered from Wicklow nettles by a friend.

People, too, were extinguished by the summer of 1985. 'He turned his hay for the twenty-seventh time, went indoors and hung himself.' The story, from somewhere inland, arrested conversation with its eerie exactitude. Here on the coast it needed a farmer's eye to pick out the uncut, falling meadows, a farmer's step to feel the impossible softness of the soil. Meadows were abandoned in the middle of their saving: a dozen hand-cocks sagging in the rain and the rest in swathes of rotting hay. As for the bog, it waited for Bergman, sepia and black beneath a ragged drift of cloud. The banks were as the people left them, covered with turf still in footings, turf as it was thrown from the *sleán*, the moorgrass growing up around it. Even machine-cut turf was abandoned, melting where it lay. As winter closed in, the unfamiliar smell of coal-smoke drifted on the wind.

The West's cattle survived in those years on hay bought from the midlands. In the second miserable May, all silage gone, the growth of grass postponed, the big hay lorry made endless sorties down the hill, its horn blaring at cattle turned out to the verges. While we, on our trivial acre, tried to coax seeds to grow under cloches improvised from plastic and sheep-wire, our neighbours were buying hay at their gates – twenty bales, then twenty more, and so on each week into June. The first tourists found a fresh greenness in the fields and a brilliant flush of buttercups: they were looking at silage meadows, grazed in desperation and mortgaging the growth of summer.

In '87, when spring arrived on schedule, the lift in morale was shared like a conspiracy. 'We're going around kicking *tortógs*,' said a man in Kinnadoohey ('a tuft or clump,' says Dinneen, as of sedge or heather).

The swing of a scythe must follow the curve of the earth. Imagine the land raised, ever so slightly, there in front of your feet, as if you stood on a great grapefruit and were shaving it. By this sleight-of-fancy the scythe miraculously finds its arc and angle, its sector of a circle embracing earth and man. The blade leaves down its parcel of grass, neatly at the left, retraces the arc as if on a spring, muscles unwinding with the steel. Slide a foot forward, slyly, and the blade surprises another swathe of grass, content with an advance of inexorable inches. When you've got the rhythm, the trick is to stop for nothing, not your name, nor distant gunfire, nor even, if it must be, for the dog's tail.

I have mowed rushes and thistles, barley and rye, serving a solitary apprenticeship to this deceptive implement. No – that's to deprecate the tool, when it's the eye that insists on pulling and chopping and hacking. The secret of the scythe is in slicing. If only you paused to listen to the word, the way it sounds . . . sli–cing . . . the hands might begin to get it right.

Sharpening a scythe is something else again. I have a knife on my belt: a folding knife cased in ebony and brass, a bit of macho. I learned to sharpen it by listening, tilting it on the stone until it whistled at a certain pitch, whistled and whispered (the words again making the right sounds). It is the same with the scythe, the rasp of the sharpening stone softening to a hiss and a whir.

When I first sharpened a scythe with a neighbour watching (Michael, Paddy's father), he said: 'You do it like that, do you?' – as if the options were infinite. At this courtly hint, I surrendered the stone and watched as he whetted the scythe to a razor's edge with short, soft strokes across the blade, not the coarse flourishes which I had addressed to its length. When, later, I left the stone down on the grass, he picked it up and stuck it in the back pocket of my jeans: 'A wet stone isn't a whetstone!' – smiling as I worked it out. An artificial sharpening stone, slick with rain or dew, slides where it should bite into the steel.

Scythes have changed and I wanted one that fitted me, not the soulless sort, of tubular steel, that everyone buys off the shelf. This was not a whimsical idea. In the days of long-handled, wooden scythes and men with long, strong backs, the fitting and hanging of a scythe was a matter of course: you had to be measured for it, as for a suit. Estyn Evans, in his *Irish Folk Ways*, gives the essence of it:

> The lower handle should be at arm's length from the bottom of the sned, the upper one distant from the top by the length from elbow to fingertips. The two handles should also be a cubit apart. The angle of the blade is determined by swinging the left leg and adjusting the blade until its point comes within a nicely determined distance of it when the sned is held upright against the right leg.

I once had the use of such a scythe, fitted to a man of my own height and frame, and found this such a perfect conspiracy of movement that nothing would do me but the length and balance of a wooden shaft, and a blade to be taught where my left foot was. I found them in Westport, together with the *dúirníns*, the side handles, the last pair left in town. My mistake was to imagine I could put it all together myself, and the sned, that lovely, curving shaft, was quickly shattered by an ill-considered swipe at nettles. I dumped the wreckage in the shed and went back to stooping over tubular steel and the shaving of half a grapefruit.

Barley was the prettiest crop I ever grew, the most pleasurable from start to finish. A patch of twenty square perches was all we had room for, the size of a generous suburban lawn, but it gave

us winter grain for hens and ducks, and a brief taste of skills only
lapsing now in Mayo after something like five thousand years.
The most important skill came in May, in the simple act of sowing. I knew this to be a tricky one: a half-bushel of grain to be
broadcast evenly, and matched in density to what the land
would grow. Michael, who had been sowing odd corners of
fields with oats and barley all his life, was pleased to take the
bucket and show me how. With measured pace and an easy flick
of the fingers, he rained barley into the air like a lawn-sprinkler.
It fell with astonishing regularity – no islands of bare soil, no
clumping of seed, just an even scattering, lengthways and crossways, which left not so much as a hand's breadth of ground un-
sown. I followed on with the rake, burying the seed in the clean,
velvety tilth I had prepared for it.

It sprang up like a coarse grass, then tillered and rose until, in
June, it made the brightest, greenest plot in the landscape. At full
height in July, it took life from the wind, the whole patch moving in waves silvered by the awns, the long whiskers on the ears
of barley. In the early days of ripening, green and gold chased
through the crop like colours in shot silk; I was awed at having
organised anything so beautiful. And then, after mowing it with
the scythe and tying sheaves and stooking it (the two of us
aching and pricked with barley stems and thistles), a sun setting
over the ocean would light a cameo, a miniature harvest scene,
as fetchingly Arcadian as anything painted by Holman Hunt.

I saw, without knowing it, the last journey of the last threshing machine to the last farm along this road that grew any oats
worth threshing: such is the unremarkable way things trundle
and clank to an end. That was late in the seventies. With our
couple of stacks, our three or four bags of grain, we were never
in the threshing league. Before threshing machines there was
scutching, and this is what we did.

Everyone over sixty remembered scutching – usually with a
grin. You cleared and cleaned the kitchen, took the table up to
The Room and hung a sheet across the dresser. Then you dashed
the sheaves hard against a stool, so that the grain flew out. Or

you might clear the barn and sweep it and beat at the sheaves with a flail, a short stick joined to a long one by a leather thong. Two men would flail alternately, in rhythm; it sounded dangerous.

Old Michael, enthused, devised a safer variation outdoors: this even though the whole townland, passing in tractors on the boreen, could see him indulging me. We spread a plastic silage sheet on the grass as an instant threshing floor, stood a kitchen chair in the middle and put a rounded rock on it. Then we stood at opposite sides, each with a sheaf, and took turns at smiting the rock. Three or four whacks would empty the sheaf, each followed by a little shake so that the loosened grains fell from the ears and were not flung back over our shoulders. The barley pattered onto the shiny black plastic, made rivulets along its folds and gathered in golden pools. When we scooped it into hessian bags, the dense weight of the grain was almost sensually delicious.

Rye, too, is a crop of enlivening beauty. I grew it by accident: that is, I sowed it as a 'green manure', to cover the soil in winter as a rich sort of grass; it was then to be dug under in spring before it could leap up. But I missed my cue for the spadework and then, suddenly, it was waving shoulder-high. Visitors came in from the boreen to fondle the whiskery ears and admire the length and sturdiness of stem. What excellent straw for thatching! This, indeed, and stuffing horse-collars, was rye's limited destiny in Ireland – never the use in mixed-grain breads perfected elsewhere in Europe.

We fed the grain to the hens and bedded the pony on the straw, but also found a source of rye flour for experiments. Rye dough is low in gluten and has to be coaxed into rising over a period of days. Even with hands-on advice from a visiting Finnish matriarch, it remained an exacting and uncertain process, soon abandoned for our regular, yeasty wheat loaves. Once, also, we tried malting our barley for beer, but the basinfuls of moistened, swollen grain went mouldy while waiting for the oven.

Ducks will eat barley only when it has been winnowed; otherwise, fragments of the awns stick in their throats as they shovel up the grain. This made more work for Ethna, who had to pour barley from one basin to another, standing at a corner of the house in just the right weight of wind. Ducks, as Praeger said, 'understand their own business so thoroughly and know their own minds so well'. Like him, we formed great admiration for their independence and anarchy, their comic talent.

They lived in The Hollow, where the stream runs in through an arch beneath the road. I built them a shed on the bank – the 'little housheen', as one neighbour called it (it was also to shelter goats, as will emerge). In May, when the ducks' egg production reached its peak, it became important to close them in the shed overnight. But the domestication of ducks is a fragile discipline, effective only in deep-litter stalags. Given a habitat in any way natural and free-ranging, even the most matronly Aylesbury will follow her unofficial instincts.

Thus, as the evenings drew out, the drake would lead his harem on long expeditions, under the bridge and up the hill, with detours round the waterfalls; or downstream into the dark, tangled canyon beneath the willows. They might or might not return by sunset, and their numbers dwindled, one by one, as they made secret nests in the brambles and meadowsweet. Once, roused at midnight by an anguished quacking from The Hollow, Ethna found a duck running up and down in a fugue of dismay and a hedgehog with nose deep in its nest of seven eggs. She lifted him out with the turf-tongs and imprisoned him overnight.

In the early days, when raising and killing our own meat seemed a logical consequence of any oath of self-reliance, we followed the book's instructions in rearing a dozen ducklings for the freezer. They were to be killed at ten weeks old, at the optimal point for conversion of barley and boiled potatoes into duck-meat. The young birds ate and grew at a prodigious rate, tilting a bright eye to greet us every morning. It seemed a pity not to let them continue. Eventually, in the fifth month, I was running out of excuses. On the appointed day, I proceeded in the manner prescribed. Dangle the duck until its neck rests on the floor. Lay a broomstick over the back of the neck and put a foot on each end. Then pull, but not so hard that the head comes off.

When you catch a duck, pinning its wings with spread fingers, its feathers are cool, dry, glossy as taffeta. Then, as your fingers sink into the down beneath, they meet the duck's warmth, feel the spring in its muscles. If it knows you, it retains its poise without struggling, head up, neck turning inquisitively like a young girl's.

I got through six of the ducks; only one of the heads came off. Ethna was waiting in the kitchen, to pluck and draw. We worked together, and the kitchen billowed with bride-white feathers and down; they covered the floor, hung in our hair like garlands. 'We're not going to do this again, are we.' It was not a question.

May was the month when pet lambs were brought to us by neighbours, for fattening on the lawn and in the hen run and The Hollow, and then killing at Christmas. A pet lamb is an 'orphan', which may mean merely that its mother has rejected it, a hungry waif to be assuaged with bottles of Golden Frisky. The bleating near feeding time can be hard on the nerves. Once, driven to distraction by the orphan in The Hollow, we accepted a second lamb to keep it company. It was all black, so they became Ebony and Ivory, a breach of our policy never to give names to livestock on death row. As they filled out and quietened down, they disconcerted me by developing an eager pleasure in being alive and in each other's company; sheep, it seems, with some encouragement, can be almost as personable as goats. Ivory, the Cheviot-cross, was a large and handsome ewe-lamb of questing disposition. Ebony, a runty little Black-face with a limp, asked only to follow where Ivory led. There were hectic evening processions, as the lambs galloped back to their shed (and a basin of nuts), preceded by Meg, the dog, and followed by Cinnamon, the ginger tom. But this is not that sort of book.

About killing, then (relax, this is the Irish countryside, mild-mannered, a wave from every driver). Few farmers, even those with capacious freezers, have any ambitions to be their own butcher. Think of the pig-sticker, visiting every farm until the fifties ended (Ethna in her Cavan valley, peeping from the gable window, fascinated and forbidden). Before tractors and trailers for carrying beasts to slaughterhouses, even cattle were killed and cut up in the townland: a ring, set in concrete in the floor of our shed, turned out to have been for the rope that pulled down a bullock's head for the sledgehammer.

Thirty years on, at this side of the hill, the killing of sheep was all that remained, this by the method now more usually associated with the world's Jews and Muslims: no preliminary stunning, but a sticking, as with the pig, of the great artery of the neck. This secured 'a good bleed' into the waiting kitchen bowl, a process deemed essential for the tenderness and flavour of the meat. The hunting knife from America was borrowed from my belt for the purpose: not a stab but an attentive severing, as of an ivy stem. My function was to hold the trussed sheep still, fists clenched into its fleece, through the time it took to die.

With such an interest in skills of the self-reliant sort, I did want to know how to butcher and skin, and watched closely as the sheep, now strung from a rafter, was emptied, or hulked. Entrails dropped into the wheelbarrow in a glossy avalanche; breastbone was split and prised ajar to lift out liver, lungs and heart. Bladder, a frail, full condom, was carefully excised; bung cut loose and tied. Skin and fleece were not cut off but levered away with blunt thrusts of the fist. The sheep now emerged as on a butcher's hook, hollow and prettily flushed with pinks and purples. It was washed and wiped down tenderly and wrapped in a muslin shroud, for me to take home.

I could see myself doing all of this: there was nothing grisly or objectionable about the dismantling, not even much of a smell if you left the shed door open. My neighbour clearly anticipated some development in my apprenticeship. There came the day when, passing over the knife, I found it offered back to me. 'About time you tried?' In the shake of my head, all pretensions evaporated. 'No, I can't.' And that was the difference between us. Ebony and Ivory were the last lambs we reared, and they were sent down the boreen alone.

JUNE

The house breathes gently, all doors and windows open to whatever breeze there is. Raised up on the hillside, we seem besieged by light. It burnishes the ocean, bleaches the islands to a distant slatey blue. Temperate people, at home with the cool, moist and luminous, we step out reluctantly, and stoop among the crops in wide-brimmed Italian straw hats.

Just for once, just for now, there is a glossy perfection to everything that grows: to the crisp whorls of sweet corn, to the grape-sheen on red cabbage, to the polished green spikes of onions and shallots. You could put them in a gallery, each on its plinth: plants posing as themselves. But also, just for once, there is point and satisfaction in the hiss of the hoe, stroking away grass and groundsel. Some weeds I leave, to shade the soil and save its moisture: cool fleeces of dead-nettle and jostling chickweed. Others I spare because they are beautiful. Fumitory, *fumus terrae*, the wispy 'smoke of the earth', wreathes the Welsh onions in lacy stems, waxy bells. Pink stars of cranesbill and herb Robert infiltrate the cauliflowers. ('You remember all these names,' Ethna says, 'but you won't remember people or who's married to whom.' She is right: the parish goes on without me.)

Even the grasses have names: old names we are forgetting because 'grass' is what farmers grow, and of one sort only, meant to be mowed for silage before it flowers. We are missing nothing – the flower of perennial rye-grass is a ratty little pigtail. But in June, in any sheltered spot away from grazing animals, the true grasses of Ireland find their own stature and magnifi-cence. Across the stream in The Hollow, where I have not yet penetrated with the scythe, cocksfoot, red fescue and Yorkshire fog join with flowering sorrel in a rampant, rosy meadow.

Cocksfoot is an easy one to know. Its flower-heads are spread in fat, spiky lobes, smothered now in anthers of pale purple. This is the grass for the human nibbler. Pulled at the right time, the stalk comes away with a squeak to offer a white base full of sugar; later, as the seed-head develops, it uses up the sugar and leaves only a crunchy stem to chew on. Yorkshire fog is also worth a bite, and the velvety, purplish fox-tail of its flowers worth brushing on one's cheek, for softness.

Looming presences beyond the ditch, heavy breathing through the hedge: the closest I get to cattle is when we can't see each other. On my side, grunts and mutterings as I lever up the weeds; on their side, coughs and tummy-rumbles and that dis-concerting, calico-ripping sound which is a cow wrapping its tongue around a tuft of grass and pulling. Eamon Grennan, who spends weeks in a cottage across the bay when he is not teaching English at Vassar, has written the most evocative poem about cows that I know (the only poem about cows, if I am honest). A sample:

> I love the way a torn tuft
> of grassblades, stringy buttercup and succulent clover
> sway-dangles towards a cow's mouth, the mild teeth
> taking it in – purple flowers, green stems and yellow
>   petals
> lingering on those hinged lips
> fringed with spittle . . .

I do stand and watch cattle sometimes, struck by the sculpture they make lying down, or the bits of paintings they compose, clustered at the lake or strung out, backlit, in procession across the strand. I call them all cows, even though I know better: they are usually bullocks or heifers. I know an 'elder' is really an

udder, I know – now – that a cow isn't bellowing because she's
hungry.

There are cattle right up on the ridge today, a jotting of little
black marks along the skyline. Only a very dry spell would let
them up that high; only a very fine day would keep them there
so long, glad of the breeze on their rocky prominence. Left to
themselves, cattle seek out variety; they like landscape with
hollows and hillocks and out-of-the-way places. On this side of
the hill, their groups are small: cows and their followers, and
calves bought in for stores. They are the sort to be herded slowly, by one boy with a stick, or a tractor creeping in bottom gear.

A young friend over at Drummin, a blue-cheese-maker of some
accomplishment, used to take his flock of dairy goats for walks
on a little-used road through the mountains. More accurately,
they took him, since goats have a dominant nanny to make decisions about stopping for a browse, or moving on. As honorary
billy, his role was that of consort or guardian, and the leisurely
meander from whin to bramble, bells tinkling, suited his medi-
tative nature, or so he claimed.

Our own goats, while we had them, were not a flock, but a
succession of mothers and daughters, shrewd, self-willed and
teasing. Even two goats are too many on an acre given over, at
the same time, to gardening, ducks, hens, bees, sometimes a
pony. The shifting and untangling of tethers two or three times
a day did not suit either of our natures.

Milking, however, had its moments. I find my fingers curling
at the thought – that special, two-part squeeze that traps the
milk and squirts it in the pail. I felt sure I would never learn to
use both hands at once. But, 'Barby stands still only while she's
eating' was the message that came with our prize Saanen, so
milking became a race against time. As she chased the last nut
around the bottom of her bucket, her rear, offside leg began to
twitch, and a few seconds later, if the milk pail had not been
snatched up, one dainty but shitty hoof was plunged into it.
But there were times when knack and rhythm coincided. A

great calm would descend in the shed as two jets of milk converged and foamed in the beam of the flashlamp. This is remembered from dusk in winter. Outside, a smoky blue afterglow above the islands: in the cave of the shed, goats and milker rapt on a mattress of rushes; in the shadows, black cat and white ducks. Sounds: hiss of milk, munching goat, muttering ducks, whispers of stream and wind.

June was when our second goat, Sally, gave birth to twins, ejecting them in pink balloons in a moment when my back was turned. They were silky and winsome, and within a week were butting at my wellingtons and leaping up and down from the boulder in the hen run, a most engaging display. Part of the charm in a kid's appearance are the two tight curls of hair on top of its head. Within a few days of birth, two bumps can be felt at the centre of the curls. Left alone, these erupt in sharp little horns like those on the classical Pan. We forget, in a countryside of hornless cattle, that calves which are not of a naturally polled breed are routinely disbudded at a couple of weeks old. Dairy goats, too, must conform, for the sake of human comfort in small spaces.

The disbudding of kids at a few days old is not yet within the casual competence of the average Irish vet. Our goat-keepers' manual seemed to anticipate this, since it described the technique of using a red-hot disbudding iron, to be applied 'briefly (six seconds) but firmly to the horn buds, searing down to the skull ...' Even with the kid properly anaesthetised, the book confessed, 'the human operator is often in agony'.

We did not own a disbudding iron, but an expert consulted by telephone was happy to describe an alternative contrived from copper tubing. 'You stick it in the fire, and while it's heating ...' He went on to detail the anaesthetising of a kid with chloroform, sprinkled on cotton wool inside a cocoa tin. 'You can't really go wrong,' he reassured me. 'You're an intelligent chap, good with your hands and all that. You won't burn through the skull.'

In thanking him, my gratitude already fought with dread. The more I rehearsed the scene in my mind, the more unthinkable it became. Ethna, on the other hand, while every bit as humane, has a dogged, stoical streak which she attributes to a Catholic childhood. Confronted with an unpleasant solution to a problem, she will put her head down and go through with it while I am still procrastinating. Fortunately, in our marriage, we each do what we can. Ethna cannot go very far up ladders and I cannot cauterise a kid with a red-hot iron. Thus, as we knelt together on the kitchen floor, giving the first kid whiffs of chloroform, it was Ethna who was bracing herself for an ultimate ordeal. I would merely be holding the little animal 'firmly between the knees'.

In the event, her nerve was not to be tested. It took much longer than expected for the chloroform to take effect. Each time we decided the kid was asleep, and withdrew its little muzzle from the cocoa tin, it would raise its head and bleat for its mother. By the time Ethna reached for the home-made disbudding iron, left to heat between the bars of the range, the copper tube had gone soft and collapsed. I could, perhaps, have made another, but the excuse was too providential. We abandoned the surgery (later completed, not very well, by a vet with a red-hot screwdriver) and got tipsy together, rather quickly, on home-made parsley wine.

A friend lives among trees beyond the village. We were standing at his door at dusk, making farewells after a convivial evening, when a cuckoo called from somewhere close at hand. My friend wet his palms with spit, then cupped them together and blew between his thumbs to mimic the fluting call to perfection. At once, the cuckoo's hawk-like silhouette arrived above us, full of territorial angst. Finding no intruder, it vanished again – then returned to a second summons. I was most impressed.

On our side of the hill, I more often see than hear the cuckoo, my eye drawn by the procession of meadow pipits the big bird trails behind it, like a sky-sign towed by an aeroplane. The little birds mob and harass the cuckoo whenever it rests, teetering, on a wall or wire. Yet, when the damage has long been done, and the baby cuckoo is out of the pipit's nest, the same birds will follow and fawn upon it, feeding it titbits like a fat young prince. Across in stony Connemara, where such scandals are even more in the open, an ornithologist watched eleven pipits and one skylark feeding a young cuckoo as it rested on a fence-post. The birds took turns to perch on its shoulder, and it accepted their insect offerings with a languid turn of the head. Such triumphant perversion of parental altruism deserves a special footnote in the record of the selfish gene.

Europe's cuckoos are divided into races, according to the species they habitually choose as foster parents to their young. Thus, most of Connacht's birds are pipit-cuckoos, while those in other regions and habitats might be dunnock-cuckoos or reed-warbler-cuckoos. In each race, the cuckoo is faithful, if that is the word, to the species that reared it, but we do not know if this happens through genetic inheritance or by imprinting when the cuckoo is a chick. In any event, the female flies in from Africa already programmed with its host's identity, ready to mimic the size and mottling of its eggs. How this pattern is maintained between generations of cuckoo, when male cuckoos mate across the races, is still a mystery.

The whole story of the cuckoo's parasitic lifestyle greatly troubled my early, plain man's grapplings with evolutionary biology. How many million chances did it take, after all, how many solitary and random repetitions, to build this bizarre con-trivance and deceit into normal behaviour for one species? But of course it is not just one species, merely the one we are used to, and we are always more ready to accept the bizarre if examples can be multiplied. Across the world, brood parasitism is practised by some eighty kinds of birds, fifty of them various sorts of cuckoo. In Africa, rather than heaving fellow nestlings over the edge, the baby honey guide hacks them to death with a specially sharp, hooked beak. In India, the male koel approaches

a crow's nest with loud cries and lets itself be driven off; the
female koel, meanwhile, nips in to lay her egg. Thus I can go on
believing in the neo-Darwinian ordering of chance. But I have
yet to see how life is made much easier for the female cuckoo,
which has to hang about for hours, watching for the critical
moment to swoop in and lay – this, at anything up to twenty-
five different nests over a period of seven or eight weeks. Nor
can it make much odds to the eventual survival of her chick,
since the world is scarcely overrun by cuckoos. But nature
abounds in different ways of doing everything, not all of them
efficient or economical.

Our fuchsia windbreaks, barbered every month or two to keep
them thick and vigorous, carve out quadrangles of calm from
the hillside breezes. Flying insects congregate in these restful
spaces, sampling unexpected flowers (chives, chicory, strawber-
ries) or hovering, bright as beads, like fixed points in a quantum
diagram. Midges, unfortunately, like to dawdle here too: clouds
of them dance perpetually above the water tap.

Midges can drive strong men from the bog and scatter hay-
makers homewards. The sweet little trout of the mountain lake
are safe enough from me, for any day dark enough to fish them
is a day when the midges are biting, too. They make the cotton-
grass bogs especially their own because their larvae can live in
peaty mud, low in oxygen, but there are midges for every niche
and contour. Some sorts are for heathery slopes, others for
mossy flushes and the high springheads among the rocks. 'Fistigruffs' is one name for them in Connemara, as in 'them bloody
fistigruffs have the cow's elder ate – it's all swelled'.

Does it help to know that the intensity of biting is governed
precisely by the level of the light? As radiation from the sun
declines below a critical level of 260 watts per square yard,
clouds of midges take wing. Hence the special torment at dusk
and on dark days.

Three or four crossroads towards Louisburgh, at Carrowniskey, hidden among bushes, a thatched cabin with tiny windows and green-stained walls is waiting to fall down. The bushes are elders, rampant. In June their flowers reflect the sunshine, like mirrors, into the sooty interior of the house, and the scent of them, on a dry day, is medievally sensual. It has to be a dry day, the flowers fluffed up like lace, if the blossom is to carry its fragrance into the wine: an hour on tiptoe, with scissors and buckets, stretching up through the creamy light.

Elder needs phosphate and feeds greedily on bones and ashes, which is why, like nettles, it thrives outside back doors. Once this side of Louisburgh, however, human habitation and the elder both begin to peter out. The Carrowniskey bushes are a lonely grove on moorland and there is one more thicket, in a ditch, at a crossroads near the sea. But for the last five miles towards the mountain, *Sambucus nigra* (*Sambucus* for a Greek penny whistle, *nigra* for the ebony berries) has no roothold. In our vestigial spinneys, its absence among oak and hazel is proof of their wild antiquity.

Wine-making explains this intimate knowledge of the elder's biogeography. For years it was the queen of the flower wines we mashed in the big red dustbin, five or ten gallons at a time. Gorse was, if anything, mellower, and could be started in spring, but the prickles made the harvesting a diffident investment: half a gallon of golden petals for a mere half-dozen bottles. Honeysuckle seemed a good idea, but yielded wine with a cloying bouquet, like cachous or old dressing tables. Meadowsweet, frothing into bloom on the damp bank beside the stream, carried aspirin-like principles into the wine along with the fragrance of almonds: we sipped and – later – sweated.

Flower wines are a pleasant illusion; they marry a summer bouquet to Christmas alcohol conjured chiefly from the added sugar, raisins and oranges. Almost any sugary vegetable, too, can be persuaded to ferment. Once, harvesting peas for the freezer and finding ourselves with basins of pristine pods, we were happy to discover pea-pod wine in the manual we keep on the dresser. 'Like a light Sauternes' was the promise, so we made five gallons of it. Every six months we sampled a bottle and the flavour was of pea-pods. The wine became increasingly smooth and clear, and found great favour with a cousin home from the Gulf. But the hoped-for miracle never occurred: it remained pea-pod wine, even if you weren't told. After three years, we smuggled it in cupfuls into the gooseberry wine, to which it brought a subdued (and anonymous) gravitas.

Of all our vintages, the best have been the berry wines, fermenting their own sugars along with pagan flavours. Blackberry is probably the finest, the wine sneaked by druids in the vestry. Rowan and rosehip, mashed together, make a bitter, addictive elixir in small glasses. Blackcurrant, from bushes we share with the birds, has been the *vin ordinaire* for parties and the droppers-in of summer. 'You're really very comfortable!' they beam after the second glass. The labour has been Ethna's: hours – no, days – on her knees in the perfumed blackcurrant thickets, juice dripping down her wrists; hours of boiling kettles for the mash; days more of squeezing, straining, bottling, heaving in and out. Thirty gallons in some years, and she doesn't even drink it.

'A June Day' was my *Irish Times* column for 14 June 1986 – one of the difficult summers. It belongs here, warts and all:

'You write about the odd things,' a reader says, 'but try giving us an average, boring old day – then I might know if I'd like it.' Yesterday will do.

4.45 a.m.

We beat the alarm – must be in training. Ethna sits up in bed to write, lost at once in her story. I pad out to the studio, to catch up on letters. A still, pewtery morning, islands stretched out in a haze, the surf silent. I write to Norway, to a hut above a fiord, where a young German is translating 'Another Life' for a book the Greens might like. What, he needs to know, is a JCB? What are sea rods? Some of the headings come out well in German: for 'Wimp of the West', read

'Softe Des Westens'.

7.15 a.m.

Short jog before breakfast – just as far as Paddy's silage pit.
Jeered by grey crow on an ESB pole.

Try the new batch of rye bread at breakfast. Well-risen but
still a bit soggy; Ethna quite put out. Radio tells about a plan
to put mailboxes at the ends of boreens, to save the postman
time. Michael Fergus, just retired, used to wade the channel
to the last house.

8.15 a.m.

Feed hens, collect two eggs; feed ducks, steal one egg. 'Steal'
because it feels like that: the duck has a drake, covers her egg,
has obvious hopes. I sidle by as they shovel up their mash, the
egg palmed. Measure the rain in the gauge on the lawn:
0.5 mm. Better than May: 167 mm, over twice normal.

8.30 a.m.

We are a two-wheelbarrow family. Ethna takes the small one
to Báinín's field, to shake nitrogen on the bare bits. What isn't
bare he has dunged on, and thus won't eat. We tether him at
the gable to eat the lawn until the rain has melted the nitrogen: he'll have to spend his nights in the hen run.

With the big barrow, I start shifting the last ton of cow-
muck we tipped outside Michele's window. She is in Paris,
au-pairing to improve her French. How're we going to keep
her down on the farm, after she's seen Paree? We're not, if she
can help it.

Meg runs at my heels as I trundle down and up the path
(thank goodness for the slope: the heavy, wet manure almost
runs away with the barrow). The cats laze among the
strawberry flowers, watching. Bimbo and her kitten got into
the cold frame last night and slept on the sweet corn seedlings.
They see all the plastic cloches as summer pavilions put up
specially for them. Cinnamon gives me less trouble, but he
does piss on the turf.

Take off my anorak – about time! It's June, but where are
the flies? Three bumblebees burrow into the catmint, grateful

for a decent drop of nectar.

10.30 a.m.

The postman's van at the gate. Among the mail, a Dublin
housewife wants to say how much she enjoys WWOOFing –
'Working Weekends On Organic Farms'. WWOOFers would
shift this muck for me, but we're not the hospitable,
outgoing kind. I should have a beard and play the tin whistle
until two o'clock in the morning.

11.00 a.m.

A young neighbour arrives with an American cousin: could
they take Báinín to ride? Keep him for a week, we say (but no
one has that much spare grass).

Noon

A farmer and his collie gather sheep in the rocky field across
the road. I lean on my fork to watch, taking pleasure in the
work of an intelligent dog. But the sheep are uncooperative
and keep breaking ranks as they near the gate. Another
neighbour, passing in his car, pulls up and gets out to help in
the last push. I feel mortified, as usual – I was just standing
there. Nine years alongside farmers and I still never know
when to offer a hand.

1.00 p.m.

Egg salad for lunch. I could eat fresh-laid eggs at every meal –
before cholesterol, did people worry? The hens have another
two when I take them their feed. Rooks and jackdaws perch
on the fence, waiting their turn at the bowl.

3.00 p.m.

Finish the muck at last and turn to planting out winter
cabbage. On my knees, scooping holes, when a strange sound
rasps out from the field-bank beside me. Not quite a belch,
not quite a growl, but a beastly, mammalian sort of a sound. I
creep close and peer into the dark behind the nettles. It comes
again at intervals, but its source eludes me. Settle for a
hedgehog – perhaps a family. Creep away again, delighted.

3.30 p.m.

Ethna has been trying to mow the steep bank of The

Hollow, across the stream where the pony won't go. She is using our new Italian machine, but the growth in this sheltery place keeps choking it into silence. I am appealed to: 'I've been waiting for years to mow that grass!' I take down the scythe and open up an arc into the soft, green stuff. Finding my rhythm, I begin to enjoy it . . . swish . . . swish . . . The sun comes out and sweat begins to drip from my eyebrows – which is, I suppose, what they're for.

4.30 p.m.

Fish van at the gate: spotless, well-iced, worth a medal. Our own ray in the freezer is almost gone and we can't start fishing with the spillet until I'm on top of the planting. We buy plaice and cod and fresh mackerel. Do we eat the mackerel or freeze them for bait? Prudence wins.

5.00 p.m.

Too sunny now for planting (the seedlings wilt). Start hoeing weeds off a bed to plant out French beans under plastic, but decide the hedge needs cutting back first. Get out the electric hedge-cutter – not the luxury it seems when you have six-foot hedges within hedges, like Hampton Court maze. Plug in two hundred feet of cable, bring end over right shoulder where it won't get cut, and prepare to concentrate. Goes through fuchsia like butter – 'Magic!' as Selwyn Froggitt would say. Get carried away and do the next hedge as well.

6.00 p.m.

Dinner. 'How is it,' asks Ethna, 'that however many potatoes I do there are never enough left over for potato salad?'

7.00 p.m.

Night chores. Bring in sack of turf to fill the box, and bucket of clods to bank down range. Take Báinín down to the hen run, close in hens. Lure ducks into shed with bowl of mash. Passing belt of infant spruces (for more shelter), start pulling grass from around them. Stop me, somebody.

8.00 p.m.

Nothing on RTÉ – is there ever, in summer? Take Meg for walk round the boreen. Thorn hedges still withered by the

Big Wind, willows barely in leaf, ferns just uncoiled above
the primroses. The fields are green, but cattle come running
to me, mistaking my figure. The hay lorry swoops down the
hill, blowing its horn like a French *camion*.

'I don't see any dead beasts,' I said to a neighbour a week or
two back. He looked at me quizzically. ' "Not a drum was
heard, not a funeral note" – do you know that one? "We
buried him darkly at dead of night, the sods with our
bayonets turning".'

9.00 p.m.

To bed, with the *London Review of Books*.

The first big sailboat of summer clears Renvyle Point and glides
northwards, so slowly that its white triangle is a presence like the
shadow of a sundial, tipping the islands one by one through the
long afternoon. Working at weeds, I keep straightening up to
see where the yacht is now. I'm reminded how, alone on an
island, one comes to sense if the sea is empty.

There was an old stone sundial on Inishvickillane, one of the
Blaskets off Kerry: an island that helped, you could say, to set
my own course, all the way here to Thallabawn. I camped on
the island alone for most of June, thirty years ago. It was an
exercise in solitude, a small adventure all my own. I weathered
a train of summer gales, shot rabbits and cooked them over
sheep's dung; swam naked and uneasy in the grey seals' cove;
braved the midnight petrels that crashed into my tent; kept a
diary. Day Fourteen takes a typical tone for posterity:

> This evening I climbed the sea-crag to watch the sun go down: for
> once there was no low, leaden bank of cloud to snare it prema-
> turely. A theatrical clarity of light lent the islands new perspec-
> tives: deep avenues of cliffs like vistas in a Piranesi, gleaming and
> gold-enamelled (slow bursts of spun-glass spray). I stayed on the
> crag until the gulls flew black against the afterglow and the wind
> grew unfriendly. Walking back along the fringe of the southern
> cliffs, I found a colony of puffballs shining white in the dusk, and
> picked the youngest of them to slice and fry for breakfast . . .

The gales had a few people worried: among them Ethna, then beginning to have 'notions' of me, as her mother might have said. She drove to Dingle, and organised a trawler on the first good day to sail the twenty miles to Inishvickillane. In a cove wheeling with excited puffins, she was left to hold the throttle while the skipper rowed in to get me.

Islands, thereafter, seemed to celebrate so much of what we had in common. Our mutual immersion in the West's more rugged effects seemed to speak for some sort of choice between the natural and the sophisticated, the real and the ritual; there was a general lack of interest in the details of living it up. We honeymooned (in a hotel) on Clare Island, just round the corner from us now, and spent our next holiday marooned on Caher, an empty island on the way from Clare to Inishturk.

Camped on Caher among the seals and peewits and early Christian crosses, we drew the curiosity of the lobstermen of Inishturk. They circled us in currachs and landed at last to brew tea and talk. It puzzled them that we should have cast ourselves away on this bare wedge of rock and grass, when a couple of sea miles further would have brought us to their own, more hospitable, isle. 'There are days,' said one enticingly, 'when the smell of the flowers comes out to meet you. It would do your heart good.'

Inishturk now reclines in our kitchen window, all hips and hollows like a Henry Moore sculpture. Close up, the obdurate toughness of the rock, the way the island twists along its Ordovician grain, is a matter for some awe. The people could be dour, but are not. They do know their own minds. When the gold in our ridge was tracked down to the sea and out under the waves, surfacing again in Inishturk's switchback strata, the islanders thought about it and talked together, and then they asked the mining company not to call again. The island has no signposts, nor a single public notice: it seems to know all it needs to know. Once, following a track from the northern cliffs, we came unexpectedly into the heart of a farmstead. Cocks of hay were being hauled bodily to the rick with a rope looped behind a pony. Father was up the ladder, children led the pony, a heroic line of washing flapped brightly in the breeze; Dev's Ireland, smiling and waving in a clean check shirt. More than once after settling here, we thought of taking that last step westwards, out into the ocean. But we shrank from drawing such a tight and final knot around our lives, and from the fretful improvisations of island living. Now I wish we had been braver and less practical.

Our daughter, if not quite conceived on an island, chose one on which to make her presence known. To the south of Inishbofin, at the left of our horizon, is Ardoilean, High Island. In winter it is hunched amid huge gouts of foam, but in summer it calms down for the nesting of sea birds, which wheel in and out the black shadows and cave-echoes of the cliffs. Ethna and I were delivered by trawler from Cleggan and set up camp high among the sea pinks, where the old monks built their hermitage. We caught a lobster in a pot we had brought with us, a huge creature studded with white barnacles. We ate all of him at one sitting (the weather was hot). When Ethna was struck with nausea that refused to go away, we grew anxious and hailed a passing half-decker. It used its new radio in a garbled and overexcited fashion. Our return to Cleggan drew black-shawled women to the skyline, like figures from Synge, and Ethna, who was feeling much better, had to lie down and look sick all over again. Later, there were bills from boat-owners who had put to sea to rescue us, or so they said.

Michele, reared on this and other stories about islands, had her turn at the Crusoe caper when she was twelve years old. The island was Inishdegil, straight below Mweelrea and just far enough out from the mouth of Killary to be foam-girt and mysterious. It is no bigger than St Stephen's Green in Dublin, but fits into its few acres a hill with lazy-beds, a rushy valley, a web of grassy roads. On the lee side the harbour is just big enough to swing a currach, and right beside it are the ruins of two tiny cabins, home of the O'Tooles until they were coaxed ashore in the 1920s. They had lived with a currach at the door, like a gondola in Venice, and when a stormy spring tide swirled into the house, the fire was scooped into a cooking pot and hoisted up the chimney.

We camped at the harbour, a creek between rocks embroidered brilliantly with lichen. A tarpaulin lashed over driftwood spars made a kitchen in a corner of a ruin. We gathered more driftwood for a fire and cooked periwinkles picked from the harbour bottom, where they grazed among shards of stoneware, glazed crocks, and fragments of sepia willow-pattern plates.

There were hundreds and thousands of periwinkles. Michele would clear a square yard of them for our supper and find it carpeted again at the next low tide. I have this image of her, kneeling, the shadowed water glowing where the sun shone through her hair. She was never more of a red-head than among the island's greens and blues, a maverick gene that last cropped up in a Cavan great-great-grandfather, Ned Mhice Rua. It was one more mystery for the questions that suggest themselves on islands: who is she? who am I? how did it come to this?

Michele, watching the winkles' slow perambulations underwater, took her cue: 'What are they for?' Stuck in the rucksack was a book still in its wrappings from the post, one that seemed to have sought out its perfect occasion: *Life on Earth*, by David Attenborough. What winkles are for, and why the question is improper to evolutionary theory, took us beautifully into Chapter One, 'The Infinite Variety', and on into the magic shapes of trilobites and feather stars. The island seemed made for the performance of my life as father, guide and reader-aloud. We hung over rock pools, watching scenes from primitive life among the prawns and sea urchins. We set a lobster pot in the sound, where the big compass jellyfish drifted like art nouveau lamp shades. We discussed the crabs before we cooked them.

All this really had less to do with explaining life on earth than with explaining me to my daughter. When I took up a curlew's skull, with the long, curved tweezers of a bill, and used it as a prop for a sermon on adaptation, she had other things to read in my face and voice: why any of it mattered to me, why I cared if she were interested. At twelve and a half, the reason for our change of lifestyle must still have seemed deeply mysterious, a thing of constantly shifting focus and enthusiasm, of unassuagable curiosity and finding-out. This was, if I could communicate it, the state of grace I wanted her to share.

Expecting that solitude meant silence, she was a little appalled by the clamour of the island, disconcerted by the manic alarm of the gulls that nagged at us night and morning from their colony across the sound and by the unrelenting boom and boil of surf. Even the engines of the fishing boats, echoing among the reefs, were noisier than the few cars and tractors she was used to.

There is a special sound we both remember, a tremulous hooting that seemed to fill the air above our tent in the half-light just before dawn. It was the sound a child makes with a sheet over its head, playing ghosts, but had a tense vibrato that spoke of something not human. For a second, dragging awake, I shared Michele's clutch of alarm; then recognised the drumming of a snipe, the 'heatherbleat', the 'goat of the air'. I explained to her how the bird rises up in towering circles, then shoots steeply down, spreading its tail-feathers stiffly against the rush of air. She was interested, but less so than in the novelty of being frightened, in a tent on an island, with her father's arm around her.

The snipe of Inishdegil now has an almost heraldic presence in our family album. For Inishbofin, too, there are bird-sounds of a summer's night to be cut out and pasted in, these all the more poignant because, just like a photograph, their moment is utterly lost. There were nights not long ago on Gustin's island when, walking home late from Dea's Hotel through that magical, rocky defile between the two harbours, you could hear two, three, even four corncrakes calling in the little flaggy fields at either side. Listening to their ratchety mantras floating out of the dark, I had just one face to go with the voice: a corncrake glimpsed beyond the hedge of our home at the edge of Dublin (we bordered on a wheat field, rich farmland now concreted over for a suburban shopping centre).

Nothing has changed in the damp little meadows on Inish-bofin; they still wait for the scythe in July. Yet the corncrakes have deserted the island, crashing from eleven pairs in 1991 to two to none at all – part, it seems, of the wider crisis in the species.

> Why go on chiselling mottoes for a tomb,
> Counting on a scythe to spare
> Your small defenceless home?
> Quicken your tune, O improvise before
> The combine and the digger come
> Little bridegroom.

Richard Murphy, whose life as a poet has been so much bound up with these islands, wrote his 'Song for a Corncrake' almost twenty years ago. But the story of decline goes back long before the words 'combine' and 'digger' took on their mechanical meanings. For a century in Ireland, longer still in Britain and France, almost everything that changed in grassland farming had some baneful significance for the corncrake: 'reclamation' of moist meadows, the switch from haymaking to silage-mowing, the coming of bigger and faster machines. Now, in a flurry of concern, a few scores of farmers are being paid to delay their mowing for a month, then to start in the middle and mow outwards, to give the mother and her chicks a chance to run. It is as if we are trying to unwind the past.

But there was always something about the corncrake that suggested a species pressing to its limits. Take the mere fact of its migration from East Africa: how absurdly taxing a venture on those stubby, rounded wings! The corncrake is not one of nature's flyers: on its breeding grounds, at least, it hides and skulks, that rasping *crex-crex* its only sense of community. When Irish lighthouses had keepers, they would sometimes find dozens of corncrakes on a spring morning, newly arrived in the night and lying exhausted under rocks: was there, on passage, some transient togetherness?

Once, in our early days here, days when I was full of my own

manly pioneering, a neighbour's children arrived at the gate
with a shoe box. Pressed together in one corner were half a
dozen balls of trembling, ashy black fluff. I could see the forage
harvester still at work in a meadow at the edge of the strand, its
red neck spewing minced-up grass. The children wanted advice
on how to rear the chicks. I was not encouraging. 'Are you really going to be able to feed them on squashed insects, every
fifteen minutes from dawn to dusk, for weeks?' This was only
approximately, hastily, true, but as much as I knew at the time.
The children turned from the gate, their faces closed. Thus the
corncrake was lost to Thallabawn, probably for ever.

JULY

Clambering over ditches with a farmer friend, in pursuit of a bulling heifer, we arrived in a field he named as Ruadh-muing na Scamall, or the 'field like a rough red mane in which the sailing clouds are mirrored'. Such subtle imagery squeezed into five syllables made it somehow less remarkable that the 'red' cow we were seeking turned out to be quite black, her distinguishing dab of paint having long since rubbed off. We retrieved her from a boggy corner and let the dog trot her off to the gap, taking her cloud of flies along with her.

Seeing my delight in his place-naming, my friend (also the one who can call a cuckoo through his thumbs) pointed down the hill to Ait-shuidhe a' Phearsuin, the 'place where the parson sat', and two further, traditionally ill-favoured fields, the one Gan Famainn, 'without herbage', and the other, worse still, Gan Móin . . . 'A farmer with no Irish,' he concluded resonantly, 'is a stranger in his own land.'

The intimate topography of farms, townlands, coastlines, unimportant to the military or political designs of map-makers, is vanishing with the language. Each generation knows fewer place-names and fewer meanings, so that the whole fabric of ordinary, neighbourhood history has faded like the paint from the cow's hide.

In one of the last thatched houses on this side of the hill lived a man who could put a name to every headland and inlet, from the *súmaire*, the point where the tide turns in to the fiord, to the

sruthair where the salmon ran, when they were let, up into
Carrowniskey Lake. Most of the names are simply descriptive
– the head of the strand, the fairy fort, and so on – but others
bear the stamp of remembrance. Did a red-haired John drown
in the cove of Uaigh Sheáin Rua? Was Uaighe a' Chait, where
wrack was hauled up in a *cliabh*, so deep and slippery-sided that a
cat could not climb out of it?

Without the language, what is all this to me? Even to shape
the words in my mouth I must be nursed along by Ethna, must
be discouraged from intoning some melodic stage-Gaelic of my
own. But something in these fragments does move me power-
fully. This also happens when I go browsing in Dinneen's Irish–
English dictionary, a work of gifted obsession and surreal effect,
compiled by a Kerry Jesuit and fitting somewhere between
Ulysses and *The Hobbit*. I take it down to check on a flower or
unravel a place-name and half an hour later am still in thrall.
'Churchyards have suffered through your not dying in time'
(this to illustrate one nuance of *measa*, or 'worse'). Among the
usages of *mol* (a heap): 'the protuberances of the calves on his
shins ... making the dough into lumps ... money in heaps and
basketfuls'. Among the meanings of Máirtín or Martin: 'a
vampless stocking worn against wind-gall'. Such incongruities
were mocked to great comic purpose by Myles na Gopaleen,
but they arose from the living vernacular as Dinneen collected
it, at parish level and from one dialect to another (he used to wait
outside the station in Dublin's Westland Row and crossexamine
the Irish speakers as they arrived from the West). Such richness,
anyway, as I wander past the hay-ropes and finger-stones, the
suds and urine (*maothachán*) stored for the felting of new woollen
flannel ('the consumption of cabbage,' noted Father Dinneen
with a small smile, 'affected its emollient qualities').

Where I was heading, actually, was *meitheal*, a word that still
jumps into my mind in July. 'A gang or party,' says Dinneen,
'esp. of reapers, a number of men employed at any special work,
as haymaking, turf-cutting, etc; a number of young men,
brothers or others, a concourse; in modern times *m.* seems to

include the idea of *comhar*: A. has B. C. D. etc. at his *meitheal* for turf-cutting, say, B. in his turn will have A. C. D., etc., C. will have A. B. D. etc., and so on.'

Comhar was all about co-operation – 'alliance, reciprocity; society, companionship'. *Comhar na gcomharsan* was a 'system of reciprocal labour among neighbours'. Get a bunch of rural ide-alists talking about the way society should be run, and *comhar* will soon be on somebody's lips, with *meitheal* soon after (for Americans: say it meh-hill, but quickly).

When we came west, the *meitheal*s were for silage-making. There seemed no better way to prove my neighbourliness than to arrive unbidden at the nearest gathering with a hay-fork over my shoulder and to pitch in with a will. This, indeed, was what I did, each July for a number of years. It produced some uncer-tainty at first, since, having no silage to make myself, there was no way in which A. B. C. and D., etc., could reciprocate my day's labour. To the brothers, nephews and in-laws arriving from dis-tant townlands, my presence seemed puzzling: even, perhaps, a bit of a damper on the day, since, being a quiet man when sober, I was not much value for *craic*.

Everyone knows *craic*, that inventive, convivial drollery so typical of the Irish in high spirits. 'Ah, it was great *craic!*' 'He's great *craic*, the same man!' But what does Dinneen have to say about *craic*? Nothing at all. *Cracaire* is as near as he gets: 'a boaster, a jester, a talker', all of which fits very well; but of *craic*, there is no sign. The word was English from way back – 'crack', as in joke, or 'cracked' as in mad – and then modulated by the Scots to mean 'someone full of conversation'. But *craic*, spelt like that, is a modern transcription, an Irish word that never was.

Much of the *craic* at the silage clamp might as well have been in Irish, for all I caught of it. 'Have you ever tuned in to the voice of a Mayoman?' enquired Paul Durcan,

> In his mouth the English language is sphagnum moss
> Under the bare braceleted feet of a pirate queen:

> Syllables are blooms of tentativeness in bog cotton;
> Words are bog oak sunk in understatement . . .

Add to this a delivery compressed into a code of half-sentences, strained through whoops of laughter and a tractor's close and constant rumble, and my difficulties become clear.

Occasionally I would intercept a strand or two of some soaring web of conjecture (about, say, a plan to divide the *duach* into tennis courts – no, pool tables! – or why you'd call the AI man to a windmill farm) and I would mourn my own unreadiness of wit. So I worked all the harder, tossing the grass about with great flourishes in the effort to earn my keep. Only later, at dinner in the crowded farmhouse kitchen, prompted by questions about the strange crops we grew, or the swarming habits of our bees, could I feel myself unwinding to some small intimation of *craic*.

It was mere chance that all our *meitheal*s were for silage, rather than hay. Even now, in any moderately sunny July, I can stand above the post office and look north across a patchwork of meadows saved for hay, each mounded haycock with its knotted handkerchief against the rain. But on our side of the hill, where the meadows are larger and more regular, the shroud of black plastic came early. The grass it encases ('ensiles') is not always up to the highest nutritional standards: it is usually cut too late, when the meadow has bulked up and the grass has spent its energies on flowering and seeding; it is full of wild herbs, any fistful a bouquet. It is lovely hay, or would be if it were dry, but it is not what the books would call silage.

The story of silage in Ireland goes back to the first tower silos of timber or masonry, built on the big farms of Leinster just over a century ago. Later came the 'horizontal' version in which the mown grass was clamped between two strong concrete walls, trodden down by men in heavy boots to press out the air, then covered with old sacks and a layer of earth. Much of it still rotted, rather than fermenting. The coming of polythene plastic offered a cheap and certain way of sealing out the air (black polythene, so that birds should not discern seeds or insects and be tempted to peck holes in the cover). Now a clamp could be made in any corner of a small farm, gathering up the grass that would have made thirty cocks of hay, and squeezing it with a tractor into a dense mattress of fodder no more than a yard high. 'The first time I made silage,' said a man at my first *meitheal*, 'I was worried looking at it. I was sure it wouldn't last past Christmas Night.' But haystacks had their troubles, too: 'The wind would lift them, or the cat would go up on top and piss, and no cow will eat what a cat's pissed on.' We were sitting with the dogs on the ditch at tea-time, each man with a bottle of Guinness from the bag.

Now, even the silage *meitheal*s are vanishing, giving way to a machine that travels the windrows of mown grass, moulds it into uniform bundles and bandages each with plastic so tightly that the stalks must squeak. One finds these corseted bales everywhere, secreted behind hedges and dry-stone walls to the very ends of the boreens on the remotest headlands of the West. They are bulging, black and shiny, like misplaced props for some rural pornographic movie.

I like the way the freshly mown meadows open up new shapes and bright, transparent colours in the landscape: chevrons, lozenges and rhomboids of lime and lemon. The rest of the hillside is muffled in heavy greens, or glazed with the beige of seeding grasses – shades to make a mess of any watercolour.

My own boundary hedges are beginning to bristle with Umbelliferae of the hogweed and hedge parsley sort. Their flat white flower-heads tower above the vegetable beds, providing landing pads for carrot root flies: for that alone, perhaps, I should dig them out. But there comes a point in July when I simply abandon the battle with the weeds.

The last big operation of the sowing and planting season is to set out the seedlings of winter brassicas – whole squads of Brussels sprouts, winter cauliflowers, savoys and sprouting broccoli. I choose strange weather for it sometimes, delighting in mornings of fog and drizzle, even frankly pouring rain. What matters is to move the plants at the right size and in the right conditions, keeping them pert and sturdy in their journey from the seedbed. For that satisfaction, in otherwise droughty summers, I have spent whole days kneeling in oilskins, water dripping from my cap, kept company by a loyal and sodden dog. To neighbours on the boreen I must have offered a picture of misery; only a dedicated gardener might guess at the truth. There is weather for making hay, and weather for planting brassicas: the 'soft' western day with intermittent showers from the sea.

Mayomen in general do not seek too close an acquaintance with the soil. They are herdsmen and stockmen, never so fulfilled as when striding the hill after sheep, or walking tall, like nomads, behind their cattle. They keep the soil at spade's length, and a long-handled spade at that. They stoop perfunctorily to drop a town-bought cabbage seedling into its slot, or will sow, surreptitiously, a ridge of carrots and onions in a perennially temporary vegetable patch wired off in a corner of a field. But they are not cottagers by nature, as Bretons and Devonians often are; their proper pose is upright and angular, like the Masai (see them leaning on their spears at a silage-making).

On my knees, like any good Hobbit, I receive the full shock of a phenomenon quite special to this landscape in early July: a sudden *whoosh!* – a torrent – of dark wings above my head that makes me duck away, heart pounding. Even though I know, now, what it is, I react more quickly than my brain can think.

This is the time when young starlings leave home and form into gangs – flocks, I should say – which roam the coastal meadows, putting the heart crossways in ordinary decent people. The flocks are rarely big (fifty or a hundred birds is typical), but their hedge-hopping, wall-skimming rush of flight is alarming to people and animals alike. I have taken up their behaviour (how earnest of me!) with Christopher Feare, the biologist who studies agricultural bird pests for Britain's Ministry of

Agriculture, Food and Fisheries and has written a whole book
on the starling. He knows all about these unruly summer flocks
of juveniles: or rather, not nearly as much as he would like to
know.

What is it that takes these young birds away from their breeding areas in the farming lowlands – where their parents remain –
to congregate on coastal meadows and saltmarshes, and on
rough, grassy uplands far from people? Are these places rich in
some specially nutritive food, or are the adult starlings so much
better at cornering the food supply at home? Dr Feare finds this
a fascinating ecological riddle, and regrets that MAFF seems unlikely to pay him to solve it. Either of his alternatives makes
more sense, I am sure, than my own wild conjecture: that the
young starlings seek out these wide-open spaces as practice
grounds for aerobatics. In some regions, apparently, the summer
flocks grow to many thousands, which must make their
whooshing a menace to life and limb.

The starlings would send Báinín galloping in fright, tail and
mane flying, hoofs chopping divots out of his rocky little
meadow. It is time for his part of the story; Michele's, too.

A young girl's passion for horses remains deeply mysterious,
whatever the theories (mostly male) that are offered to explain
it. Nothing in the genes on either side could account for the
rapture which overtook Michele when, at two and a half, she
was set on the back of a pony at a church fête. From then on,
happiness was horse-shaped – ambition, fulfilment, identity
itself were leather-grained and lanolin-scented. For puritanical
Fabians like Ethna and me, little could have been more alien
than the world to which our small daughter aspired. Not, in
Dublin, that she got very far towards it: a hard hat on the hall-
stand was for odd Saturday mornings on the smallest hack the
local stables could produce. Báinín was a tenth birthday present
after we moved west; after it became clear, also, that our
daughter could be facing a peculiarly lonely childhood.

Part of this was my fault, but I did not realise it at the time. I was writing the weekly column about our new, 'alternative' lifestyle, and its episodes inevitably brought in references to real people, often only casually disguised. They were always amiable and often most appreciative references, pointing up my own lack of rural skill or common sense. But their content was unpredictable, and sometimes joky or ironic, a tone not always comfortably received in print. For the local community I was an unknown quantity, an Englishman, a Protestant or worse; no one could be sure what turn my chronicle might take. It may have seemed wiser, to some people, not to talk to any of those Vineys or you could end up in the paper. Michele, in her new primary school across the hill, was already marked out by a Dublin accent and city 'forwardness'; even by her flaming red hair. It was a small step to ostracism, a regime at which young schoolgirls seem especially adept. To buy a pony for her to come home to seemed the least we could do. He learned the sound of the school bus as it swooped down the hill, and would be there at the fence to meet her.

Báinín was (and is, for he lives on happily near Clifden) a burly Connemara, self-willed and sweet-natured. Watching him gallop and frisk, I could scarcely credit our good fortune in possessing him. I liked the warm hay-fragrance of his breath as we stood, nose to nose, communing in the field at dusk or across the stable door. 'Where were you?' 'Snogging with Báinín.'

He came of champion stock in the limestone country of east Galway, and his friendly, even giveaway, price was contingent on him being gelded. This affront was carried out in his second year, in the middle of a wide, soft meadow. Afterwards, struggling to his feet as he came out of the chloroform, he began a strange, high-stepping walk like that of a circus pony – or rather, as the vet recognised, like that of a nineteenth-century thoroughbred trained to pull a carriage in style. Whatever genetic time-slip this bizarre behaviour betrayed, it was Báinín's last gesture to the Big House stables; he had fallen on humble times.

For all its open demeanour, this is not good country for a small novice rider with a young, untrained mount. The hillside is webbed with barbed-wire fences; the roads are narrow, often stone-walled, much travelled by tractors and impatient delivery vans – in summer, by reckless tourists who do not know what to do about a child on a horse. There was the *duach*, yes, and the strand, of course, but only for a rider already quite sure how to check a headlong gallop over rabbit-holes, or a sudden move to roll in the sand for the cool pleasure of it.

Only one or two people for miles around knew anything about schooling a pony and we could not presume on them too much. We scraped together the money for a week at a riding school, we built rough-and-ready jumps in Báinín's field and he cleared them with style on the days when he felt like it. Borne on by her adamant enthusiasm, and the occasional clear round, Michele had certainly earned her Thelwellian dreams, but she was fast approaching the limit of the possible. We had never aspired to the league in which families set off, horsebox in tow, weekend after weekend, so that daughters might jump for cups and rosettes in horse shows all over the country. Now, not merely did we lack a horsebox – we had, for some years, no car. It was as well that Báinín and I were on such fond terms, since I sometimes had to fetch a bale of hay with the bicycle and trailer, pushing up hills and battling into the wind.

This dogged but quixotic course came to a climax one Sunday in July when Michele was about fourteen. There was a horse show in Louisburgh. She could not jump in it, because that would have meant transporting the pony halfway across the county to have him identified for registration, and paying money we didn't have to the Show Jumping Association of Ireland. She elected, instead, for an entry which at least would let her ride him around the ring – not realising that, even in this, she was straying right out of her class.

He did look beautiful that morning: as white as the family shampoo bottle could make him, his mane combed all the one way, his tail floating on the wind. We did our best to live up to

him, Michele's red tresses wound up in a hairnet beneath her
hard hat, my own tweed cap tilted well towards my nose. I took
the lead on the bicycle, an arrangement which always put Báinín
on his best behaviour. We had picked a quiet time between
masses and travelled an almost empty road through gusts of
honeysuckle and new-mown hay and the sweetbrier roses of
the moor beyond Killeen. Those eight companionable miles
were the best part of the day.

I don't think I want to go into it, really. The loudspeakers
were dreadful, setting Báinín on edge. A fresh pony barged into
him and he bucked Michele off, her fingers twisted cruelly in the
reins. As her class inched closer, we scrutinised the competition.
Beside the nearest horsebox, a father knotted a snowy white
stock about his daughter's throat. Mother was using a stencil to
brush the pony's rump into a chequerboard of diamonds, and its
mane was already plaited and knotted like the edge of a mantilla.
It was a small pony, like all the others in the class, burnished and
nut-brown with fine bones and neat quarters. I looked at
Báinín's burly shoulders, his coarse white mane in a tangle again,
the sweat-stains from his long trot creeping from under the
saddle. What on earth were we doing here? The judges obviously wondered the same thing: they managed not even to look at
Michele as they waved her pony aside, out of the running.

I bought us all ice creams – Báinín, too. Then, on the way
home, a car with a rattling trailer passed too close and sent him
plunging off the road into a slough of wet bog. I spun round, to
see Michele flying over the pony's head and landing with a
splash. Báinín was lurching and heaving like a drunken rocking
horse, trying to find solid footing. Here, I thought, is where he
breaks a leg and the light of the world goes out. But we managed to lead him from the morass, black to his oxters, and
Michele resumed her saddle only a little smeared with mud.
We had gone another mile when I heard her say: 'Next year, I
think I'll plait his mane.'

But I've been forgetting again: this is not that sort of book.

★

Such calm for so long has refined new colours in the sea. The surf has quite subsided, leaving the ocean rimmed with pale, wine-bottle shades of turquoise and aquamarine; beneath them, a dance of sea-light on white sand.

The strand has gone unruffled for weeks by anything stronger than a zephyr, so that the sand above high-tide mark retains an increasingly intricate palimpsest of tracks: otters crossing nightly from the sea to the dunes; a fox trotting daintily at dawn; the curlicued tracks of a pair of ringed plovers; the firm, asterisked prints of gulls. Most delicate of all, and scarcely perceptible except in a raking light, faint and feathery tracks like those a zip fastener might press into one's skin. They wind like toy-town railway lines through the lower hummocks of the dunes, erased here and there by the shell-craters of trudging cattle, or the morning water bombs of dewdrops falling from the tips of the marram grass. Some, I am sure, are the tracks of nocturnal dung beetles, advancing ponderously on tiptoe; others show a faint keel-mark made by a tail and are more appropriate to fieldmice.

By mid-afternoon there are other beetles crawling out across the strand: big tin ones, with alien markings, glittering in the sun. One of them, inevitably, creeps too far towards the sea and starts to bury itself, whereupon its pink-shouldered occupants emerge to scurry anxiously around the stranded carapace and try to dig beneath it with children's spades. Watching through binoculars from my study window, I fight down tremors of eremitical relish. I know their tracks, their tyre marks and their fallen arches. I will send wasps and dragonflies to plague their picnic, and a tractor to haul them out only just ahead of the tide.

We cannot complain. For fully three hundred days of the year (in some summers, many more) we can be confident of walking the strand without meeting another living person. For the remainder, the early morning is a free and innocent time. In the summer heat wave of 1995 we were out before six o'clock. The strand was still cool in the shadow of the ridge and the sky was latticed with the gilded vapour trails of aircraft we had no desire

to be on. We walked beside little, glassy waves, discoursing like
Greeks, until the sun cleared the ridge and cast our shadows
headlong.

When the wind went west again, raising a chop on the sea and
reviving it to a proper, oceanic blue, it seemed to round up
every jellyfish between us and the islands . The tideline gleamed
with their discs, large as dinner plates or small as paperweights.
Four purple rings at the heart of the bell, the sex organs, marked
them as *Aurelia*, the common moon-jelly of coastal waters all
over the world. From the air, they can sometimes be seen in
hundreds at the intersections of currents, or congregated at a
gyre, a swirl of water shaped by the coast's topography. At the
bend of Killary, a marine biologist friend found himself diving
through a dense mass of *Aurelia*, pulsing in every direction, but
it was the laws of physics, not any volition of their own, which
had gathered them there.

A litter of moon-jellies along the shore has the look of something spent and finished with, but while it is true that in autumn,
when they have spawned, they hang more passively in the
water, they may be swept ashore at any age and size. *Aurelia*'s
life is a double, or alternate, one, like that of so many aquatic
animals. As a larva, freshly hatched, it swims about among the
plankton and settles finally on the sea floor, becoming a tiny,
plant-like wisp – a polyp – attached to a rock in shallow water.
When the first storms of winter break its parent apart, the little
polyp sways safely on the sea bed. In the following spring it
changes shape, growing buds like a pile of saucers. Each saucer
splits off as a tiny jellyfish, or medusa, which swims away and
grows rapidly, reaching full size in July.

There is a fascinating range of 'directedness' among the
creatures that spend their lives drifting – not, like *Aurelia*, in the
shallower reaches of the continental shelf, but out on the surface
of the deep blue Atlantic. Once, among the rocks at Allaran
Point, I found the battered wreckage of a Portuguese man-o-
war, *Physalia physalis*, a floating *meitheal* or assemblage of hydro-
zoans which sometimes reaches Ireland in the Gulf Stream. It

trails long and dangerous stinging tentacles and sails along with
the help of an iridescent, gas-filled float. Rachel Carson took
one of these home in a bucket (a very big bucket, it must have
been) and returning it to the sea next day, was struck by its abil-
ity to adjust its 'sail' as it scudded before the wind. 'This was no
helpless bit of flotsam,' she wrote, 'but a living creature exerting
every means at its disposal to control its fate.'

Come right down the scale from *Physalia* and you find its
little relative, *Velella velella*, commonly called by-the-wind-
sailor. What you actually find, as a rule, often washed up in hundreds on the western strands of Ireland, is a two-inch oval disc,
often prettily rainbowed, with a small, transparent flap set diag-
onally across it. This rubbery little disc, which soon dries out in
the sun, was once embedded in the top of a bright blue 'jellyfish', a simpler miniature of *Physalia* with far less potent
tentacles. The flap acts as an upright sail, to keep the jellyfish
moving in the wind and improve its chances of bumping into
fresh supplies of food.

Velella cannot move its sail, but it has a further and subtle refinement. On some discs, the sail is set NW–SE across the float; on
others, NE–SW. In the same wind, one will sail leftwards, the
other to the right, either of them veering as much as sixty
degrees away from the wind's direction. Both models of *Velella*
occur in all the big oceans, and the biological consequence of
their two different paths (I almost wrote 'purpose') is to disperse
the species as widely as possible. In the northern hemisphere,
where the ocean winds are twisted clockwise, it is most often
the left-sailing *Velella* that end up on our beaches, while the
right-handed sailors are whirled away into the centre of the
ocean. In a fit of scientific diligence I once gathered handfuls of
the little floats and sat out in the garden to sort them. Two hundred and twenty-eight were left-sailers and forty-two were
right-sailers: a random sample, proving nothing, but at least
not at odds with probability.

The story of *Velella* takes me on to an even stranger one, and
for this I produce a beachcombing treasure that no one is

encouraged to handle. In a Perspex box, and cradled in cotton wool, lie two seashells. They are the size and shape of common garden snails, but their colour is stunningly different – the deep violet-blue of periwinkle flowers. They are translucent, and so featherlight and fragile that a pinch would crush them – any tumble in the surf, too, which is why they are so seldom found intact. Rachel Carson once saw one in a shell-shop in North Carolina, but it was the store's only specimen, and not for sale; years passed before she found another one herself, resting in the coral at Key Largo. When Ethna and I came upon our two snails, set down at the very top of the tide on a gentle day in autumn, it was almost as good as getting a message in a bottle, signed 'Rachel'.

The snail is called *Janthina*, a pelagic gastropod that belongs on the surface of the ocean, far from land, suspended from a raft of silver bubbles. *Janthina* makes the raft itself, lifting its foot to trap morsels of air in a film of mucus; this hardens into something that looks and feels like cellophane. Each bubble takes a minute to make, and the snail has a rest after every dozen. So while *Helix aspersa*, the snail of gardens, leaves a silver trail across soil and stone, *Janthina* travels the ocean on a scrap of silver froth. Even the gradations in the colour of its shell are selected for survival. It hangs 'upside down', as we might think, and the deeper blue of its lower whorls help to hide it from gulls looking down on the sea. Its topmost whorl, on the other hand, is of palest blue, to disguise it from predators looking up from below.

What has *Janthina* to do with *Velella velella*? Whenever it meets it, it eats it. The snail is eyeless, so that all its food arrives within reach by the same rootless chance. It feeds on whatever it comes across – planktonic crustaceans, floating insects, and so on – but *Velella*, bobbing against the snail blindly like a toy boat on a park pond, becomes its most substantial meal.

These two marine creatures, a snail and a jellyfish (very well, then, a 'free-floating, colonial hydrozoan'), express so much of what I love and hate about the Darwinian scheme of things. They are each sufficiently primitive as organisms that one can imagine the infinitesimal steps of mutation and selection that brought them to these shapes and colours, these particular paths on the ocean. And their lifestyles and destinies might almost have been designed as a parable on the workings of indifferent chance.

It did not occur to me, when I chose to live closer to nature, that natural history and biology would come to be so much the fabric of my thought, and that I would end up exploring my own existence along with the rest of creation. How odd it was to feel so much more rooted in 'nature' once I had accepted the accident of human evolution, once I could visualise the planet working perfectly well – if not a great deal better – without us. It felt good to have that piece of Christian hubris out of the way. But the next step is to live with the supremacy of chance, the absence of purpose in the entire fabric of nature – and that is not so easy or comforting.

What I admire in Darwinian thinkers like Stephen Jay Gould, Richard Dawkins, Edward O. Wilson, Richard Leakey, is that unravelling the random history of genetic mutation and selection seems to bring them no sense of loss or impoverishment: rather, a deepening of intellectual excitement; even, sometimes, a near-mystical exaltation. 'How elegant!' they exclaim, as the cogs and wheels of some puzzling adaptation at last fall open to their view. *'Wonderful Life!'* exclaims Gould, for a book which shows how easily our species might have missed its turn.

'Isn't nature *marvellous!*' more ordinary people murmur, as they rewind the video tape of *The Secret Life of Plants.* Well yes, of course it is, and no one gets more pleasure than I do from enthusing about it: even – and sometimes especially – when what excites me is the 'elegance' of some conjuring trick organised by chance. But the intellectual buzz is never quite enough. It doesn't make up for the emotional loss of any sense of purpose in my existence. I still feel the self-regarding, totally human demand to know what things are 'for'. In his book *River Out of Eden*, Richard Dawkins finds this desire perfectly natural in an animal surrounded by things it has designed and made itself.

'What is it for?' is simply an inappropriate question for anything to do with the creations of nature, including our own species.

I am not humble enough to be a mystic. But I draw defensive lines around some of my humanity, resisting all efforts to tame it or explain it away biologically. Love and altruism may, indeed, be devious slaves to Richard Dawkins's 'selfish gene', but our instinct for beauty, our creation of art, are the last manifestations of mind I would want to see decoded to the digits of DNA.

When I produce *Janthina* from its shady corner on the piano, I know that my visitors' faces will light up with pleasure at the colour of the shells, even before they know a thing about them. My windowsills silt up with beachcombers' bric-à-brac: shells, stones, beaks and skulls; driftwood fluted, gnarled or full of holes; a twining section of liana stems, chopped by a machete somewhere south of Florida; a little, wave-worn slab of teak with a brass lifting-ring like a tiny door. What makes these useless oddments precious to me? What aesthetic is at work in this relish of bleached and weathered textures and shapes, of things pared to the core? Whatever it is, my friends from the city seem to share it.

The broad agreement within social groups on what is beautiful or ugly, the very existence of 'beauty' as a universal human idea – this fascinates me. Has 'beauty' some adaptive value? Is there a biological origin to 'art'? There he goes again, Dawkins might say, asking what things are 'for'.

Desmond Morris, who studied us as 'naked apes', wrote a book, *The Biology of Art*. That was in the early 1960s, when captive chimpanzees and gorillas first displayed their startling enthusiasm for painting and drawing. The famous chimpanzee Congo produced hundreds of pictures, progressing in pattern and complexity like those from very young humans. Today, this sort of art is regarded as a variation of tool-using behaviour, a simple extension of adaptive ingenuity not far above the use of a stick to pull a banana through the bars.

Art as exploratory behaviour makes a lot of sense, but it does not go far towards explaining the *isn't-that-lovely!* rush of pleasure that can accompany the act of beholding, whether a work of art or a spray of flowers. Efforts to explain the aesthetic experience have ranged over disciplines as contrary as psychoanalysis and mathematics. Many have speculated, for example, on the link between the structural ratios of plant forms and our instinctive recognition of ideal proportions in everything from paintings to pottery to architecture. 'From the logic of form,' as Herbert Read put it, 'proceeds the emotion of beauty.' But if there is an aesthetic instilled in us by the way the natural environment is 'put together', a sense of beauty that echoes the mathematics of natural shapes and structures, it is now filtered through cultural fashion, personal metaphor and symbol.

The new trophy on my windowsill is not worth trying to draw. No line or shading could do justice to its purity of form, no pen-point keep track of its myriad divisions and random, pearly nodes. A perfect globe (but then not perfect, having an apex and a base) all suffused with a pinky orange light.

It is the largest of the Irish sea urchins and the biggest specimen of *Echinus acutus* we are ever likely to find, being quite the size of a Californian grapefruit. It tops by an inch the row of ruddy-coloured *Echinus esculentus* put up for safety on the pelmet-board and is hugely bigger than the smallest of the purple *Paracentrotus*, due to disintegrate any day between somebody's finger and thumb.

All of them scrape away at seaweed with five white shining teeth mounted in a five-sided 'lantern' of rods and muscles first described by Aristotle. The figure five, and its multiples, keep turning up in the structure of the urchin (and of all echinoderms – starfish, sand dollars, sea cucumbers). The tube-feet project in five rows around the shell; the roe sits in five clusters and is ejected through holes in five petal-shaped plates. The coloured, globular skeleton of the urchin is beautiful to contemplate, but so is this . . . um . . . quintessential number.

AUGUST

Dinneen offers winds for many occasions, among them *gaoth an tsonais*, the 'wind of good luck', and *gaoth ghaibhtheach gheintlidhe*, the 'perilous, magical wind' that blows from some unimaginable quarter. No one seems to have told him of *gaoth ruadh*, the vengeful 'red' wind of the Atlantic coast. It swoops in upon the decadent growth of high summer, scourging the hollyhocks and laying lupins low. Alders are blackened, hawthorn browned (reddened, then), the fuchsia left grey and curling. All this comes not, as we might think, from the salt in the wind, but a forced evaporation dragging water from the leaves. Their overnight withering could, indeed, seem perilous and magical.

Before our hedges grew so tall, the first stirrings of a summer gale would send us out urgently to lash peas to their fences, weave webs about the sweet corn, shackle sprouts to their stakes. Even now, there can be sensible precautions: garden netting, stretched across potatoes, calms them in a wind like a flock of nervous geese.

'How are your stalks?' The progress of potatoes used to be a staple courtesy of wayside conversation. Now, as one house after another slips into the cash economy, it may be more tactful not to ask. A season or two of blight is often the last straw: half an acre's hard work, sometimes, rendered into stinking embarrassment. Paranoia about blight has been part of my more visible eccentricity: Viney out with his sprayer again, stumbling along the ridges even as a gloomy drizzle thickens into rain.

Thus, when blight finally sneaked up on me, the blotches on the leaves were unreasonably shocking. Half of the crop was gone within a week, charred as if by fire. The old gourmet varieties went first: La Ratte from France; the pink-fleshed Himalayan Burgundy. Records and Golden Wonders did better, and the old-fashioned red-skin, Land Leaguer.

If the poor cottiers of Connacht had been more loyal to their round and red-skinned Apple, they might have fared a lot better in the Famine. The Apple was a well-favoured, floury potato which kept extremely well. But early in the nineteenth century it began to lose ground to the Lumper, a tasteless, watery variety grown originally in England for cattle feed. Migrant labourers ('lumpers') brought it home to Connacht. It gave big crops on poor soil with only a little manure, so it was grown by families tilling the worst of land, high on the mountainside or on the edge of bog. When *Phytophthora infestans* drifted in on the wind, the Lumper was the first potato to succumb. To stoop in this landscape now, digging up sample forkfuls of tubers, squeezing them, rubbing them, peering at them, sniffing them, is to feel at least a hint of *imní*, which is one step down from dread.

Blackbirds rummage under the fruit bushes, rake through my mulches of mowings in search of worms: the mess they make! But the acre in August gives a fair simulation of the litter on a woodland floor: they feel at home. We are all so familiar with blackbirds, so used to the idea of them living and nesting virtually outside the door, that we forget how recent is their intimacy with people (more a daring, really). Not until the growth of suburbia did blackbirds venture to build their nests away from woods and hedgerows, but now, in most of Europe, town blackbirds far outnumber those left in forests.

Here in Connacht, they took their time prospecting. It is hard for us to imagine just how inhospitable to songbirds so much of the 'human' terrain was in the last century (how inhospitable to humans, too, for that matter). Outside the estate walls, no sycamores or shelter belts; no fuchsia, no gardens. Plenty of willows, yes, along the streams, but these were heavily cut for weaving, from *cliabh*s to lobster pots. The whins on the ditches, similarly, were cut at any time to stop a gap, clean a chimney or keep the hens off the corn-stack. There were few hawthorn hedges: just isolated fairy thorns that no one would touch. No blackbird would nest in them, either, without some good cover nearby. Whole hillsides, like our own, were a bare, black quilt of lazy-beds, dotted with rocks. Thus, the final spread of blackbirds, to Connemara, to the islands, to the bleak spit of the Mullet, may have waited on the thickets of brambles that sprang up in the wake of the Famine, and the emptying out of the land.

On our little patch of hillside, the output of young blackbirds can never have been higher in postglacial history, an awesome thought. On a fine August morning, a dozen at once are bouncing on the lawn or swinging on the branches of the blackcurrants. I catch them, even, sunbathing in sheltered corners, wings spread and beaks agape. Halfway through their first moult, they have comically scraggy necks; 'vulturine', a word the bird books use, seems far too solemn.

The holiday cottages have child-sized fishing rods leaning beside the door, and swimming trunks pinned to windowsills by ostrich eggs which are really beach pebbles. Within the house, the same bouquet of flowers redeems the plastic on the kitchen table: a sturdy twig of fuchsia, lanterns dangling; spikes of rosy purple loosestrife; a froth of meadowsweet; flaming orange sprays of montbretia. The sumptuous marriage of purple and vermilion imprints itself on young minds: a perennial emblem of August in the West.

Only two of the flowers can call themselves natives, and both depend on the moister margins of hay-meadows, ditches and banks. Meadowsweet was in great demand when people and plants were closer. Its leaves and flowers, said Gerard, 'farre excelle all other strowing herbs for to decke up houses, to strawe in chambers, halls and banqueting houses in the summer time, for the smell thereof makes the heart merrie and joyful and delighteth the senses'.

Loosestrife, also, carries a benign message: bunches tied to the yokes of oxen would keep away flies and make the beasts less fractious. That, at least, is what was said of *yellow* loosestrife, a quite different plant. All I know of the purple sort is that, introduced to America, it has become an invasive and beautiful weed, springing up by the acre in marshes and smothering all its competitors.

Something similar is true of our own two beautiful aliens, fuchsia and montbretia, since, where a habitat suits them, they assume a triumphant ascendancy. Being hybrids, they do this not through seeding, or only rarely, but through proliferating shoots in the one case and multiplying corms in the other. We should be grateful: at least they can be dug out or hacked back. The sandy banks of The Hollow give both plants just the sharp drainage they like, and here the fuchsia makes rampant bushes on the scale of its wild originals in Chile and Argentina. In August some parts of the stream quite vanish beneath boughs of scarlet bells, and others are flanked by thickets of fiery trumpets – all 'from nowhere', as a gift.

To spell fuchsia without a dictionary, it helps to remember the name Fuchs, pronounced *fooks*, the sixteenth-century German herbalist thus immortalised, if ultimately garbled. The original stock from which most Irish fuchsia hedges came, from Cork to Donegal and right round to Antrim, was originally planted in Kerry in the middle of the last century. It was a new cultivar, hybridised at Riccarton in Scotland in 1830. Hence, the full name for it: *Fuchsia magellanica* 'Riccartonii'. In the breeding of plants, the words 'hybrid' and 'vigour' are always clasped together, but there can have been few hybrids so possessed of explosive energy. At just the right distance from the sea, the right rainfall and humidity, the right range of winter temperature, *F. magellanica* 'Riccartonii' grows with a crimson passion: even a twig, thrown down in a moist place, will root itself and flower within a year. This generous, even feckless, habit made it possible for farmers to grow hedges without being seen to stoop

too much or make finicky motions with their fingers: just snap a
bit off, and ram it in.

Montbretia is more genuinely 'a garden escape'. It was bred in
the 1870s by a French nurseryman who crossed two irises from
southern Africa. *Crocosmia* had the size and brilliant colour,
crocosmiiflora the hardiness and vigour. Together, they made a
plant which has wandered like a gypsy, setting up camp in
rough places all over the west of these islands, from Cornish
cliffs and heathery Scottish roadsides to the rocky river-banks
and lake shores of Connacht. Here it is the poor man's gladiolus,
brightening small farms where no other flower has ever been
sown. On the moorland road to Cregganbawn, one thicket of
montbretia grows all alone on a rocky verge just opposite a
farmhouse. Early in autumn, as the flowers light up, the farmer's
wife goes out with baler twine to tie them against the first big
wind; nowhere else in her world is there any colour quite so free
and fiery.

Moorland, rock, wind . . . code words for the longings of the
summer people. Theirs are the cars with field-guides on the back
seat (birds, flowers, rock pools) and, in the boot, green wellingtons for all the family. Meeting the children sometimes, setting
off bravely in their anoraks across the great spaces of *duach* or
mountain, I think of the beach at Brighton in the last years of
the trippers, so crowded in a fine August that you had to thread
a maze of arms and legs to find space for another towel. The
misery of the masses in a rainy summer, pressed like crabs into
every crevice of the seafront, was deepened by convictions of
injustice and loss: a holiday *ruined*. Crowding now around the
swimming pools of the Spanish *costas*, they are spared all that.

At least, you might say, they have time for their own society.
Writing about flowers excuses me from writing about people
and confronting their sprawling, hybrid vigour. Once profes-
sionally ready to engage with almost anyone on any subject, at
the drop of a press conference or panel show, I now shrink from
telephone calls or strangers at the gate. After some months of not

going anywhere much, or meeting anyone new, a train journey
to Dublin amounts almost to a fresh encounter with the species.
I am then riveted by the individuality of the human face, the
infinitely variable Identikit of eyes and ears and noses. I think
of Darwin, staring surreptitiously at strangers' faces for forty
years, on and off, in preparation for his book *The Expression of
the Emotions in Man and Animals* (1872): 'The great zygomatic
muscle is sometimes variable in its course, and I have seen a
young woman in whom the *depressores anguli oris* were brought
into strong action in suppressing a smile; but this by no means
gave to her countenance a melancholy expression, owing to the
brightness of her eyes.' In such manner, perhaps, should a naturalist refine his powers of observation, on the 7.25 a.m. from
Westport.

One of Darwin's fellow scientists, reviewing his book on the
emotions, remarked on his 'insatiable longing to discover the
causes of the varied and complex phenomena presented by living things' and he suggested that, for Darwin, 'the restless
curiosity of the child [seems] never to have abated its force'. Just
as, in some reaches of molecular physics, observation is said to
change the thing observed, does the habit of great curiosity set
the enquirer at a necessary tangent to the world? Darwin found
human society difficult, and the stress of scientific controversy
did his stomach no good at all. On the other hand, Carl Jung
wrote of his own childhood: 'Nature seemed to me full of wonders, and I wanted to steep myself in them. Every stone, every
plant, every single thing seemed alive and indescribably marvellous. I immersed myself in nature, crawled, as it were, into the
very essence of nature and away from the whole human world.'
But then he emerged from this schoolboy solitariness to engage
with the whole of humanity.

In August I swing about between avoiding people and wanting more of them: they are very addictive. Some curious cultural
eddy has gathered a colony of kindred professionals to identify
with this corner of Mayo, and as we revolve around each other's
supper tables, the talk is of writing and film-making, publishers

and newspapers, life in the law or on campus. Sometimes I think of all the similar conversations going on at the far rim of the ocean, in the summer houses of Cape Cod and Martha's Vineyard. What have they got that we haven't? A better label on their chinos, perhaps, and a yacht in the marina. 'You live like millionaires,' we're told again. In August, dressing wild salmon in a froth of green herbs, we can even act the part.

The natural abundance of a good summer embraces even the grains of sand along the shore. Long calms reverse, as it were, the habitual roll of the waves, so that, instead of gnawing at the strand, they spin discreetly the other way, sweeping fresh sand towards the land and piling it higher and higher. Thus, a whole new selvedge, soft and fluffy, overlaps the old, worn fringe of the tideline; one's feet sink deeply into it.

To trudge there in early morning is to hear eerie whistles in the sky, mad yelps from the lake behind the dunes. The whistles slide down through seven notes, the wistful signature of whimbrels on migration. I spot their little squadron (like neater, swifter curlews) flying purposefully south. The yelps are from red-shanks, rising from sandy shallows to resume their own passage to Africa. On both sides of Ireland, intimate little parties of wad-ers add up to thousands, then hundreds of thousands of birds, all streaming down from Iceland or Greenland. I imagine the si-lence of their deserted breeding grounds, the berries left to the foxes, the tundra reddening in the first frosts.

It was at this time, in the summer of 1987, that I came home from Greenland, from what was grandly but quite properly called the Irish Biological Expedition. There were three of us. Our leader (if three are enough to need such) was Dr David Cabot, the entrepreneurial zoologist whose venture and achievement it was, and who lives for some of the time in a cot-tage between the lakes at Thallabawn. Among David's contri-butions to science has been a study, stretching over decades, of the barnacle geese which winter on the uninhabited Inishkea is-lands, off north Mayo. For a number of years I accompanied him on his sorties to count the two-thousand-odd geese, and net and ring some more of them – hair-raising journeys, at times, in an inflatable dinghy outrunning January storms. We lived in a deserted fisherman's cottage, and my principal job was as goose-herd, walking the cliffs of the islands to nudge the flocks closer to David's telescope. I could also carry things, and express doubtful or timid sentiments on which he could practise reassurance. These essentially Sancho Panza qualities, plus some skill at putting wildlife films together, earned me a place on his two expeditions to north-east Greenland in 1984 and 1987.

In the 1987 expedition, much longer and more ambitious than the first, our companion was Dr Roger Goodwillie, botanist and ecologist and a former colleague of David's. In the delicate chemistry of our three-month encampment, his laid-back forbearance was a soothing and stabilising influence. He was also an excellent teacher, on such matters as stone-sorting, the linking of streams, and solifluction (the downhill creep of saturated soil).

But our main preoccupation was the geese, the voluble, vulnerable barnacles, who protect their genes by behaviour that has to be seen (and filmed) to be believed. In 1984, on pinnacled cliffs above the tundra of Jameson Land, we had captured the moments in which the barnacle goslings, at the urging of their parents, jumped from their nesting ledges to fall as much as six hundred feet to the rocks and scree below. About half of them die, bouncing off crags or boulders or snapped up by waiting foxes. The other half, miraculously, survive the fall and the foxes, and are gathered up by their parents for a long march to the nearest lake.

Here, with the water as refuge, the adults can drop their wing-feathers in their annual moult. And at this time, with nets and stakes and a good sense of strategy, quite a small team of people can round up a great number of flightless geese for ringing. Our 1984 expedition to Jameson Land had herded about six hundred geese to a final, thrilling torrent into the catching-pen (it then took more than twenty hours, in which the sun dipped to the cliff-tops and rose again, to ring, weigh and release them; but that is another story). Sadly for David's hopes, only three of the birds carried his rings from the Inishkeas, and most of the birds we ringed in Jameson Land turned up the following winter in Scotland. The bulk of the Irish population must breed somewhere else.

By 1987, David had pinned his interest on a valley in Germania Land, at seventy-seven degrees north, twenty degrees west. Here, in 1970, a passing Sirius patrol (then Denmark's token armed presence in the Arctic) had glimpsed 'three to five hundred' barnacle geese. We studied three-dimensional aerial photographs, in which the cliffs looked unspeakably bleak. The only human settlement for many hundreds of miles was a Danish weather station at Cape Bismarck, fifty miles away as a gyrfalcon flies. No oilmen, no mountain climbers, no Italian skiing parties: this was one of the last really 'empty' places on Earth.

The barnacles decide to leave the Inishkeas about the end of April. They wag their white cheeks at each other in mounting excitement and lift up in long skeins, yelping like puppies. They head out above the sea towards Iceland, to the first spring grass in that island's northern valleys. There they mate and fly on, paired for life, another six hundred miles or so across the torn and crumpled ice floes. We followed, at the end of May, hoping that, as some reward for rashness, our destinations might precisely coincide. Behind this hope was the fact that, in many migrant populations, a 'leapfrogging' effect takes the southernmost birds to the northernmost edge of the breeding territory; thus the Irish barnacles should be found somewhere beyond the Scottish ones.

It was a long-odds gamble, even so. As we flew steadily polewards, the corrugations of the Greenland coast slid away under the wing: ridge after ridge of snow-covered plateaux, one deep valley after another, each with its dark threads of meltwater rushing to the fiords. Inland, above this coastal maze of rock and snow, loomed the brilliant waste of the icecap and its glaciers. The untrodden emptiness of it all was intimidating; also deeply stirring with its promise of adventure.

We reached our chosen valley and lost height to inspect it. The cliffs towered up like blank prison walls along featureless corridors of snow. Our engines boomed against the rock, and little parties of geese, a few half-dozens, fled away from under our shadow. Was that all? Would there be more? The promise of 'hundreds' of barnacles seemed suddenly terribly slender, and the cost (at twenty thousand pounds or so) a huge amount to risk on it. But there did not seem, at that moment, to be any very good alternative.

The timing of our arrival was crucial. A week early, and we could be sitting around in soft and sticky blizzards, watching and hoping for geese to arrive. A week late, and the frozen fiord could be too soft to land on. The climate of the High Arctic is notoriously erratic. ('Up there,' said the Sirius captain on the phone, 'there is nothing normal.') As it was, the ice near the shore began to buckle under the skis of the laden Twin Otter as we taxied in, and it needed full throttle, both engines roaring, to drag us clear again. We circled and landed more circumspectly, in the centre of the fiord. When we had unloaded and shaken hands, and the plane had gone – irretrievably gone, back to Iceland – the silence settled back around the three of us and our jumble of cardboard boxes, all suddenly quite tiny in the middle of the whiteness. We improvised a sled and towed the first boxes to the shore.

Between the banks of snow higher up and the marshy mud lower down, there was a patch of bare gravel big enough to camp on. As we pitched our tents, more groups of geese flew in from the south; they banked low to have a look at us, their craning black necks crisp and glossy in the sharp Arctic light. And once we had calmed down and were sitting on rocks with mugs of soup, we could pick up distant echoes of squabbling in the shadows of a cliff across the valley. Irish or not, the barnacles were coming in, and in numbers enough for heated arguments about who should nest where.

The summer thaw is one of nature's grand crescendos: billions of tons of snow and ice dissolving steadily, round the clock. Tricklings become rivulets and then torrents, and silence finally surrenders to the roar of rivers, churning and grey with silt. For weeks the rush of water was a background to our lives, like city traffic. Trekking over snow, we would break through again and again into an icy flow. Bare soil above the deep permafrost was, for these weeks, a yielding porridge under our boots. Everywhere, we confronted a primary law of the planet: water, when frozen, expands. A hairline crack becomes a wedge, slowly, irresistibly widening through one winter after another. Enough cracks, enough water, can topple mountains and crumble rocks to dust.

Thus, the sides of the valleys were hugely banked with scree, great slopes of broken rock precariously settled at forty-five degrees. Every morning in the thaw we stirred in our sleeping bags to the rumble of avalanches, as more pieces of cliff came unstuck. We found bedrock cracked into crazy paving, granite boulders disintegrated into powder, powdered rock settled out into glutinous clay. Whole slopes were creeping downhill to the sea (Roger's 'solifluction'). And repeated again and again, in peaty tundra, in pebble-fields, in plains of clay, was the polygon, the honeycomb geometry of Arctic ground. It is generated by tension cracks and ice wedges, formed sometimes over thousands of years. However it is explained by physics, the precise repetition of the polygon pattern remains, like the laws of crystals, movingly mysterious.

This primal theatre of erosion, the topographical work-in-progress, held me fascinated. In the naked moraines and eskers, the roughly piled drumlins, I could see Mayo after the glaciers, ten thousand years ago. But in north Greenland the retreat and reassertion of extreme cold is a yearly cycle, leaving scarcely three months for the urgent greening and blossoming of the valleys. Most High Arctic plants take many years to come to flower, nursing their buds beneath the snow. On our first trek out of camp, we found purple saxifrage in bloom, clustering like amethysts in a flow of icy water. Later came yellow poppies (bright candle-flames in the midnight sun) and carpets of mountain avens, white and gold, even richer than those one meets in the Burren in May. It was a rock gardener's Eden, tufted and cushioned with dozens of different species of the plants we treasure as 'alpines': starry *Drabas* and moss campions, white buttercups, dwarf heathers, rhododendron blossoming at an inch or two high. For trees there were the prostrate arctic willows, rarely taller than my ankle.

Dead willow-leaves carpet the little pools that linger for half the summer among the sedgy hummocks of the tundra. Everything lasts and accumulates. Among the leaves were masses of 'sheep droppings'. Hundreds of hoof-marks pitted the narrow passages between rocks. Massive old skulls lay about in the pastures of the inner valley. All these belonged to musk oxen, the primeval-looking herbivore that roams the Arctic tundra in little herds, each with its guardian bull. It is a compact, sheep-like mammal, *Ovibos moschatus*, but the great bulk of its thick woollen coat and the sweep of its pointed horns make it look as big and fierce as a buffalo. It is not especially aggressive, until it feels threatened: then the herd forms a ring, facing outwards, ready to charge.

A group of six arrived in the valley in mid-June: a bull, three cows and a new little calf, and an older bull who kept to himself. Like Thallabawn sheep which have been left past shearing-time, they were moulting their coats and using rough corners of boulders as what, in Mayo, are 'itching-posts'. David, ever intrepid as a cameraman, went off with the tripod and CP-16 to see how close the bull would let him get. He reappeared an hour later, somewhat pale and out of breath: the bull had charged him. As poet laureate to the expedition, I commemorated the occasion:

MUSK OX, TAKE THREE

Disreputable, caught in his old coat
On a Sunday, snagging wool

On every rock along this piebald valley,
He pauses, sullen as an aborigine,
Bending upon Cyclops his own evil eye.
His cows crowd the frame, frowning,
A hat stand of horns,
Rags like pennants in the wind:
A band of shuffling Cheyenne
Down on their luck.
Sheep in bison's clothing, bull in skirts,
He snorts, stamps, wipes his eye.
A bum's rush routs the wolf with five legs
From the frieze at Altamira.

Real wolves were once quite common in north-eastern
Greenland. They were almost wiped out by Norwegian hunters, whose traps for the Arctic fox they were scavenging, and
by the extinction of the region's reindeer a century ago. With
Denmark's protection of the north-east as the world's biggest,
least-visited 'national park', the wolves have gradually advanced
again. A week or two after the musk ox charge, one wandered
into camp, drawn by the smell of a curry supper. It stopped a
short stone's throw away and regarded three seated humans
with spoons halfway to their mouths. I was both enchanted
and confused. A wolf, yes, but how dog-like just the same, a
lean and silvery Alsatian with golden almond eyes. Should one
say, 'Here, fella!', and spoon out the rest of the curry? Any
movement, as it turned out, was too threatening: it retreated
slowly, with pauses for looking back. It was still hungry, for
soon we saw it at some distance, under the cliffs, skirmishing
with the musk oxen and trying to cut out the calf. On its own
it hadn't a hope: the oxen took turns in rushing out of the circle,
horns ready to hook. At length, the wolf gave up and loped
away, a grey dot dwindling between the snow-banks.

The polar bear, when it, too, came into camp, was almost a
relief; we had been watching and listening for so long and won-
dering what size and temper of beast would initiate us. Even

before we landed, that last steep tilt around the mountains had shown us several bear-tracks stitched boldly across the snow. Our first treks discovered more. Some were old and weathered, impressed like escalators into the snow of the hillsides; others were a lot fresher, and preserved the shape of the claws in pawprints of daunting size (two made the length of our rifle).

The bears were probably safely out on the ice, catching seals, but they often retreat to land in summer, scavenging for food. Along with all the good advice about keeping camps clean, not cooking fragrant meals, not keeping the clothes you cook in beside your sleeping bag, one could not help imbibing the salutary horror stories of people scalped at a swipe. When we saw our first bears, out on the ice at the mouth of the fiord, my excitement at their beauty was well-tempered with what the Inuit call *ilira*, the fear that accompanies awe.

They were a mother and daughter, blond-white against the blue-white of the snow and bounding along like borzoi from one seal-hole to the next. Even at almost a mile away (we were watching from a cliff-top at the tip of the peninsula), the mother's casual power, the rangy grace and speed, were of an order quite unguessable from the pacing, half-mad robots of zoos. There was further drama in her behaviour, for she was trying to discourage her daughter, about two years old, from following her around (her daughter, because male cubs are the first to be weaned). At every hundred yards or so, she would wheel about and charge at her offspring, driving her to some distance before turning back to her tour of the seal-holes. These pursuits left the soft snow inscribed with great spiralling curlicues that only an Inuit hunter, perhaps, would readily have understood.

The spectacle of the bears, thrilling as it was, gave us a nervous night or two. For individual defence, we had packs of hand-fired miniflares, and David, creeping up to my tent to growl, was warned that repetition might fetch a rocket up his gansey.

It was the banished daughter-bear – or so we supposed – that eventually came to call. We'd had a day of wind from the glacier, which blew the scent of our supper far out to sea (soya bean curry, again). Any passing bear, following its nose, might also have become curious about the little Irish tricolour flapping away above the fort of cardboard food boxes which was our kitchen. At one o'clock in the morning, the sound of toppling boxes set David reaching, not for the gun, but the camera. His reward, as the animal took fright, was a minute of film of a bear with very clean paws, skipping and splashing onto the ice and retreating down the glittering path of the sun.

> What chance despatched this prim, loquacious bird
> To the last and loneliest cliffs on Earth,
> There to hatch chicks and fly them forth
> Wingless, from the precipice?
> In a hawk heroic, mythic in a swan, this
> Desperate device, in merest geese, absurd!

To read the barnacles' mind – that is, to seek the key to the immemorial print-out of their adaptation and selection – it helps to have handled another of the many kinds of geese that fly to the Arctic to breed. The pink-footed goose, for example (which winters mostly in Scotland), may sound somewhat effete, but actually has the bearing of a Mafia bodyguard, dark and powerful. In a mixed lot of geese caught for ringing, it takes the lead in the break-out from the catching-pen; pinned under one's arm, it ripples with a muscular resentment. Its nests are spaced widely in the heather on the tundra, daring any fox to come near.

The barnacles are smaller and daintier, pack less of a punch. They lose fewer of their goslings in the jump from the cliffs than they would if they nested on the ground. And if they choose (as they did in our valley) to nest on a cliff with a gyrfalcon's eyrie right in the middle, there would be odds to prove the sense of that, as well. Yes, the falcons fed their young with goslings at the time of the jump, but for the rest of the breeding period their presence kept away ravens and glaucous gulls, both with a notorious appetite for eggs. On balance, it paid the geese to have nine of their goslings fed to the four young of the gyrfalcons, screaming and beating their wings as they waited for meat (headless leverets, half-chewed plover chicks, oven-ready ptarmigan).

In the days before the jumping began, the sun's heat on the bare rock and mud made the air in the valley rise, and fog was dragged in from the sea, still clotted with ice, to replace it. The fog precipitated its moisture as heavy, gentle snow. This settled in Roger's beard as he perched on a crag of rock across an abyss from a dozen pairs of nesting geese: the special study group. Every five minutes, hour after hour, he noted what the geese were doing, fumbling to note the data (Sleeping, Head On Back, Head Up, Extreme Head Up – tick one) in the columns of a card inside a plastic bag. I knew the numbing monotony of this computer-fodder fieldwork, having shared with David a week of similar cliff-top vigils in Jameson Land. Watching Roger reappearing at the rim of the cliff at four in the morning, dusted with snow like the ghost of Darwin, I struggled with my sense of guilt, only slightly assuaged by feeding him curry and boil-in-the-bag rice at my little kitchen in the rocks.

I had opted out of the goose-watch as one of the comforts of cowardice. The crag overlooking the nests projected from a frost-shattered, six-hundred-foot cliff. To reach it meant a slow descent over large, sharp-edged rocks, wedged together in a scree above a precipice. I am not very agile, have a poor sense of balance, and I especially hate scree – the hollow sounds it makes, the grating and wobbling from one step to the next. 'Michael would die, wouldn't he, Roger?' said David, after their first trip down together. 'Some of it is a bit woolly, all right,' said Roger briefly. 'Roger doesn't like it at all,' said David to me later, 'but he's a great chap, never complains.'

To film the gyrfalcon nest and the jumping goslings, David found a camera position halfway down the cliff, on an outward-sloping rock, and had the tripod and camera lowered to him on a rope. 'One pebble under my foot and I'm gone!' he exulted, as he rehearsed me in the procedure for injecting him with morphine, in the buttock. If he did slip, indeed, or if that section of

the cliff gave way in one of the thunderous collapses that we
heard almost every day, it seemed unlikely I would find much
of a buttock to inject.

There is, I suppose, a great deal to be said for throwing down
the gauntlet to fate like this – for marching straight through
rivers instead of mincing up and down looking for a better
way. Every bold day one has enjoyed must seem a vindication
of daring and winning. Timid and paranoid people like me do
waste a lot of what ought to be the good times in our lives, just
as I wasted a lot of the expedition thinking bad thoughts of
David Cabot. But he was quick to reassure me about opting
out of the cliff. 'Even *I* am frightened,' he said, his blue eyes
wide.

He stood for many hours at a time on his sloping ledge, waiting for the falcons to fly in with some food, and then for the
goslings to jump. This they did, on average, forty-one hours
and twenty minutes after breaking out of the egg. They flut-
tered down, little wing-stubs whirring, to bounce off a rock or
glissade down a snow-bank at the bottom. David followed
them in a smooth and unhesitating tilt of the camera. Eye
pressed to the viewfinder, he might so easily have leaned forward past the tripod's centre of gravity; he could have had a
rope round him, tied to something, but chose not to. The jumping shots make everybody gasp.

In the final stages of the expedition we had the help of a Swiss
doctor, a precise and sometimes impatient man whose great
pleasure in life was to fly his own helicopter in skilful but
dangerous ways. At home he specialised in mountain rescue
work, hovering alongside cliffs and daring the winds to nudge
him to disaster. But for real freedom and exhilaration he made
these summer trips to Greenland, where he could take off and
land as he pleased, and fling his machine around a totally empty
sky. It had no flotation tanks: 'If there is risk in flying over the
sea, then that is the risk you take.' But he would help any serious
expedition – archaeological, biological, geological – for the cost
of the paraffin, flying far out over ice and wilderness, often

without his young mechanic, and risking a breakdown hundreds of miles from any help.

He was trapped in fog at the Danmarkshavn weather station and came to us rather late. For days, every passing bumblebee had us hushing each other, to listen. These were days when we should have been driving the geese and goslings off the lakes and ringing them. As July passed into August, more and more of the adults were testing their new wing-feathers; soon, they would be able to escape from us. David grew fretful and spent a lot of time on his own, checking the nets for holes, and polishing the primus. If we lost the geese, it was only half an expedition.

But Peter came eventually, and lifted us about between the valleys, crammed in with the nets and heavy bundles of stakes. His flying was assured, aerobatic, like a hunting gyrfalcon. He enjoyed skimming cliffs and rushing low through ravines, or banking and side-slipping to look at geese on a lake. I stopped being nervous. There was nothing to do but enjoy this culmination of all the flying dreams I ever had.

Just once, Peter let his own composure slip. It happened at Danmarkshavn, as the expedition was withdrawing. He and I had been listening to Beethoven together in the station's recreation room (an enormous polar bear skin stretched on the wall). Then we left separately, I to my tent on the perimeter and Peter to the helicopter parked nearby. He was refuelling it with a hand pump and forgot to take the bung out of the nozzle. It was suddenly expelled, beyond reach in the helicopter's fuel tank. I heard distraught crying, an unrestrained human anguish, and looked out to see Peter pacing up and down, holding his head. '*Ach, nein! Nein! Nein! Nein!*' He had done this once before. Now he had to call out the station bulldozer, which lifted the helicopter and tilted it, like a child that has swallowed a penny. The bung slid down to the sump.

Our ringing had been moderately successful – one hundred birds, rounded up in catches at half a dozen lakes. A lot more escaped, under the net or over it: they were starting to fly again after their moult. Just one of those we caught was 'Irish': it had been ringed in Donegal two years before. Almost all the rest, as it transpired, were more geese from Islay, the island on the west coast of Scotland. Thus, as David noted for science, 'the likelihood that "leapfrog migration" occurs in the barnacle goose is small'.

Flying south in the Twin Otter from Germania Land, somewhat gaunt but deeply tanned, we found ourselves travelling into night. The last coppery glints of sun on the icecap were swallowed up in dusk above the sea between Greenland and Iceland, and at Keflavik we stepped down into the first darkness we had known in three months. I shrugged it around me, gratefully. The human need for darkness, rooted in the circadian rhythms of our bodies, is psychological as well. A world without the night's punctuation becomes a deeply uneasy place: we need the chance that things will, indeed, seem better in the morning. I had written some lines about it:

> This circling light demands a double shift:
> Youth begun and done with by the first frost,
> Flowers on short stalks, brief songs and couplings,
> Judicious fruit to measure out the past.
>
> Veteran of twilights and fresh starts
> I am too old for sleeping on hard ground,
> Or hints at this brash latitude
> That while I sleep the world is going round.

The tundra we left behind was a tight, heathery carpet already smouldering with autumn, the willows lit up with seed-plumes like fiery candelabra. How lush, by comparison, our 'bleak' Mayo hillside, how sprawling and coarsely tangled and seething with flies and bees! But down on the *duach*, at the margin of the lake, there was an echo of the spare and precious flora of seventy-seven degrees north. For eleven months of the year, the close-bitten sward is a sodden green carpet mostly innocent of blossom. And then, in August, its wettest parts put up a flush of chaste and beautiful white flowers.

Like Arctic buttercups, like alpine saxifrage, they are actually neither. Even their true name is what they are not, for grass-of-Parnassus is neither a grass nor ever grew on that Greek mountain; it is a flower all its own. Each stem is clasped by a single, heart-shaped leaf; one blossom to each rosette. Five overlapping white petals, delicately veined with green, make a honey-scented chalice for the stamens. Every other stamen is fringed with golden filaments, but only a fly, perhaps, could say exactly what they are for.

The social whirl is almost over. As August winds down, and the last wisps of turf-smoke curl up from the holiday houses, we are lured away from freezer bags and pickling jars to long, convivial evenings at other people's hearths. And since this keeps us up long past our usual bedtimes, it brings us the novel pleasure of being abroad in the summer dark. Most people relish August for the brazen indulgence of its days, but, remote from town-lights, we have known something very like Lawrence Durrell's 'moth-soft darkness of the Aegean night'. Cycling home across the *duach* with the Milky Way unveiled above us to the furthest mote of a star, we have felt the sea breathing beyond the dunes and heard its uncertain tumble onto sand. Or, gliding through the hedgerows in a hollow of the moor, black bats and shooting stars have rained upon our heads from a whirling, necromancer's sky.

All this, of course, needs bicycles, with or without lights, and silent tracks or boreens leading nowhere of worldly importance. And once, I remember, lacking enough wheels, we arrived below Mweelrea with two squeaks of brakes and a clatter of hoofs.

Riding home again, after the party, was a little more problematic. Michele had never ridden Báinín at night: how well could he see? And what would happen if we met a car on the twisting, narrow road? It seemed sensible to leave before the pubs turned out in distant Louisburgh. We travelled in procession,

bracketing the pony between the fitful lights of the bicycles.
I led the way, alert for cattle or donkeys in the shadows, or a
distant glow of headlights round the hill.

But the pale ribbon of the road led us freely on, steeply down
to the bridge across a mountain stream, up again to a view of
mist-blurred lakes and the sprawling black calligraphy of the
islands. As confidence grew, the pace of the convoy quickened,
from a jog to a trot to a canter. A warm wind from the mountain brought us rich night-scents from cattle communing in
corners and newly made haystacks rustling under their nets.
The rhythm of hoof-beats at my back lifted me, too, behind a
flowing white mane and ushered me on between stone walls,
daring the dark.

The home straight was a race against the first car, its headlights brushing the sky as it climbed from Killadoon: a safe race,
with half a mile to spare. How little the driver made of the
distance to the mountain. But in the darkness that closed again
behind him, there was still a tremor, a remembered hoof-beat
and heartbeat, from our thrilling passage through the night.

SEPTEMBER

Almost from the first day, September is not August. The summer people have driven off abruptly, over the hill, and the tyre marks they leave on the strand soon wear to a spiralling enigma, like the kerbstones of the Boyne. It seems impossible that the absence of these few dozens of cars could account for the tangible quietude that settles from one day to the next, a stillness even the weather conspires to. Yet suddenly here are all the 'normal' sounds: *kronks* of passing ravens, distant shouts to dogs. Travels of tractors and minibuses become noteworthy and local again.

Without the swirl of summer cars and jeeps and camper vans, it is the birds that bring movement to the hillside. Their restless traffic speaks of a good summer for reproduction: full quotas of nestlings, second or even third broods. In the open terrain, every little flock catches the eye, and their characterful passage has me coining new collective nouns: a skip of linnets, a sift of starlings, a swirl of curlews. The sudden fall of young starlings into the hedges around the house gives us close-ups of young birds caught in *déshabillé*: brilliant waistcoat of speckles and greeny purple gloss, but, above it, unmoulted, the drab, brown head and shoulders of the feathers they were fledged in.

The house on its acre of trees and shrubs is also a magnet for passing swallows. 'Chitterlings', a fond Scottish name, perfectly evokes their discourse along the eaves, the flicker of their wings outside the window. In this unaccustomed, even intimidating, intimacy, a detail of plumage can suddenly catch the eye with something like the significance it has among swallows. Thus, as the adult birds hover against the sky, pale patches in their spread tail-feathers light up in a vivid pattern, a signal not visible at any other time. Strangely, it echoes exactly the white patches which chequer the wing-tips of red admiral butterflies. These insects, too, in a generous summer, dash darkly about the walls of the house in challenge or amorous pursuit, and the chequering is what catches the eye as a pair of them soar up in the twining column of the courtship flight. There are evenings in late summer when fluttering chitterlings and twirling butterflies are held, so to speak, in the same frame. There is nothing to be read into this but coincidence.

The swallows are on passage south, caught up in the great river of migrant wings that begins to flow down around Ireland in early autumn. I am reminded of it each August by the whistling of whimbrels over the strand and the little squads of sanderling quartering the tide's edge. These first parties of migrant waders are odd birds out, those that failed to breed on the tundra of Iceland and Greenland. Their arrival is a token of the wheeling flocks to come, just as the young gannets out beyond the third wave, smiting the sea like flung axes, are local outriders of a great southern movement of sea birds: shearwaters, kittiwakes, fulmars, auks, streaming past Ireland by the hundred thousand. Just once, it is worth trying to be in the right place at the right time: Annagh Head, say, at the north-west of Mayo, on a September day when wind and rain are pressing the birds nearer to the land. The images, however blurred, are of great numbers, implacable happenings. They include the watcher crouched among the sea pinks on the headland, awed and in tears.

The full harvest moon of September rises colossal and coppery, stirring great oscillations in the sea. The big spring tide the other evening also felt the push of a north-westerly wind, so that, once gathered at the channel's mouth and heaped above its sandy corrugations, it surged landwards in a flood to which there was no checking or end. It lifted the long baulk of timber that has rested on the strand since spring and swept it on like a battering ram through the first fences on the shore. It spilled across the grass of the *duach*, erasing the lines of the otter-runs and filling the lowest rabbit-holes and the hollows of the summer larks. It reached up the river and joined the lakes in a vast and alien configuration of silver water, and, finding the swans at the furthest corner of the reeds, carried them further still, bearing them like emblems above the drowned pastures.

Next day, in the wake of this inundation, I walked out across the salty grass and, reaching the new, smooth sand, printed my first steps upon it. This traverse of the cleaned and rejuvenated strand has become something of an autumn ritual. There is nothing proprietorial about it, nothing that would be too dismayed if my neighbour John had already set his mark on the virgin tideline: indeed I now saw him, far off across the channel, too distant even to wave to, and the sun found a glint of bright blue in his burden of beachcombed fishing net.

What draws me to the shore is the clean sheet these big tides make of it, erasing the last runic vestiges of car tracks and shriving the very air of summer sweat. The wet strand is a huge mirror to a sky laundered of haze, full of blue, rinsed distances and shining clouds; the wind off the sea is cold and fresh, the surf has a wild white glitter and an altered sound. In these bare, gleaming surfaces and atmospheric changes are intimations I find deeply affecting.

Yet this time, for some reason, the magic was slow to work. As the long tongues of foam seethed around my feet I found myself preoccupied with pessimistic thoughts and images. Watching the shadows moving on Mweelrea and the Sheeffrys, I could think only of the thousands of State-subsidised ewes engaged in grazing the uplands bare. The arrival of another plastic bottle had me troubled with visions of the deep, marbled strata of plastic beneath the strand. And that, by sad association, took me on to questions of aesthetics and 'appreciation of nature'. What if, rather than signifying a wider sense of our place on the planet, the present middle-class passion for wildlife and

ecology is some sort of desperate distraction from the dire state
of human society? If Pope was right, and the proper study of
mankind is man, then perhaps the obsession with birds and dolphins is part of a betrayal: we have not, after all, had one worth-
while new idea about organising the lives of our own species for
the whole of the past hundred years.

From voicing a heresy, it is only a small step to losing one's
faith. What is the beauty of wild landscape but a Romantic construction scarcely two centuries old? Before Rousseau, when
mankind was still hewing down the forests and clearing the
rocks for farmland, what was beautiful in the countryside was
the evidence of fertility and the worth of human endeavour:
fields of cattle, stooks of grain. The Romantic revolt was one
of educated individualism in a world of stultifying peace and
quiet and its symbols, in Bertrand Russell's summary, exalted
'wild torrents, fearful precipices, pathless forests, thunderstorms,
tempests at sea and generally what is useless, destructive and violent'. As a criterion for beauty, 'wildness' has survived and still
holds its promise of individual fantasy. In tamer landscapes,
'wildness' is what offers peace and quiet, and the concrete cliffs
of the Spanish holiday coasts are where to head for passionate
adventure.

But what is landscape (I am back on the shore and framing the
Twelve Bens, all bunched-up and jagged in a long shot across
Killary) except one of nature's accidents? A mere accretion of
geological thrusts and faults, a vegetation conditioned by man
and climate – a trick of the light! In the echoing valleys of
Greenland I found it difficult to make a drawing, so chaotic
and 'shapeless' was the raw debris of the wilderness, so uncouth
the frost-shattered rock, so drab its colours in the unblinking
sun. Since that visit to the brash beginnings of landscape, I have
had to beat down a scepticism of what we admire as scenery,
aware of the veneer of order we demand for nature's chaos to
engage the eye. Even the waves that churned beside me as I
walked would have to be composed in a painting, some
aesthetic pattern made of their unruly molecules of water. It is

memory and culture, Simon Schama insists, that impress the retina with beauty: 'Landscape is the work of the mind.'

Too much science, on the other hand, is not good for artists and poets. It makes them uneasy, subverts their innocence. Once they acknowledge the randomness of landscape, what becomes of the struggle with its forms and colours? Science has given us ecology, which stresses our oneness with nature, yet science is also what separates us from it. 'We know quite enough facts now,' says John Fowles. 'Nature is a sort of art *sans* art; and the right human attitude to it ought to be, unashamedly, poetic rather than scientific.'

At the end of the strand I climbed up over the dunes and descended to the lawn of the machair. I was still depressed about the sheep-worn hills and the sham of painting disorder into order. A flock of mallard lifted off the lake and I counted them: twenty-five – or was it twenty-six? A flock of golden plover lifted from the machair and swung about. A longer count, with binoculars: seventy, was it, or seventy-five? A group of four swans flew across the flank of the mountain from Killary: mutes, not whoopers.

It was the swans that fetched me out of it: their shining, rippling lines and the spaces they carved in the air. And the plovers' flight of arrows, changing bronze to silver in an instant as they wheeled around the sun. Seventy? Eighty? It was not what mattered!

Late in August, a young friend from England came to spend a week or two with his grandmother, over at the foot of Mweelrea. After he had roofed his fort on the mountain with hazel boughs and heather scraws, after he had dammed a few more streams for bathing pools and harassed the rabbits on the *duach* with a bow and arrow, he remembered that I had an eel net somewhere I didn't seem to use. I passed it over on an equal-shares basis and in due course received one limp and slender specimen that was much appreciated by the dog. Before my partner returned to the city, however, he called to say goodbye and to apprise me of the net's new location in the lake, at a place where another young friend had once caught an eel 'seven feet long'.

The net is a fyke net (from the Dutch word *fuik*), of a kind now used to catch eels all over the world. In my variation there are two long, conical traps of netting, rather like the windsocks at an airstrip, supported on tough plastic hoops of successively diminishing size. The entrance hoops, a couple of feet across, are linked by a long, shallow curtain of net, weighted at the bottom and fitted with floats at the top. When an eel meets the net it turns along it, rubbing against the mesh as sensuously as a cat, and is guided into one or other of the long cones of netting. These have internal funnels that lure the eel on and on, past the option of retreat, into a bag at the end that is tied with a draw-string and a bow.

We bought the fyke in the early days, when we were still giddy with all the things we were going to do. As we discovered the finite nature of the day, eels and the smoking of them receded in the order of priority. The net had occasional outings, usually when the sea got too rough to fish in autumn, but never with enough result to encourage perseverance. One day, I resolved, I would do the thing properly.

The lake is a peaceful place at any time, sheltered by ivy-hung cliffs and rocky pastures, but to approach it in a still September sunset, past flocks of curlews, lapwings and starlings becalmed on the grass, past shining rings of mushrooms and puffballs, is to know the intoxicating solitude that sweeps in upon this place at the end of summer. As I crossed in from the dunes, the low sun picked out a pair of stakes in the lake between which the fyke was stretched. They turned the net into a 'fixed engine', of the kind fishery boards like to sanction – or not, as the case may be. (Once, in my early sojourn across the bay, I was introduced to an even less equivocally illegal device, the 'otter-board'. This is like a crude, flat-topped toy yacht, with its keel set at an angle, thus exactly counterpointing the diagonal sail of the jellyfish *Velella*. The board is attached to the end of a fishing line, furnished at intervals with hooks and trout-flies. When it is pulled along by a walker on the lake shore, this undistinguished piece of wood will draw the line out to its fullest extent, drifting the flies seductively above the lake's most promising depths. I have sometimes wondered how far, given a good long beach, one could float a spillet of baited hooks out across the ocean.)

At the boggy margin of the lake, braided with streams, the scent of crushed wild peppermint rose up at every step. Dashing ahead of me, the dog flushed a party of snipe – a whole dozen, one after the other, jinking away across the bulrushes – and then a hare, bright chestnut in its first summer coat, bounded off in a glitter of spray. Meg whimpered from the bank as I waded out.

Slim shadows were twining in the pockets of the net. Not counting the two that slipped through my fists, there were half a dozen substantial eels to pour from one bag into another. Each had the bronze back and silver belly that marked the mature fish, ready to swim seawards on some dark and rainy night in November.

Superb eel recipes abound in the books by Jane Grigson, Alan Davidson, George Lasalle and others, but while such writers agree that 'eels should be bought alive', they do rather pass the buck when it comes to killing them. The difficulty lies in their amazing muscular power (like that of a kicking fire hose), their secretion of slime, and the galvanic simulation of life after death. Many commercial processors kill their eels by letting them thrash about in trays of salt for a couple of hours, or by passing a high-voltage current through the tank. Others cram the live eels into polystyrene container blocks and put these straight into the freezer.

The largest of my catch, at something over two feet, shot out of my grasp, caromed off the kettle and almost made it to the gap at the back of the cooker. It was pinned down under a rough towel, beheaded, and shut up in a big saucepan for the night. Skinning an eel is, happily, very much less of a problem: once you have a corner started with the pliers, it pulls off as smoothly as a glove. In the days when eels were caught with mud-spears (those recovered from *crannógs* have long shafts and multiple flat tines, like Neptune's trident), the skins were in great demand: they were used as thongs and flail-hangings, as charms against rheumatism; even, perhaps, as penis-sheaths in copulation with mermaids.

September finds the acre under siege: from parachuting thistle-down, from helicopter squads of cabbage whites, from grapnel-lines of bramble shoots tossed over the boundary hedge as if by some invisible army. Invasion is clearly on the cards, for each slender green briar, dropping to earth, takes root at its tip to seize a new bridgehead for its parent plant. Next summer it will arch on again – and again. In fact, said Pliny the Elder (thinking, perhaps, of the country estate he was neglecting for his scholar-ship in Nero's Rome), blackberry briars 'would fill up the whole place if resistance were not offered by cultivation, so that it would be positively possible to imagine that mankind is cre-ated for this service of the earth'.

Some of the briars I do, indeed, chop back, and tug from the soil if they have rooted. But others, springing out from plants with the biggest, juiciest berries, are carefully woven back into the hedge, for next year's crop. *Rubus fruticosus*, the blackberry, achieves its many forms through variations in its seeds. Each suc-cessful variation, spread in the droppings of starlings or foxes, is potentially a microspecies, adapted to particular conditions of temperature or soil chemistry and cloning itself repeatedly by the arching of its shoots. There are at least seventy sorts of black-berry along the hedges of Ireland now, some hauling themselves about with briars the thickness of my thumb and armed with hooked prickles of a medieval ferocity. The rooted arches of briars figure in rural 'cures' (like a hole in a rock or a split in a tree, it was one more natural loop or orifice through which to crawl from one state of grace to another) and some microspecies of *R. fruticosus*, threatened as a remedy for boils or hernia, must have added elements of genuine ordeal.

Pauses to straighten one's back and sample the blackberries are the prerogative of the potato-digger. The job takes a good many days (a few together now and then) and can't be hurried. Nothing suits the new silence of the acre better than the hiss of spade in earth, the small whispery sounds as I search out the tubers and lob them gently together, the whir of a robin darting to snatch a worm from my shadow; above all, the measured buzz of working bumblebees. They fumble the last few holly-hock blossoms, stuck to the tops of their stems like stubborn pink butterflies, and the purple sheafs of Michaelmas daisies sprawled beside the pond. Sometimes, the very pointlessness of their industry overwhelms me: they will all die. Only the queens will live past winter and there will be no more queen bumblebees in Connacht next year than there were this: perhaps even fewer, as more field-banks are bulldozed away. I go back to the potatoes, digging blackberry pips out with my tongue, even less ready to die than I was before.

I had forgotten the very voice of autumn, a whistling descant that wires me directly to the old, grassed-over potato ridges on the hill: *cour-lee! cour-lee!* There is no deconstructing the 'cry of the curlew', a singular notion if ever there was one. Yet what is wist-ful to others is comforting to me. A lone and unemployed curlew along the shore in summer is a link with the 'real' Thallabawn, waiting for us when the cars are gone; and the first flock, gathered on the strand after breeding on the moors, is the seal of reinheri-tance. They fold away from me nervously, lifting and settling, lifting and settling in a drift of down-curved wings, then rising at last with a guttural *whaup!* of alarm and a flash of white rumps.

How far has wariness been bred into the curlew? I get into terrible fixes in thinking about this, never quite sure when I am stumbling into the heresy of 'inheritance of acquired character-istics'. It makes sense that, where curlews are regularly hunted, a hyper-alertness and nervousness would be pooled among the genes of survivors. The curlew sold in the markets of Dublin a century ago were shot among great winter flocks along the mud banks of Clontarf and Malahide. These were notoriously nervous birds: a shred of seaweed scurrying in the wind might put them all up. Here in the West, the assiduous wildfowler Sir Ralph Payne-Gallwey recommended crippling a curlew (*'if you can'* in arch italics) and fastening it to a peg as a decoy, so that others in the neighbourhood would 'pay a visit of curiosity or condolence to the noisy captive'.

Today, the habit of fear among Thallabawn's curlews ought to be substantially diluted. Notwithstanding the minister's permission to shoot them in season, they are not among the countryman's favourite game ('fishy' is the word that saves them). Perhaps the fact that they allow me to approach them at all is a sign of a slow ebbing of apprehension, generation by generation. But the habit must still be strong in the flocks of migrant birds with which they are mingled in winter, when Ireland holds at least a quarter of all the curlews in Europe. It is usual, when anathematising the excesses of continental hunters, to single out the French and Italians, but for curlews the image that stays with me is one from Denmark, a notable crossroads on the flight paths of migration. There, after an autumn weekend's shooting, the market in Copenhagen is, by some accounts, stacked with crates of waders, the long bills of the curlews sticking out at all angles.

A fine week in September is a time for fixing roofs, moving walls and making roads through marshy places. Between here and the mountain, all these are in train. On the acre, with the stream in The Hollow reduced to a companionable babble, these were days for building a new footbridge.

The alternative was to move the clothesline from its corner behind the big willow on the far bank of the stream, a corner so sheltered that bed-sheets, caught out in a gale, merely flutter, and many showers never find it. Pegging out the wash there on a sunny morning, with a willow warbler singing in the branches overhead, one would have to describe it as a clothesline with ambience; relocation is unthinkable.

Over the years, footbridges have come and gone, sometimes swept away in the spates that have torn at the banks and worn the stream bed to a canyon in the soft yellow clay. As the span grew wider and wider, we forgot about planks and took to scrambling across between the boulders: not, in prospect, an exercise for pensioners. Thus, a matter of building up new foundations, proper steps, solid footings; of getting to grips with Earth's primal fabric; of splashing around in wellingtons with buckets of cement.

Almost anything to do with the stream is, I find, immensely therapeutic. Whether or not it has positive ions (should that be negative?) to excite my molecules, there is the play of light on underwater pebbles, the engaging anarchy and music of the water's flow. Then, the delicious unwisdom of interfering with it, of predicting how it will react to some boulders put here or taken from there. The stream wants to go down the hill to the sea: would carve for itself, if it could, a dead-straight, U-shaped chute with sides of glass. It is pure, formless energy, pushing and twisting down the path of least resistance. Narrow it, and it will speed up and push harder; block it, and it will start to burrow under, around, behind. In a spate, its dynamics change, spinning and churning, and bowling loose rocks, like cannonballs, at everything ahead. One's only hope, really, is to give it as much room as possible, then weld a lot of rocks together with cement.

A sign of grace in these matters is finding use for an essential material already in one's keeping. One autumn a decade ago, enormous planks, fifteen feet long, began drifting ashore on the strand. I was their first discoverer and should, by all the rules, have cached as many as I could in the dunes until surprised or betrayed. Instead, I settled for one, and spread the word.

A plank fifteen feet long and handsomely wide and thick has few everyday uses, but once cut in half it is no longer remarkable. I hoisted it up with ropes beneath the roof of the shed until the right day should come. With what satisfaction I now took it down and sawed it through, soaked its dry fibres in creosote, and bolted it together for our bridge, may be imagined only by readers of *Practical Self-Sufficiency*.

★

When I have stored up enough virtue in September, and the first dozen bags of Records and Golden Wonders are safely in the dark of the shed, I make my autumn pilgrimage to Derry – my Derry, of the hundreds of places in Ireland with that name. To reach most of them, you head for an island in a bog, a hillock of glacial debris on which a grove of wild oaks survived. To reach the Derry I mean, it is necessary to circumnavigate a mountain and seek out one of the most remarkable paths in Ireland. (As I write, this is easier said than done, since a highly contentious farm fence, resolutely defended, checks the explorer right at the beginning, but my purposes must suppose an ideal world, free of all trespass.)

The path begins beneath the southern wall of Mweelrea, where the mountain spills down into the fiord. At this point, already remote by two white strands from the end of the nearest road, a stony track leads up, promisingly, through the bluffs above the shore. Quite early on, however, a twisted holly tree, bleached silver by salt and wind, leans over a wall like a signpost to gesture up the hill. What looks, and feels underfoot, like the bed of a stream ascends to a new level of the mountainside.

Here, astray on a broken slope of rock and bog, one feels in need of a landmark. But the sound arrives first: on this bare slope, an insistent rustling of leaves. Perched upon a low cliff, feet wedged firmly in a crack, arms spread-eagled across the warm rock, ten whispering aspens cling side by side. They are worth a detour.

To survive on their narrow ledge, beyond the reach of sheep, they have sent roots searching *through the rock* for minerals flushed into its cracks. On a rainy mountain, water constantly leaches the minerals from one place and deposits them in another, and a cliff below a sheer slope, and the pocket of soil below that, is thereby enriched. The ten whispering graces are, in all probability, clones of a single seedling (for aspen grows by suckering, as well). What set out as the first soft filaments of roots, testing the crevices for moisture and nourishment, are now limbs as gnarled and thick as your thigh, embedded in the hard Mweelrea gritstone. As if to make some point about strength and fragility, speckled grey spiders have chosen to spin great webs across the base of the cliff: a gossamer curtain, billowing and glinting in the wind.

Even the path, when you discover it, has something to say about the survival of species, about the adaptation of organisms to their habitats. At first sight, there *is* no path, just long ridges of smooth bedrock lifted up above the bog, one ridge succeeding another, one slab taking over from another in an endless, uneven pavement across the bog. And then one begins to notice worn and dusty places, like the hollows in the steps of old cathedrals, and stretches of rocks laid down into the bog, like setts, to link the natural terraces.

In this way the path becomes peopled by ghosts long before it arrives at Derry, the deserted village, the 'Famine' ruin in the wilderness. This fortuitous rib of sandstone, running for a mile along the marshy flank of the mountain, was the clachan's highroad to the outer coast at the mouth of the fiord. Another, more substantial, track ran eastwards to Bundorragha, clinging for much of the way to the rocky, seaweedy shore of the fiord.

The dramatic location of Derry, on its narrow shelf of land below the mountain cliffs, and its utter isolation today from roads and modern houses, invest its ruins with an almost operatic sense of doom, if you are in that sort of mood. A paragraph in Cecil Woodham-Smith's *The Great Famine* resists all revisionism:

> The revenue cutter *Eliza*, making a visit of inspection, on June 22, to the Killeries, a wild district of mountain and deep ocean inlets in the far west, was implored for food by a boatload of skeletons ... One man, stated the officer in command, was lying on the bottom of the boat, unable to stand and already half dead, the others, with emaciated faces and prominent, staring eyeballs, were evidently in an advanced state of starvation.

In 1841, sixty-nine people lived along the Derry shore; ten years later, none.

But this is not what I rehearse on a sun-filled afternoon in September, or at least not this alone. Threading my way along the high terraces, I am taken up with pleasure at the peace of it all: cloud-shadows moving on the Maumturks, wind-patterns texturing the fiord (we will accommodate the mussel-lines, the salmon-rafts, the *putt-putting* work boat). Coming at last to the crooked oak trees of Derry, and sitting level with their branches on a rock overlooking the clachan, I can quite happily suppose that, pending the Famine, it was not at all a bad place to live.

The houses, with their elaborate weave of stone-walled animal pens and 'gardens', bask around a hollow facing south. Storms from the Atlantic, while rushing noisily enough along the mountain behind the village and sending waves splashing among the currachs arrayed in front of it, would scarcely have rippled Derry's oaten thatch. There were streams outside the door; turf-banks at the end of the street. Above all – or below all – there was seaweed, layer upon layer of dark bladderwrack lifting and swirling: ten miles of it, on Derry's side alone. The potato was indeed what supported the huge surge in population, the seething vivacity of Connacht's coastal slums: but the seaweed, to manure it, came first.

The fiord was full of food, each in season: scallops, mussels and lobsters, runs of salmon and sea trout, shoals of herring and mackerel (in his commentary to *Letters from the Irish Highlands*, Kevin Whelan rebukes the easy cliché that 'in pre-Famine Ireland, coastal communities avoided fish eating'; scallops were 'a very favourite and esteemed luxury'). Young Derrymen would have been among the ten thousand fishermen who converged on Inishbofin in summer to fish the herring in seine boats, each rowed by seven men.

But that was in the boom years, with the money flowing out from Napoleon's wars and trickling all the way through the cattle marts to the young calves of Connemara. Ulster's linen-weavers, too, wanted oats for their porridge; oat-growing farmers joined the gentry in a taste for untaxed *poitín*. Derry was almost as good as an island when it came to keeping watch for strangers, and any smoke from the still was lost against the mountain. In such times, Dr Whelan says, 'Connemara must have seemed like a poor man's paradise'.

But after 1815 everything collapsed like dominoes: wars and weather, farm prices, cottage weaving; even the herring deserted the coast. The clachans, trapped in their togetherness, bred on; potato ridges crept higher, to those extraordinary levels on the mountain above Leenane, and out along the shore to either side of Derry: every headland, every cultivable corner. A slow squeeze of hardship leads to the final reduction of the Famine: they'd sold their nets. *Still, living beside the fiord, you'd think . . .* You'd have to be there, I suppose, as the days passed: all those people, all those days, skidding on the seaweed, flipping it over frond by frond, looking for mussels, crabs, winkles, anything . . .

In my first winter in Ireland, that sabbatical time for 'finding' myself in a cottage under Tully Mountain, I lived on mussels and potatoes four or five days a week. I picked them in the estuary down at Derryinver, where the tweedy anglers catch their salmon. Sometimes, with more in my bucket than I meant to collect, I'd take some in to Patrick and Maria, the elderly brother and sister (more like a couple) to whom I paid the rent. They were always sharing something with me: bowls of beestings and carrageen jelly, fresh eggs, slices of brack. They baked bread for me in a pot oven with turf embers heaped on the lid, and made butter for me in a hand churn on the kitchen table (I caught them at this once, on an evening the milk was slow to turn, and was appalled by the beads of sweat on their faces, their stooped exhaustion at the handle of the churn). They admired the mussels and thanked me for them, several times, and threw them out under the sycamores when I'd gone.

Today, their house has acquired a bizarre thatched roof, with 'eyebrows', of the kind seen in Constable paintings – for summer people, I suppose. When I sit among the crooked oaks in Derry, I reinstate Patrick and Maria in the best of the old ruins. A glitter off the fiord beams in through the doorway, catching a

curl of turf-smoke and turning it bright blue. Maria has a besom
made of the bushy Mediterranean heather that, shoulder-high,
is slowly engulfing the clachan; her tall, gaunt figure, her
hollowed eyes, her moustache; indignant chickens flapping out
the door.

OCTOBER

Old Michael called it the 'green dawn': that state of the light, long before sunrise, when the brightest grey below the sky is the chalky line of the surf, and the glimmer of the fields is green only because that is the colour of grass. It is the time of the robin's first warble, of its first flight to my lighted window to snatch a daddy-longlegs buffeting the glass. It is also – and this is the reason why Michael had a name for it at all – the time when the rooks lift up from the trees around Bridie's house and go marauding.

The only time I saw him seriously discomposed was in one of those appalling autumns in the eighties. His field of oats had been rescued from disaster by a swift, heroic *meitheal* of men with scythes, but the crows would not leave it alone: he woke to see them flopping and slithering across the wet stooks, stuffing their craws with grain. He came to my door: 'God damn it, Michael! Have you a trap?' But, of course, I had not. The best he could do, until the oats were dry enough to cock, was take a barrel to the field and install his youngest dog there, on a rope. 'Didn't the buggers perch on the barrel!' he stormed next day.

In those same soft dawns, the rooks in ragged lines fly out to loot potatoes – not one here and there, or even a dozen, but in a wholesale plundering and spoiling that would break your heart. It begins, as a rule, with the first heavy rains of autumn, which hose away the thin soil from the shoulders of the ridges. White and yellow are the rooks' favourite food colours, and a few glimpses of ivory skin are quite enough to cue them. One would not grudge the poyeens, or even the creamy half of the sunburned spuds, of which there are always a good number. But I have come down the path, after a week of inattention, to find the ridges littered with scores of the biggest and best potatoes in the crop. Each is drilled with beak-marks: half-hollowed at most. A hundred more have tumbled into the mud of the sheughs. The ridges are deeply pitted where the rooks have *dug down* for their harvest (rooks are great diggers for worms and grubs: hence their featherless cheeks). One can only, with resignation, gather everything up into bags and, in the kitchen, thriftily chop the good bits off for boxty.

In the early years we tried realistic scarecrows: more, perhaps, for art than science and certainly to no lasting effect. Then, tall bamboo poles (boat-hooks, from the strand) planted at an angle and bearing long, fluttering shreds of black plastic, like prayer flags: these disconcerted the rooks, but depressed us as well. Finally, in a belated burst of lateral thinking, we have pegged out garden nets, of the sort sold to keep birds off fruit bushes. With this protection, and a concealing green froth of chickweed, the crop can be left safely in the ground all winter. But there is no substitute, really, for lifting potatoes when the job falls due.

Choughs are crows, too, but of a more enlivening kind, with none of the bullying coarseness of rooks or magpies. Their ringing *kee-aw!* gets my attention instantly, so pleased am I to see them. The acre itself has no interest for choughs, but sometimes a party will pitch down on the rocky pasture across the road, where they stab at the turf with their curving coral bills like thrushes on a lawn. They never stay long: a quick sampling for insect grubs and they're off again, fingers spread, like a gang of children playing aeroplanes.

The thin turf of 'unimproved' hill pasture corresponds exactly to the birds' more usual terrain down at the shore. There, from October onwards, I meet choughs in their little winter flocks, a dozen or two at a time, feeding among the sheep or bobbing in updrafts from cliffs and creggans. A low sun dyes their bill and legs an even more intense red, and glosses their black feathers with highlights of purple and green. I plan a pastel, or something Japanese – commas for those wing-tips, in black ink (it doesn't get done).

Choughs are fastidious specialists: you would never catch them consorting with the jackdaws, pecking at greasy wrappings outside the village takeaway. By original instinct they are mountain birds, but they have adapted to one of the better compromises between nature and man as farmer. The sheepwalks of the Celtic seaboard (the Hebrides, Wales, the Atlantic coast of Ireland) have matched certain wild things they need with an abundance of suitable food. Thus they have caves and crevices to nest in, plenty of airy, private space for their busy social lives, and a short, wind-dwarfed turf full of dung-loving insects. Celtic Cornwall had choughs, too, but after long maligning them as thieves and fire-raisers (the red bills as embers), it finally ploughed them off the cliff-tops.

Anyone who studies choughs seems to become very fond of them. A pair of choughs, the ornithologist Ian Bullock wrote to me, 'are much like humans – they walk shoulder to shoulder, fly at the same moment and close together, and often feed each other or preen each other – very obviously in love. They have suffered under the stigma of being a "crow", yet hard work and honesty mark their lives.'

I have been saving the otters: they deserve the more spacious days of autumn, quiet intervals in which they reinstate their patterns on the shore. August was scarcely over when, walking the strand together early in the day, we found no fewer than five separate otter-tracks across the freshly washed strand, all of them heading to the dunes.

We were together thirty years ago – in fact, on our honeymoon on Clare Island in October – when an otter appeared to us, buoyed up in a curling wave ('like washing on a line', as Ethna often sees them now). It was the first revelation of the life style of our coastal otters. 'You mean sea otters,' people say, thinking perhaps of the Californian sort, seen on television, floating on their backs and bashing urchins with stones, on their stomachs. But no, we mean the ordinary Irish otter, *Lutra lutra*, as happy chasing wrasse and butterfish around the seaweedy rocks as catching trout and eels in lakes and rivers.

One morning back in January (you may as well have the atmosphere) I went splashing out after a gale, to beachcomb. The breakers were curling with that minty blue light of winter, inexpressibly cold, and the foam went on spilling and churning and looping up the beach as if to see how much sand it could cover at a stretch. Blobs of spume were skating even further, each on its cushion of wind.

Here and there the last tide had almost touched the face of the dunes, so that any tracks on the sand were as fresh and crisp as cats' paw-marks in fresh cement. And what tracks there were! I was expecting the usual two-way passage of otters where the dunes come closest to the sea, but not this exuberant traffic. It crossed and recrossed the strand at several points thereafter and garlanded the high-tide line: one, two, three animals abreast.

The prints of otters do, indeed, share with those of cats a rounded precision in the toe-pads – but there are five of them, not four, and set in an arc, not tightly clustered. One line of tracks was noticeably deeper and bolder: a female, perhaps, with two well-grown cubs. I neither expected, nor even hoped, to see them – when it happens, it happens and I am glad. Between encounters, the tracks are enough of a link between the animals' lives and my own.

In the event, it was one of those – very occasional – happenings that make a naturalist wonder if he has become invisible. There I was, quite unconcealed, a large and solitary person plodding in wellingtons and swinging a stick (but without the dog, for once) in the middle of the strand at high noon. The first otter emerged from the foam a mere stone's throw ahead of me, a small fish in its mouth, and ran, with the usual, ungainly hump-and-skip, across the strand and up into the dunes. I waited still for a while, picturing the otter curled up in a hollow between the clumps of marram grass, munching on its fish. But then a raven arrived out of nowhere and hung above the marram, a few feet up, claws dangling, and uttering a bullying *caa! caa!*

All comfort gone, the otter ran this way and that, its course betrayed by the fluttering raven. It appeared on the crest of the dune, twisting and lolloping in the soft sand. It paused, and the bird touched down nearby, wings lifted, neck stretched. This was too much; the otter swung away and bounded down the face of the dune and kept on going until it gained the foam. The raven wheeled away backwards, letting the wind take it.

It is not at all excepional for mammals to be mobbed by crows – think of cats and magpies. In Greenland, the Arctic fox would wince away from the swoops of a harassing skua, and on this strand I once met a red fox, hunched in resignation as it trotted along, a pair of hoodies rasping away at either side. But ravens do cross the line between instinctual mobbing of a preda-tor and a calculated piracy: Bernd Heinrich, the American raven-watcher, quotes a Koyukon Indian in Alaska who saw an otter haul a fish onto an ice floe and then be bullied off its prey.

This exotic detail is flattering, the Koyukon Indian adding, so to speak, a notch to my bow, but we are not finished here at Thallabawn. The first otter had departed, gliding away along the slope of shallow foam, and I walked on. Then, oh my good-ness, there was mother-otter and – I would think – the second of her cubs, lolling together at the edge of the surf. Each had a floun-der and was taking bites at its leisure, as from a slippery sandwich. My binoculars were, of course, in the knapsack on my back, so I was denied the whiskery close-ups I have had from time to time. I was content to stand, two stone's throw distant, and wait until they had finished. Then they went off to catch more fish, swim-ming in tandem along the trough of the breakers, diving and reappearing. Coming abreast of me, they moved out one wave, and, having passed, swerved in again, travelling south.

Such insouciance in otters, such daytime casualness, must seem extraordinary to those who know the animals only from glimpses and ripples, or signs on river-banks. In the eighties a young scientific couple from England, Peter and Linda Chapman, toured the whole of Ireland in a minibus, surveying the 'status' of our otters for the Vincent Wildlife Trust. When I met them they had been months on the road, stopping every few miles at a likely bridge or ford, to check for spraint (the otter's droppings, distinctive and musky), or tracks in mud or sand. They found these traces almost everywhere they ought to be – Ireland is exceptional in Europe for that – but not until they reached the coast of Mayo did they actually catch sight of an otter.

Once, making a documentary film, with David Cabot, about Michael Longley and the imagery he finds in the Thallabawn landscape, I persuaded the poet to roll up his trousers and paddle in the surf. It was November: there was a ravishing, broken sky beyond him, with shafts of theatrical sun among the islands, a mood that seemed just right for his 'Sea Shanty'. As we finished the shots and released Michael from his stoical position, we were mesmerised to see a pair of otter cubs travelling fast towards us, along the line of the tide. The camera was still on its tripod in the foam and, with David's usual luck, there was unexposed film in the magazine. The cubs kept coming, dramatically black and glossy in the brilliant sea-suds, and only at the last moment, within yards, did they swerve around us, out of frame. It was, I have to say, the first time otters had shown themselves in quite this intoxicating manner.

> An upturned currach at Allaran Point
> And a breaking wave are holt and hover
> Until the otter, on wet sand in between,
> Engraves its own reflection and departure.

As usual, Michael captures a lot in a little. The corner of sand below the rocks at Allaran Point is the otters' regular pathway from the sea, and the currach berthed on the grass above it must, like any other dry cave, have attractions as a hover – a place to lie up and munch fish and sleep. But the tracks disappear into a deep gully carved in the dunes by a stream. Beyond it, going inland, is a little lake, fringed by reeds, a home to a pair of swans. It was here, on a glittering winter morning, that I saw my first Thallabawn otter swimming in its 'natural', freshwater setting. Indeed, although it seems strange to me now, years passed before I became aware of the otters' 'double life' between the lakes and the sea.

During those years of mooching back and forth across the *duach*, I grew intrigued by a network of narrow, muddy paths drawn, almost straight as a ruler, across the level sward. Sometimes, walking among the sheep that keep this common ground nibbled to the nap, I would see a few of them fall into single file along one of these paths. It defied all logic that, on a plain as open as a billiard table, where one destination was good as any other, the sheep should create and maintain such a well-worn set of trails. Then, bothering actually to follow the trails and study them, their real origin revealed itself. These are the ways the otters travel at night: a map, drawn plain as day, of their journeys between the lakes. The sheep, coming upon them, merely fall into line automatically for a while, just as they do on their own trails carved into the steeper slopes of mountains. And if their hoof-marks are 'everywhere' in the muddy parts of the trails, it is because they are everywhere in general.

The attraction of the lakes for otters would seem obvious enough: lots of eels, first of all, and the odd brown trout. But Hans Kruuk, studying the coastal otters of Shetland and the Scottish Highlands, has found an even more basic reason. Otters which fish in the sea must bathe frequently in fresh water to keep their coats in good condition: salt will mat them so that they can no longer hold air to keep them warm when they dive. It is this, before all, which brings them by night – also, perhaps, in the rooks' 'green dawn' – up through the dunes and out across the bare acres of the *duach*, travelling as fast as they are able.

'What's the closest you've *ever ever* come to an otter?' a young friend wanted to know. Was I wrong to tell him of the one I drowned in the fyke net (fur matted with eel-slime as it spun round and round)? In the old days, when these nets were made of cotton, otters would discover the eels trapped in the 'cod-end' and chew through the net to seize them. But modern plastic netting is too tough, and the otter, looking for another way, had found the entrance hoop and swum in, further and further, right to the eels at the end of the sleeve. In England, in one decade, ninety of that country's scarce otters were reported drowned in these underwater traps – probably a fraction of the real toll. It is not difficult to fit a guard-net over the entrance, with a mesh too small for otters: simply, no one had thought of it.

When October is stormy at all it is often excessively so. Long trains of Atlantic depressions pile up the sea so that spray surging high around Ardoilean gleams on the horizon like the slow, pulsing beam of a lighthouse. Tufts of sea pink, snatched from island cliffs, arrive on our tideline, and among them, from time to time, is a grey seal pup, still in the snowy white coat of infancy . . .

The pup was the largest thing on the strand and therefore tiny in so much emptiness. A high tide at dawn had delivered him almost to the foot of the dunes, along with the lightest of drift objects: feathers and bladderwrack. There he slept and woke to find the sea withdrawn. A twenty-yard trail zigzagged towards the surf, but halfway there he had fallen asleep again. As the wind dried him, his fur became fluffy: a startling white fluffiness against the smooth sand.

   He did not hear me coming. I woke him, in friendly tones, not out of meanness but to see how much energy he had. He lay on his tummy and roared at me weakly, cheeks puffed out, whisker-lines curving like the lion in *The Wizard of Oz*. He reared up on his flippers and thrust forward as I leaned too close. Reassured about his life force, I lay down, seal-like, on the sand at a companionable distance. A tractor and trailer drove past us

to the place for shovelling shell-sand. I did not stir: they are used
to me doing strange things by the sea.

The pup's eyes were unfathomably dark within, like camera
lenses at full aperture: in an adult – a big bull, say, peering past its
long, Roman nose – the eyes seem brutally carved, mere black
holes in the head. Seals, like whales, have lenses that are nearly
spherical, so that, diving deep, whatever light there is can be
brought to a focus on the retina. Out of the water, this is not an
eye for distant detail; the hunter's movement, yes, in a flash, but
only closeness would give the pup a passable image of a man
(rock-skinned, seaweed-haired).

The pup was well on towards weaning, his coat quite free of
the golden tinge of birth yolk. Soon he would begin to moult to
a sleeker, silvery blue. Fat was packed beneath his skin, would
carry him through the time of desertion, of learning to hunt
for himself. A year distant, he might not weigh even as much
as he did now.

I left for home and kept an eye on him through binoculars, a
speck on the sand, unmoving. Next morning he had gone, and
more marks in the sand told how. The overnight tide had lifted
him again, like a bottle, and nudged him up the long slope to the
dunes. For a second night he slept, waking again to find the sea
gone. But this time he followed it all the way down, and carried
on. I would like to have seen that.

The grey seals choose this precarious season for hauling out on
the shores of the wilder islands, there to give birth and mate
again. In a similarly stormy autumn, David Cabot and I camped
on Duvillaun, a small island off the tip of Mayo's Mullet peninsula, to film the seals and their pups for a wildlife documentary.

Duvillaun More is a whale-backed wedge of an island, all the
more lonely and confining for looking out to other places. On a
high point is an upright stone slab, bristling with lichens and
carved with a cross of arcs and a crucifixion scene, still potent
and legible after a thousand years. Standing beside it, one looks
north to Inishkea, east to the Mullet, south to the black cliffs of

Achill Head. At this intersection the great swells of the Atlantic are brought up short and jostle together as they swing around the island into Blacksod Bay. In a run of storms, such as David and I ... enjoyed, endured, both are true ... there are times when Duvillaun and its crucifixion are a pivot of colliding forces, wind and tide hammering it out on an encircling arena of foam.

People – not just tenth-century hermits, but warm and noisy families – lived in this place. They chose, unusually, to build their little clachan high on the windy ridge of the island, next to Christ – next also to little *lochán*s of water that pierce the plateau and mirror the sky. One would guess the damp air of Duvillaun to be rich in sodium and sulphur, a Gaian cocktail conjured from the sea. It has nourished astonishing growths of grey-green lichen, which beard the stone walls of the ruins to a depth of several inches. The whole island, for that matter, is shaggy with vegetation. Its slopes shimmer with knee-deep moorgrass, and the road from the landing place, left high above cutaway peat, is now densely carpeted with heather.

We crossed from Inishkea to Duvillaun in a morning calm, the big metal camera trunk perched like a shiny coffin between us. There was a moment in landing when the bow of the infla-table caught on a ledge of rock and the trunk and all the rest of the gear slid and tilted as the wave fell away: but it rushed back in time to save us.

We pitched the tents on grassy floors within the clachan ruins, on opposite sides of the street. As I lifted stones to anchor the pegs, a black, furry animal sprang out and fled between my boots. Black rabbits are a speciality of Duvillaun, and later, exploring their warren on the high western cliff-tops, one expla-nation was irresistible. The mouths of the burrows, tunnelling down into the peat beneath great cushions of sea pink, were as black as – as black rabbits. Among the animals scattering and ducking down from my approach, the dark ones disappeared first. Thus, it seemed to me, predation on baby rabbits by the island's fierce gulls would be bound to favour the survival of

the blackest. But zoologists prefer it a different way. Only in the
isolated populations of islands, they say, in the absence of foxes
and stoats, do the genes of 'conspicuous' black rabbits survive at
all. So much for my ingenuity.

The seals had their breeding ground at the sheltered south-east
of the island. Across the sound, the northern cliffs of Achill rose
enormous and daunting against the sun, but the seals' cove itself,
on that first, quiet day, had a tranquil sense of pleasure, a mood
of some Victorian outing to the sea. A big bull presided on his
rock, a gross, dark pyramid. Cows came and went in the shallows or hung like amphorae in the glowing crests of waves
('bottling', this is called, a dream-state perfected by seals). Up
on the terraces, young non-breeders lolled in twos and threes in
tepid rock pools. Pups lay wedged among rocks, dozing or waving their flippers like babies left in cots. They were swelling hour
by hour on the fat in their mother's milk, and here and there
struggled forward to meet the scenting sniff, the suckling roll
and sigh. A lively light modelled the lines of the animals, picking them out from the shadows and flattering their marbled
patterns, the sparkling texture of their fur. All this was laid out
for filming as if by an efficient production manager, even to
suggesting the one best position on the cliff for David's hide.
Wild creatures are not good at counting: they track movement
to and fro but do not notice if two men come to set up a hide and
only one goes away. Anxiety subsides; the little brown canvas
booth a new rock in the landscape.

The first gale rose that evening in a wall of black cloud over
Achill Head. It wrenched at our tents with a severity far greater
than anything we had met in Germania Land. The tents were
streamlined, which is to say their framing left them free to buck
and squirm, and to shake off the hosing rain like some distraught
animal. I stuffed pellets of paper into my ears and eventually
dozed. At some point, muffled or not, I registered the calling
of geese overhead: Greenland barnacles, in the teeth of the
storm, were putting down to roost at the island's boggy pools.

The train of gales continued for five days, 'a whole line of depressions', as the radio informed us, 'queuing up across the Atlantic'. When Duvillaun Beag, between us and the Mullet, began to vanish in the white sweep of rollers, we hauled the inflatable higher above the shore and weighed it down with bigger rocks. There were intervals of flooding sunshine, even of calm at night, with stars and a quarter-moon. It was then we heard the seals crooning, a soft, antiphonal chorus drifting up from the cove.

Watching the maelstrom of foam-streaked waves thrusting into every crevice, we wondered how more than a few of this year's pups could possibly survive. Then would come a lull to mere boisterousness, and the heads would reappear. In one of these intervals, we found a mother suckling her pup in a little, sandy-floored creek with a sheer cliff rising at the back. As David filmed them, the foam from the storm-swollen tide was swirling higher and higher. The cow struggled to block the waves with her body, but eventually the pup was dragged away in the backwash (the camera following steadily). Later, we saw the mother breasting the waves, towing the drowned pup by the scruff of its neck, limp as an empty purse. At some island nurseries, in a rough October, four in ten of the young are swept away like this (the watchers, keeping count, have anorak hoods laced tight around small, wet, weaselly faces: eyes, nose, mouth, a hint of beard).

The western cliffs of Duvillaun are fractured into isolated stacks. Each separated tower is capped with grass and sea pink cushions, a draping prettily at odds with the black planes of sheer rock below, sweating with spray and echoing like dungeons. Safe on the island's main substance, I lay on my back among the pillowing thrift and ogled, through binoculars, the peregrine falcon that screamed unremittingly above me. The wind tugged so fiercely at the thatch of its wings that the usual trim anchor of their silhouette was split into a fistful of dark knives.

The falcon had a regular station in the air, poised centre stage above the amphitheatre of cliffs, and returned to it again and again to hover and point like a wind vane or a compass needle. The busybody circlings and insistent, imperious screaming became slightly ridiculous. Somewhere on these ledges was the peregrine's summer eyrie, but breeding was over and the cliffs long empty of prey. The falcon's natural hunting ground now was among the autumn flocks of waders along the sands of the Mullet or the Inishkeas. But the peregrine is nothing if not territorial and sometimes defends its nest-site as a roosting place. It could reach Inishkea South within minutes; but for the moment it would stay where it belonged, at familiar co-ordinates of updraught and azimuth.

During one of our early, exhausting nights in the ruins, I discovered a fellow castaway. Beyond the snapping tent wall and the snarl of wind there came a sound I associated with summer on Inishvickillane or Ardoilean or the Bills beyond Achill. It was the unmistakeable, rhythmic purring and hiccupping of storm petrels. These are the smallest and most fragile-seeming of sea birds, dusky, martin-like miniatures weighing hardly an ounce, yet hosts of them flutter above the oceans, and thousands nest deep in burrows and crevices of our remoter Atlantic islands, venturing to come and go only by night.

On Inishvickillane I had pitched my tent, all unknowing, in the petrels' flight path to a dry-stone wall, and was woken at midnight by their little thuds and skitterings as they brushed the cloth above my head. But that was in June, when they were starting to lay their eggs. On Duvillaun now, in early October, surely, any young should long have fledged and flown? Since then, I have gone back to Ronald Lockley, who sorted out the petrels' extraordinary breeding schedule in his *Letters from Skokholm* (1947).

On his Welsh island, the petrels were still laying in the first week in July: a single large egg, often pure white. An egg laid on 6 July, for example, was incubated for thirty-nine days, the parents taking turns to sit for two or three days at a time. So the egg was hatched on 14 August – but the young bird did not leave until 21 October! The newborn petrel is weak and wobbly, a soft ball of down, and is fed just once in twenty-four hours, when the parents come in about midnight and regurgitate an oily, fishy goo for it to swallow. But this is obviously highly nutritious, because the chick ends up weighing nearly twice as much as its parents.

At about five weeks of age, in mid-September, the Skokholm parents began to lose interest. They sometimes forgot to come home for several nights together; they were moulting and low in energy and seemed to be especially reluctant to come ashore in the bright light of the Hunter's Moon. In the twenty-one days of October, the chick was visited less and less often, and not at all in the last six nights (Lockley was a dab hand with telltale matchsticks and bits of twig). Then the young bird, greatly slimmed down, crawled out between the stones and disappeared. Lockley did not see any wing-exercising, but other people have watched petrel fledglings in vigorous calisthenic sessions on a rock outside the burrow. In any event, the first flight goes straight out to sea.

A day or two after I heard the midnight churring, I crawled out in a noisy dawn to try to add another foot or two to the low wall sheltering the tent. As I hoisted slabs of rock from the debris of the fallen gable, all sharp edges and crusty lichen, I uncovered a hole, and in it a substantial ball of trembling, slaty blue fluff. The wind parted this baby-down to show feathers growing out beneath it, on the same shafts, and fragments of the terminal fluff blew away as I watched. Now I can say that this placed the chick at about seven weeks old, with perhaps another two or three weeks to wait. But on Duvillaun, putting the stone back carefully, I had only anthropomorphic thoughts, about desertion and loneliness.

By the fifth day we, too, were running somewhat low on food – a heel of bread, a little muesli, but more packets of soup than we hoped to need. However, David, while getting fretful now his camera batteries were dead, seemed unusually resigned to waiting for a reasonable sea. He had had a dream. He was in the dinghy, halfway to Inishkea, when it was swamped, and he didn't know whether to go on or turn back. There came, indeed, an overoptimistic morning forecast which could have trapped us in just this way, but, watching the sea and sky, we were uneasy and crawled into our tents again. By noon the wind was climbing rapidly back to Force 9, at which, on the Viney Scale, water being carried from a *lochán* in a saucepan is blown horizontally away.

We escaped next day between rain squalls, the dinghy pitching and banging through a cross-sea into the shelter of Inishkea South.

Even on Duvillaun it was obvious that, despite the storms, advance parties of barnacle geese were coming in early from Iceland. The calling overhead in the darkness; fresh 'cheroots' left at morning on the moss beside the *locháns*; dark swirlings of birds above the distant profile of Inishkea – all these spoke of excited arrival. Now, with a stiff wind from the north-west, we could expect a heavy fall of birds on Inishkea, their main winter refuge. In all his years of fieldwork on the islands, David had only once or twice been able to connect with the barnacles' arrival. Most of his visits were made in midwinter, when, heads down in the monotony of grazing, the geese were more indifferent to being spied on over field walls or nudged about the islands, sometimes by me, for a closer inspection of rings.

As we swung in around the pier to the gentle white sand of the harbour, a flock of perhaps two hundred birds rose from the fields behind the ruined village and banked away around the beacon on the hill. Another long skein – fifty or sixty geese – flew in from the north as we opened up a sun-blistered door and stowed our gear within. David was off almost at once, visibly ready to crouch in a second, his battered captain's telescope tucked into his armpit. I was enjoined not to show my head outside the village, and retired into our cave of driftwood and soot-blackened plaster, to boil a kettle and shave in half a mirror.

The winter visits to the geese with David had brought me some of the most vivid moments of my life: the most arresting images of light and seascape; the most stirring contact with the wild – once or twice, in stormy crossings to the mainland, four miles away, the greatest apprehension. But over all this has loomed the dour, disintegrating atmosphere of the Inishkeas themselves. At each approach, gliding in to the strand below the village, the spiky frieze of the ruins seems to have shrunk a little more. Wooden lintels sag with the burden of worm-holes; more doors stand ajar to the steady sift of sand; another grey roof is hollowed and rent like a sail in a hurricane.

The roofs of Inishkea were something special: two or three inches of concrete spread across the corrugated iron like icing on a cake and left to set into a stormproof shell, good for generations. But worm has riddled the driftwood purlins and the corrugated sheets have rusted; the great weight of the roof waits on one last gust from the ocean. All this could be expected after half a century of human desertion. But now the very fabric of Inishkea seems to have passed beyond a crucial threshold of change. The Atlantic is bent, simply, on carving the islands into slices that offer least resistance to its massive landward heave. There are, already, Inishkea South and Inishkea North, each with its ruined village. These are separated by a narrow channel, opened long ago across the waist of the original long island. On the western cliffs are spectacular storm beaches, wastelands of boulders heaped up above the shore and spilling inland. The waves that lift these rocks run seething beyond them, lapping into grass and bog and leaving bright trawler-balls stranded, as on a billiard table. Now, at several points, these driven torrents have crossed from one shore to the other, carving deeply through soil and stones and marking out the further, inevitable breaches which will make, of the two islands, an archipelago.

This increasingly primeval disorder merely makes the geese feel more at home. There are even, at the centre of the southern island, boggy areas with shallow ponds that could be lifted from the tundra of Germania Land. It is here that, on nights without a moon, David stretches nets of black nylon between black bamboo poles and catches more barnacles to ring, weigh and code.

The few times I have helped him are among my most affecting memories of Inishkea.

I don't know why the geese should be such busy birds at night. They are not like wading shore birds, which have to match their feeding to the tides – their grass and clover roots will still be there in the morning. Perhaps being born in the Arctic summer gives them habits they find no reason to change. On the open terrain of the islands they have no fear of flying in the dark. Indeed, to walk abroad at night is to move beneath a chorus of ghostly exclamations and the creaking of invisible wings. There are pinprick windows on the Mullet, the brief flare of a car, some moving, firefly lights on a passing ocean trawler – even, to the north, the sweeping beam from Eagle Rock. But here, underfoot, usually little to help. One stumbles across the old lazy-beds at the back of the village, glad even of stars. A sudden, thrilling swish of pinions makes one freeze, face lowered. The little flock swerves at the last moment, glimpsing the net against the stars reflected in the ponds, but the lowest goose is too late and strikes, sliding down the meshes. The birds lodge in pockets – not only the desired barnacles, but wigeon, oyster-catchers, dunlin, curlews, whatever's passing. All need disentangling, from meshes hooked around necks and wings and kicking feet. It takes patience and gentleness, and a helper to shine the torch and hold the bag open.

David came back from counting with a pleased, proprietorial air – eleven hundred geese so far and probably as many still to come. They were nervous, he said, as if they'd been shot at in Iceland. Released to my own walk, I found all of them crowded together on a headland at the far, southern tip of the island. They got up in an explosion such as I have never seen, a flickering eruption of black and silver between me and the sun. They broke into long chains, and circled away to the northern fields, barking and bugling. I called out to them: 'You're beautiful!'

NOVEMBER

At this point of autumn the morning sun is balanced on my shoulder – the mountain's shoulder first, and then my own. At this low angle it saturates the colours in the view from my workroom window, so that I think, just by getting a few of them right, I could paint the scene from memory no matter where I was.

That milky jade-green of a sea flecked with waves, and the clouds' purple shadows across it. A peachy white where the sun lights the tops of the clouds and the slaty blue shadows at their base. A clear Wedgwood blue high up in the sky and the lemony, Arctic blue lower down. Islands and headlands stretch out in chilly purple, to rhyme with the shadows on the sea.

And if I did get it right, even to the red splash of a barn that makes all the other colours sing, why would the picture have such meaning for me? It would be about nature, but also about me looking at it, another year on. This is the way of it every November: a cool and ruthless beauty at a given angle to the sun. So the appetite for change that brought us from the city has turned out to contain its opposite: we draw with deep pleasure on the turn of the seasons, the myriad points of recognition, year by year.

When Edmund Spenser wrote of 'the ever-whirling wheel of Change' he was talking of natural processes and the march of human mortality, not change melted down into novelty, the new imperative of humankind. The urge to explore, the capacity to adapt, these have been the great strengths of human

evolution, but now we are supposed to 'adapt' to change un-
ceasingly, even when its origin is human: an entwining spiral
of dictation and desire. Perhaps, out here on the edge, it is our
constant flux of weather and its theatre of extremes that sets us
free of the need for a daily fix of change, or the yearning for it.
Ironically, what we fear in Bill McKibben's *End of Nature* is the
loss of nature's predictable 'wildness', with its known rhythms
and parameters, and a surrender to a man-made climate with no
discipline at all.

McKibben lives across in New England, a known number of
waves beyond the horizon. A day like this would find him looking out through the last fiery shreds of maple to a steep, bare
peak in the Adirondacks. I do hope he is still in his place, still
walking in the racoons' woods, and has found his way out of
mourning that 'there is no future in loving nature'.

The annual death of chlorophyll is a wonder to poetry and
science alike: millions of tons of green pigment destroyed in a
blaze of colour that sweeps down from the Arctic tundra,
through the woods of north America and western Europe, at
about forty miles a day. From this ritual dissolution, called se-
nescence, the plants salvage sugars and proteins and stow them
away in seeds and tubers. In the leaves, the orderly dismounting
of molecules breaks down the chlorophyll to simpler parts, leaving yellow carotenoids and red or purple phenol to a brief, bio-
chemical glory.

'The hills a witch's quilt of goldrust, flushed cinnamon, wine
fever, hectic lemon ...' That's wrenched out of a poem by
Eamon Grennan, an Irish neighbour of McKibben's in the
New England fall. I wish, just once, Eamon could leave the
young essayists of Vassar to their own prim devices and spend
this semester in his holiday cottage under Tully Mountain,
across the bay. It has become a mission with me to bring our
summer friends back in autumn, to relish the lion-maned moorgrass and cobalt lakes, the bogs misted with pinks and madders
as the sedges turn. Even bracken redeems itself in dying: nothing

else has quite that vivid shade of burnt sienna, richest of all when sodden and curling into rust.

Looking the sun in the eye these mornings, just as it clears the ridge, is to catch the webs of orb-weaving spiders lighting up in the hedgerows and grasses. In this dazzling interval a whole new spatial order stands revealed. To a fly, banking and zooming through the dewy maze, it must seem as if the whole sky is suddenly strung with silver rigging and crystal spheres, like the aerial defences on Andromeda.

Down at the lake there's gossamer. Perhaps it's everywhere, it must be, but at the lake it hangs vertically in shining threads against the black shadow of the cliff; if I could walk on water, among the flotillas of whooper swans, I would be seen zigzagging, sidestepping, holding up my hands against nothing.

'Gossamer' is a word you'd fold between the pages of the book for the desert island, a poet's word now banned, like sunsets, from poetry. The *Shorter Oxford* tracks it back, tentatively, to 'goose summer', or Martinmas, when geese were supposedly in season and goosedown drifted through the air. At the lake, as if in authentication, little commas of light are launched into the air by preening swans. But I almost prefer, for once, a piece of piety: *gaze à Marie*, the gauze that fell from Mary's shroud at the Assumption (or, as some UFO-watchers were unwittingly inspired to echo it, 'angel hair').

It was gossamer that famously ensnared Gilbert White's dogs on a walk at Selborne in the autumn of 1741: 'Their eyes were so blinded and hoodwinked that they could not proceed, but were obliged to lie down and scrape the encumbrances from their faces with their forefeet.' But White had no doubt what gossamer was: 'Strange and superstitious as the notions about them were formerly,' he wrote, 'nobody in these days doubts but that [the threads] are the real production of small spiders, which swarm in the fields in fine weather in autumn, and have a power of shooting out webs from their tails so as to render themselves buoyant and lighter than air.' Darwin, ashore from the *Beagle* in South America and 'red-hot with spiders', watched one preparing to take flight from a fence-post. He noted the separate strands – four or five of them – extruded from the spinnerets and kept apart, he conjectured, by their carriage of mutually repellent electric charges. Today it has still to be decided how far these tiny aeronauts can actually control their journeys by winding in their threads or paying them out, riding the wind like yachtsmen trimming their sails.

Most of the spiders that go ballooning – and there are millions every autumn – are the little linyphiids we call money spiders. They weave their webs in sheets, not radial orbs, and it seems a sheer exuberance of chance that a breeze can weave a multitude of their airborne threads together so that they drift down to tent the ground with a silken canopy. Among the thousands of readers' observations that have come to me through the *Irish Times*, I particularly appreciated this one from a Dublin architect, Michael Fewer:

> In the Phoenix Park last week, what I first took to be the low winter sun reflecting off waterlogged ground turned out to be an infinity of strands of silk stretched across the grass as far as the eye could see. Close by, they shimmered in the sunlight like a moonlit sea, and as I watched I saw additional strands drift along over the ground until snagged on a blade of grass.

Here was the scene before Gilbert White's dogs came bounding by.

The Iceland whoopers began arriving late in October, having filtered down the coast from their first stopover on the sea loughs and potato fields of Donegal. For a day or two, working at my desk, my eye was caught by the distant ripple of white wings low against the sea, just above the line of the dunes. The swans came in threes and fours and half-dozens, swerving in across the *duach* and becoming suddenly huge above the little dots of sheep. Their reunions on the lake are noisy, demonstrative affairs, wings thrown wide, necks stretched and pumping, the calls almost wildly loud, like shouts in church.

Now there are close on thirty birds on the lake, upending daintily to grope for eelgrass; when it's gone, by midwinter, they'll move on. I sort out the families as they swim together, this year's cygnets grey and fluffy, a little gaunt, their bills pallidly pink where the parents show a wedge of yellow. Some of the adult birds have rusty-coloured heads, the feathers stained from Iceland's vivid volcanic muds. From my post behind a rock, the swans are rim-lit against the far shadow of the cliff and their beaks come up from the water dripping diamonds. By moonlight they are even more ethereally beautiful, gliding in silver haloes and raising glittering ripples as they feed.

Once I came to visit them in the green dawn, one of the 'secret' times that seem important to me, as if marvels might be going on that I should know about. Without a torch (by design), I let the Plough lead me through the shallows of the channel, and starglow pick out the otter-paths across the *duach*. The mallard were quacking already, and to fool them I took a back way round the lake, picking a grey path up across ribs of rock and squelching through pockets of bog. This brought me, crouching low, to the edge of the cliff, a precipice clad with ferns and ivy. If I slipped I would fall into a dark scrub of spindle and thorn, and end up wedged among mossy boulders; no one would know I was there.

This high rampart above the lake, like an overgrown castle wall, gives the swans' music a magical resonance. As I crept to a flat rock dry enough to lie on, the first, fluting notes drifted up.

Like a flugelhorn, it's said, but that suggests a sound all wind, whereas this has a reed vibrating somewhere in its throat. The windpipe is specially elongated to make the sound carry. There's a sad little descant of three falling notes and a whole suite of individual buglings, right up to the strident and martial. But it's the gentle, echoing, contrapuntal chords that get me: a Bach variation without end.

At first glance, the lake below seemed empty. Then I found a small flotilla, pale ghosts on pewter ripples. The rest were clustered at the marshy end, littered among the rushes like foam or flotsam. Some were sleeping with their necks folded back and beaks thrust deep into their feathers; more were awake and grooming. The flotilla turned to face the wind and their calls picked up in strength and pace. Heads were bobbing and nodding, not quite in unison, but a vigorous consensus. I thought of the geese on the islands and the subtle flick of white cheeks before the whole flock takes wing.

Taking off or landing, swan flight compels you to watch, the mechanics of lift and flex, torque and thrust, all made thrillingly obvious. The six took off in a splashing line, running like sprinters to waken the wind, and lifted away in a slow arc over the fields. When I turned the glasses back to the lake, another six swans were out in the middle, fluting in chorus and nodding to go. The rest slept on, or preened, their feathers more radiant moment by moment in the light beginning to glow around the mountain. So that is what happened on the lake before breakfast: a dozen swans got up and went somewhere.

November lets me choose how to be busy. For a couple of autumns now this has meant making more raised vegetable beds, a gardening strategy which indeed is revelatory, but a lot less arcane in process than some guru-books make it sound. Nonetheless, I will leave to their shaded diagrams the exact sequences by which earth A is shifted over compost B. What one ends up with is another long, raised oblong of soil, neat as a grave and retained by low walls of some improvised material that is not, almost ever, the ideal railway sleepers of the book (I use forest thinnings; they will rot). The virtues of such beds are many, not least that they will never need digging again and that, as one ages, weeding demands a little less stooping.

I have a huge road-mender's shovel that Ethna bought, unwittingly, in town. It suits earth-moving on a sculptural scale, the moist soil sliding and flowing. The robin darts in; a stonechat perches on the wheelbarrow handle; curlews swerve low overhead, bellies flashing, and sink to the next field but one.

In the cobwebby pastures this is the rams' month, some

purpose come at last to the prodigious, curly-coated wineskins swinging beneath their fleece. As I was digging in the quietness, I heard a noise from across the hedge as if someone were driving stakes with a sledgehammer. *Thock!* And again: *thock!* But the interval was wrong: too long between strokes. And the sound was more resonant, more ... concussive. I peered through the thorn. Two rams were fighting (that much you had guessed), but with one involuntary refinement. Ram number one, in charging his opponent, had tangled his curled horns inextricably in the wire of the intervening fence. Ram number two was now taking his time, backing off an extra foot or two before launching himself like a – like a battering ram – to collide with a massive precision, skull against skull. Between impacts, the animals nuzzled each other in what could have passed for affection, and drew dreamy lines on the turf with their delicate hoofs.

This ritualised aggression wells up with the hormones at mating-time, and its dazed and ponderous contests, where allowed, can go on for a couple of hours. They are not intended to kill; merely to assert property rights. The rams' skulls are, of course, specially strengthened for head-butting. I think of the musk oxen we met in Germania Land and the way the bulls' foreheads were pleated so massively with horn. *Ovibos moschatus* shares an evolutionary stem with both mountain sheep and goats, and the bulls become suddenly ram-like in their mating battles. They charge from twenty to thirty feet apart and 'the sound of their meeting,' says the Arctic writer Barry Lopez, 'is like the fracturing of sea ice'. Death may not be the object but, as with rams, is sometimes the result.

Blackface or Suffolk rams both have black faces, the Cheviot a pure white one, but the Blackface, squinting out through his great gnarled spirals of horns, was here first. His coarse fleece bristles with white, wiry kemp and is thrown back over his shoulder in a curve like a chieftain's cape. It is warm and utterly weatherproof, a breathing fabric made for mountains: but is worthless now to anyone but the ram. His horns are similarly marvellous and durable, winding out into space in triangular, corkscrewing circles that would drive you mad to draw. There is something melancholy about a ram kicking his heels alone in a rushy field in autumn, like a Red Indian chief sitting around in his headdress, waiting for the next tourist bus to pull in. But between now and Christmas he will jump fifty or sixty ewes, perhaps a hundred, which is more than any Red Indian chief ever got to do.

A high, closed lorry pulled onto the verge at the top of the boreen and its tailboard was lowered. A red-painted weighing machine was set up on the grass. For the next hour or so, farmers converged by some prior understanding, their trailers stuffed with bulging woolsacks hauled out from the darkest corners of their barns. They were selling this year's wool crop – no, they were handing it over and receiving money in exchange. You cannot talk about selling, when the prices have not changed in twenty years. Thirty-five to forty pence a pound for Blackface, something over fifty for crossbred Blackface–Cheviot. The last boom for wool was forty years ago, in the Korean War, when ten shillings a pound had people 'driving around in cars'. Other people's wars have always been good to farmers.

The kempy hair of mountain fleeces does not take dye and makes a scratchy fabric. Blackface fibres have very little crimp, the natural waviness that gives wool its warmth and resilience, so the yarn spun from it is hard and wiry, fit only for carpets and the pricklier sorts of tweed. The best of it goes to Italy, for the mattress the southern bride brings with her: a long-wearing mattress, quickly pounded to an irreducible thinness. I forget how I know this.

Each farmer marks his flock with dabs of coloured dye, so that shreds of wool on the briars are as likely to be cerulean or crimson as white. When an overnight gale has blown the gate open, I'm still never sure who owns the ewe on the lawn. Only Paddy's colours have impressed themselves, but then they would: the separate dabs of green and orange make a hundred national flags of his flock.

I never notice when someone has changed his car, so that for months we give offence by not waving and smiling soon enough when neighbours meet us on the road. Or a cavalcade of cars comes over the hill flashing lights and blowing horns, which means that the Louisburgh team have done something marvellous at football again. It circles the boreen where the Heneghan lads, Eric and Brendan, live, but even when the cup appears in their window, I daren't ask what it was for. There is such a big difference between the things in my mind and those known generally in the parish. I am, I suppose, 'a harmless poor creature'; at least, I hope so.

Joe O'Toole knew about nature; was attentive to it, anyway. He lived as a bachelor farmer over at Corragaun, above the lake, and herons roosted in the conifers of his shelter belt to keep him company at night. When the *Máire fhada* flew out to fish the channel (he thought of birds in Irish), he would predict settled weather. The wail of the *pilibín* from the *duach*, or the flutter of moths in his headlights on his way to the pub, meant something else again; it scarcely matters what – he was still connected, still wired to nature.

The metaphor would have amused him: he did, indeed, know about wires, or anything else under the bonnet of a car. When Michael Longley, on holiday, drove too enthusiastically through the ford a few times, Joe would go down to the *duach* and get the car started again. Once, on an autumn visit, the three of us went for a pint in Louisburgh. Coming home, the road was silver in the moonlight. A badger rippled over the ditch and made a dash for it; the cries for its misjudgement were our own. The incident was to heighten a Longley poem in Joe's memory:

> And not even when we ran over the badger
> Did he tell me he had cancer, Joe O'Toole
> Who was psychic about carburettor and clutch

And knew a folk-cure for the starter-engine.
Backing into the dark he floodlit each hair
Like a filament of light our lights had put out
Somewhere between Kinnadoohy and Tullabaun . . .

There were badgers in a briar patch where Joe's land bordered the mountain river, and a badger and he would stand aside for each other if they met at a gap in the wall. He liked to feel that he was sharing the land with nature. When the river, in a great flood, spewed tons of rocks and gravel across his one sheltered pasture, he shrugged and let them lie there. He was proud of the scrawny belt of oak scrub that gave his few cattle shelter, and liked to stand with me, looking out through the scalloped foliage, to imagine the landscape as it was in that long, empty interval after the Famine. The hazels that grew up then were still surviving in his own childhood, a wood a child could get lost in as his father cut wands for *cliabh*s and *pardóg*s. Today the trees' remnants are gaunt as gallows, mangled by cattle crashing in from the windy common. On Joe's land the oaks struggle on: a crooked gleam of grey bark in the hollow below the creggans, a sniper's tuft of browny leaves on every rocky knoll.

There is also a boggy, hummocky patch with a stream running through it, a place to find marsh cinquefoil, the lovely bronzy-flowered potentilla, blooming in July. More to the point in November, which was when a smoky kitchen prompted the knowledge, the stream ran through a pocket of fine blue clay, perfect for sealing the joints of a range or a chimney. Our first Stanley, an old one, was made whole with it. I was in love, at that time, with the use of so many 'found' earth-materials in the make-and-build culture of Thallabawn.

The rough-hewn flair for carpentry I had absorbed from my father did not extend to any confidence that I could build – a big wall, that is, or a house, or something that would hurt if it fell on you. I could only guess what, besides spiders, might be found behind skirting boards or under the floor. A drip from the ceiling would invoke a passive dread, since to do something about it could mean exploring unknown spaces and 'interfering with the structure'. As I worked with our neighbours to rebuild the tumble-down shed at the gate, and then to gut the old house to its very stones and make its rooms again, these middle-class anxieties receded. The muscular mysteries of block-laying, cement-mixing, bashing holes in walls, slowly lost their power to intimidate. Buildings need no longer be taken as given. I had graduated to the Stone Age.

Simple increments of strength had much to do with it. I had reached forty-five without ever lifting a bag of cement or more than one concrete block. In our first winter, a lorry tipped a pyramid of hollow blocks in our gateway and it took the two of us a couple of days to stack them. Only a year later, when more were dumped for the porch, Ethna worked her way steadily through two hundred of them.

The rest of the challenge was the nature of the 'stuff' itself: that is, of mortar or concrete. The men I was apprenticed to had grown up with 'stuff' since infancy, no doubt rounding up the scrapings for their first mud pie. The proper ratios of sand to cement and of both to stones would vary, of course, not only in accordance with the job in hand and its necessary strength and durability, but also with the quality of the sand and the nature of the gravel. For a small job around the house, any of the streams would give you a bucket or two of fine aggregate, ready-washed. Golden shell-sand from the shore had a great 'tooth' but was, of course, salt-laden and would draw in water unless you left it to weather in the rain (but then the dogs came and shat in it). For a really big mix of concrete – a floor, say, or a piece of a yard – the gravel came by tractor and trailer from the beaches to the north. It was worth waiting for the tide to be right at the *srutha* at Cross, when you might get a whole load of tiny pebbles, shiny-wet and sea-smelling, and not one piece of weed to pick from them.

All these products of the planet were a pleasure to shovel around, but mixing concrete, even on the big slab of plywood kept for the job, is simply the hardest work I know. It can't be skimped. Over and over it has to go, and round and round, without letting the puddle in the middle burst out and run the cement away. Now that I can judge a mix to the nearest dribble of water, I have nothing left to build. And not very much concrete is mixed the hard way any more: you hitch a mixer to a tractor-drive, or get Roadstone to arrive and pour it where you want it. Once again, I seem to have come in on the end of things.

October's round of storms began sweeping the ocean of its floating debris; November finds it bobbing ashore, wearing all the signs of a long journey. The plastic has been colonised by goose-necked barnacles or whiskery growths of hydroids. In with the seaweed at the tide's furthest fling is a loose confetti of raw plastic. This is how it is shipped around the world in bulk: tiny pellets like lentils, in assorted colours. It is virtually indestructible: who knows where it got spilled, or when? But other plastic novelties are part of the story of transatlantic drift. These are light-sticks – slim cylinders with a hole at one end, for tying at intervals to a very long line of baited hooks. When new, you just twist them and two chemicals flood together, producing a lasting, firefly luminescence bright enough to read by. Deep in the water off Florida or Puerto Rico, they attract tuna, squid and swordfish.

I prefer the witness of tropical seeds and turtles. 'What's this?' people ask about a large grey-brown object gathering dust in a corner of our living room. It's almost the size of a rugby ball, but three-lobed. Here and there, the smooth skin has split, giving glimpses of ginger fibre. At this point of scrutiny the penny sometimes drops: a coconut, just as it fell off the tree. But a coconut is a coconut and tells little of its origin – it could have been tossed overboard (but undoubtedly wasn't). Sea beans from the West Indies and the Central American coasts are, however, more distinctively exotic, and by now we have a whole wooden dish of them, their tough skins growing steadily more glossy and rich, like Morocco leather, as they are polished from hand to hand.

Most are of the sort called 'seahearts'. These have been known for centuries along the stormier western coasts of these islands and often treasured for the luck of finding something rare. They were mounted on chains and worn as pendants, or scooped out to hold vestas, pins or snuff (Charles Nelson, the botanist, who has made a special study of tropical drift-seeds and their folklore, has a seaheart snuffbox with a hinged silver lid). Seahearts have fallen from the huge pods – more than a yard long – of a tropical liana, *Entada gigas*. The other handful of seeds in our dish are exactly described as 'horse-eye' beans: round, with a rich brown case and black rim. They are *Mucuna sloanei*, from another tropical vine, this one with stinging hairs.

Were I to sift the debris that piles up gently in the innermost, sandy scallopings of the channel, there could be other sorts of peregrine disseminules (such noble words for drifters): dove-grey 'acorns' of nickar nuts, from thorny thickets along tropical tidelines; seeds of star-nut palms, like tulip bulbs; tiny morning-glories scarcely bigger than plastic pellets. But we bring home what catches the eye. Once, on Inishkea, I picked up a four-sided 'boxnut', still, like the coconut, in its fibrous husk – *Barringtonia asiatica*, no less, and the first one recorded in Europe. It arrived on Charles Nelson's desk at the National Botanic Gardens just an hour before BBC television rang to ask him to do a spot about drift-seeds in a children's wildlife show: so there was instant glory for my find.

I never got it back, but that's all right; I enjoyed the brief connection to its story. *Barringtonia* is a tree like the Brazil nut and cannonball trees and was spread across the tropics from its south-east Asian home 'by man's activities'. On the other hand it's a great voyager in tropical ocean currents and is often among the first 'arboreal disseminules' to reach a newly formed, volcanic tropical island. It can float for at least two years, but rarely arrives anywhere in a viable condition. It certainly wasn't going to do much good on Inishkea.

All the West Indian seeds have had to float for at least fifteen months to reach Ireland, but they are often still alive and viable; they have simply drifted towards the wrong climate. It is perfectly possible to rear an indoor vine from nickar nut or horse-eye bean and sometimes (not often) from a seaheart, but they need chipping with a hacksaw and some nursing with fungicides at the point of germination, and so far we have not persevered.

The wood-stove in my study gives off a steady warmth, and in the process sucks away insidiously at my oxygen; a pleasant torpor has me meditating on the distant humps and hollows of a greyish Inishturk for minutes on end ... where was I?

Yes. On the rough white wall above the wood-stove hangs a tear-shaped object like a primitive warshield of wickerwork and leather, two feet from top to bottom. It is the carapace of an adult loggerhead turtle, and would look, perhaps, less primitive if Meg, when a puppy, had not chewed the rim off it. At that point it was buried in the garden, but obviously not deeply enough.

The loggerhead was by far the biggest of my turtles, lolling in the wheelbarrow like a sinister Mafia capo, very dead and grossly smelly. As with many stranded turtle corpses, it lacked one of its front flippers, suggesting a skirmish with a shark, but the idea that this could doom it to swimming in circles is apparently erroneous. They die, a long way from home, succumbing to cold, gently, as I might succumb to the carbon monoxide of the wood-stove.

The loggerhead, *Caretta caretta*, is born on nesting beaches both along the Atlantic coast of America and around the Mediterranean. In both places it is threatened by the disturbance and glaring lights of expanding human playgrounds – this after one hundred million years. But because it can wander from either coast, and from Africa, its occasional stranding on European shores could not be taken as proving anything about trans-atlantic traffic.

This had to wait on the arrival of a little turtle known as Kemp's ridley (*Lepidochelys kempii*), a species known to nest only

on beaches around the Gulf of Mexico. In some winters, both
very young ridleys and loggerheads have been washed up in
Europe together, so now it is accepted that both of them cross
the Atlantic in the North Atlantic Drift. A ridley I sent to the
Natural History Museum in Dublin (where it swims for ever
in a column of pickling spirit) was, I am glad to say, so fresh
and wholesomely sea-scented that I could bring it home to
draw. Its carapace was black, with the little vertebral ridge of
the young turtle, and its shape was more or less round: a
twelve-inch dinner plate. This is also the size of most of the loggerheads that get to Ireland – some even, as in the stormy spring
of 1992, alive and fit for an aquarium, which was where they
went. I found one of the dead ones on a strand in Connemara,
packed it in sand in a box with a tight lid, and left this to forget
about on a shelf at the back of the shed. Opening it the other
day, I found that almost nothing had survived of carapace, body
or flippers; only the skull remained, perfect but with jaws un-
hinged. I have this skull on a windowsill, and tediously insist
that people tell me what they think it is. The parrot-like 'beak',
designed for biting pieces out of jellyfish, has sometimes suggested a bird (but *what* bird?) or even a snake. Children do
better, thanks to Ninja turtles.

There is a third kind of turtle that reaches our western coast in
summer, drawn on through the Gulf Stream's shimmering procession of jellyfish. Compared with loggerhead or ridley, the
leathery turtle is an awesome giant, often six feet long, with a
flipper span of half as much again and enormous swimming
muscles: a Johnny Weissmuller among turtles. It has no horny
carapace, but is covered instead with what looks and feels like
black vulcanised rubber, or wellington boot, and the flattened
barrel of its body has ridges running along the back, like seams
or struts, to hold it rigid; only the skull seems properly roofed
over. Add oblique, reptilian eyes and a primeval presence suggesting great antiquity, and one can understand why generations of fishermen, finding the animal trapped in a net or the
ropes of lobster pots, have winched it ashore to be stood on

bravely and photographed for the paper. And there, of course, gasping on the slipway and weeping slow, viscous tears of jelly-fish-juice, *Dermochelys coriacea* has died of respiratory collapse. One I visited at Purteen, a little fishing harbour on Achill Island, was already moribund and beginning to reek of the oil that suffuses the whole of this creature, part of the design for its thermo-regulation and survival in deep, cold water.

The ocean-wide travels of the leathery turtle make its birth-place almost incidental: those arriving off Ireland were probably hatched on the remoter beaches of French Guiana, north of the Amazon estuary. Unlike the windblown loggerheads or ridleys, they are well-equipped to turn south again when the jellyfish are finished and the water begins to chill. This regular migration had to be documented and then impressed upon the fishermen, a task that became a personal crusade for a dedicated zoologist called Gabriel King. I name him to put his efforts on the record, and also to acknowledge the otherness of the sadhu, or travelling holy man, which for a while he needed to be. Gently spoken, radiant with purpose – archangelic, indeed – he toured the fish-ing ports of Ireland to lobby the scale-spattered, stubbly men fresh off coastal trawlers in the hope of engaging their sym-pathies on behalf of *Dermochelys*. That he made some impression is suggested by a simple silence about any subsequent 'capture' of live leatheries. He went on to campaign about the perils of ocean plastic: in particular the supermarket bags which, drifting and billowing just under the surface, are gobbled by turtles in mistake for jellyfish and bunch up in the gut. Or balloons, which have to end up somewhere; why not the sea? Thanks to Gabriel, any charitable flight of a thousand gas-filled balloons, glimpsed on television, compels our private apology to the leatheries, the loggerheads and the little Kemp's ridleys.

My mental pictures of wild Connacht weather would furnish a municipal gallery, each of them hugely framed in gilt and called something like 'Tempest in Mayo'. The storm the other night would have suited Turner to a T: in the fierce headlights of a friend's minibus, it swarmed about us in flourishes of silver, in washes of ochre and umber. Only a minibus, driven with knowledge of every twist and turn of the road in all conceivable conditions (in other words, the school bus) could have brought us home at all. The road seethed with water. It poured from every gap in the ditch, spilled from every hill stream, hummocked out of boreens. Below our own gable, The Hollow echoed to the crash and grind of boulders, the hollow *thock!* so like the collisions of rams. A quick swing of the flashlamp in the run from the gate to the front door lit a dizzying rush of water just inches below the new footbridge.

I was kept awake for a long while, listening to the stream and rehearsing what I might have done with ropes and stakes to stop the bridge being swept away (it wasn't). Then, ritually for a really black and stormy night in November, I found myself thinking of the eels that, even now, must be rushing out into the ocean.

They wait for earth vibrations – microseisms – that run ahead of depressions and set the rivers tingling in the last quarter of the moon. Shortly after sunset, when these tremors are pulsing at one every three seconds, they begin to move, thronging the deepest and fastest part of the flow. They are much older than people suppose – ten at least; could be forty, growing slowly in a lean lake, an acid river. This is how life should be handed on, from a long, impossible swim at the end of our days.

Their eyes have grown huge in the change. Their chests have sprouted long, pointed fins. Their bellies flash silver, like the rain in the headlights. This is how dark it will be, one thousand feet down in the Sargasso Sea, six hundred miles south-east of Bermuda, more or less. Millions of eels in the soundless dark below the seaweed. Millions from all over Europe, and never one found there – just the larvae, *Leptocephalus*, crystal willow-leaves glinting in the plankton. Sir Alister Hardy wrote in *The Open Sea*:

It seems too much to suppose that the larvae from the eggs of (say) Scottish eels – even supposing that Scottish females are fertilized by Scottish males (and this we do not know) – should by the chance of ocean drift find their way back to Scotland; similarly it seems equally impossible that larvae from the eggs of Spanish eels should find their way back to Spain. Yet if they do not do this, how can Scottish adult eels have the instinct to navigate to a point lying some 2,000 miles due *south-west*, whereas Spanish and Mediterranean eels must navigate towards the same distant point but on a course *west-by-south?*

Discuss, or sleep. In the morning, a great arc of peaty water reaches out from the channel, its colour and scent reaching out on the trail of the eels.

DECEMBER

Half the silence of the Arctic or of deserts is in the vast amount of it you can see at a glance, headland beyond headland, dune after dune. On this side of the hill, December's silence overarches us all the way from the Maumturk Mountains at the top of the fiord to the furthest smudge of islands. The quiet subdues even the children, gathered at nine at the top of the boreen. When they break up for Christmas and the early plumes of turf-smoke disappear, cats and hens wait even longer to be fed. Porch-lights, naked in the daylight, advertise the sleeping houses and all the people not making any noise.

This is the month when our own diurnal rhythms seem so blatantly out of step with those of our neighbours. Cars coming home round the hill, from games of twenty-five or whatever it is keeps people up all night, can find us settling to a first cup of coffee and the separate chimes of our AppleMacs.

But then, the lives of so many people in the countryside are totally enigmatic to me. I wonder what joy they are getting out of living where they do. Sometimes in winter we go mooching in the car to lost-looking places on the map – a coastal headland, a wooded bit beside a lake – in the hope of discovering something that Ireland might have been concealing from us or not bothering to mention. And everywhere we find these inexplicable lives set down at the wayside, all these brand-new bungalows aligned four-square to the road. Not so much as a strand of ivy seems to tie them to where they are. You'd have to know who they were married to, I suppose, and who their mothers were – what makes them feel that they and this particular, often monotonous, prospect of Ireland have any special understanding.

Growing up in Sussex, I took for granted a countryside physically rich in the layering of the past: real Tudor beams, clay tiles, flint walls, dew ponds, field paths and stiles. In Ireland so much of what ought to have been history has been disowned; in long stretches of landscape the centuries have passed without leaving any vernacular mark. Say what you like about the fairies, wise women and the rest, they did give meaning to the countryside: particular trees, hill forts, old bridges, gables, bends in the road. Some of this lives on with the shreds of the language, but most of Ireland has broken with folklore, or was uprooted from it in the sharing out of land. So little yet exists to connect people with their landscape, to make it 'part of what they are'.

The big new roads do not help. They whisk us along at a remove from local lives, front gates and gardens, and the intimate business of the land. They overlay the countryside with a quite new matrix of time and space, a different sense of what matters. The lives they pass by seem pensioned off to insignificance in quadrants of anonymous fields, redundant webs of lanes. There was meaning in the old, narrow roads, a sense of being part of humanity's spread across the landscape, of being on the way from here to there. The world's new ambition is to be everywhere at once.

We wander inland also to be among trees for a while. They are all the more huggable in December for being bare, and honest about their age. On the limestone land around Mask and Carra there are enormous old trees that amaze me: great black candelabra looming above the white-lichened walls. Their fantastical shapes result from pollarding and storm damage, but a fine veil of crimson twigs marks them out as common lime. They were Big House trees, like the beeches we find standing guard around old ruins on winter afternoons, grey trunks moulded in the ochre glow from the west.

Once, a friend who lives among such trees, and who wanted to be kind, arrived with a vanload of glamorous firewood for Christmas: great slices of beech tree, two or three feet across and almost too heavy to lift. An ordinary axe made no impression on them but simply stuck fast until knocked free with a lump-hammer. Eventually I was introduced to something called a 'wood grenade', an object of fluted metal like the head of some ferocious Trojan spear. It is tapped into any slight crack in the timber and then bashed at full swing with a sledge-hammer. A few blows are quite enough to shiver the whole round of beech into many stove-sized chunks. The 'grenade' was forged in China, where gunpowder came from.

But my favourite tree in these winter excursions is nothing so grand as lime or beech. It is a 'white' willow, *Salix alba*, growing in a drain in a field somewhere west of Headford. In summer, its rounded form is graceful enough, and prettily silver in a breeze, but in winter its bare twigs blaze in an incandescent reddish-orange: a flame-tree. If only one willow in fifty were of this strain of *S. alba*, how winter afternoons would be transformed.

Two saplings of this magical willow light up the hen run, part of the spinney now growing close around us as we enter old age. We have reproached ourselves quite harshly for the years that were lost in taking this bare hillside at face value. Perhaps we did have to wait for a critical biomass of fuchsia to create some kindly spaces, but what was, for the most part, a desultory sticking-in of trees has suddenly thickened and flourished. A fistful of sprouting acorns, sent by a friend as a mossy parcel a dozen Decembers ago, are now a grove of sessile oaks waving above the woodshed. Alders, birches and sycamores, trees taken for granted anywhere else, are scrutinised and adored in every vigorous detail – as if, each day, we were painting a picture of them. And in odd, sheltered niches are the nonsense trees – lime, beech, sweet chestnut – none of which seems to have discovered it is living on borrowed time.

Where the last mile of road curls down between Mweelrea and the sea, the holly trees are a vestige of woods that once clothed the foot of the mountain. Further on, more hollies grow in rocky alcoves behind the shore. They are gnarled and knobbly, with few leaves, and their bark has been burnished to silver, which shows off the berries most handsomely, like an *objet* in a jeweller's window. In the early Christmases I went there armed with secateurs and amputated the best bits I could reach. There is something unreal and desert-island about coming in off white sand to dark ravines with waterfalls and fern gardens and twisted trunks of holly. Even the ivy acknowledges this special station at the ocean's edge, inscribing the sides of boulders with a slow and crusted calligraphy, its leaves like tiny arrowheads. There are prostrate junipers, and little hawthorns no more than two feet high, crouching to rocks and dwarfed and shaped by the wind. They have taken so long to grow and have made so many fresh starts that twigs and spines are woven to an intricate filigree, like the nest of a bowerbird.

I wanted one of these beautiful bonsai. I felt beneath its thorns and found the stem, no thicker than the base of my thumb. Long wrestling with the secateurs left my wrists bleeding and the shears askew. The stem would not be cut: God knows how many years were wrapped like steel within it. I left it to grow on, unfolding leaf by leaf against the press of the wind.

The mountain in summer, though it fills the same space in the window, is oddly diminished by haze and light: Cézanne, who painted his Mont-Saint-Victoire sixty-five times, knew all about the retreat and advance of colour. Of Mweelrea's summer presences, he might have coveted one: the half-hour of a late June sunset in which the whole mountain is bathed in rose and violet and the northern buttresses jut out in crimson, like the desert cliffs of Petra.

In winter the mountain spends more of the day looming at centre stage, thrust forward by the surrounding furnace-aura of the sun. I am dazzled but also tempted, convinced as usual of some secret waiting to be caught off guard. Perhaps right now, on a frosty Tuesday morning, with the *punt* standing at 1.03 sterling and the traffic heavy in D'Olier Street, Dublin, would be a good time.

I push my mountain bike to the top of the bog road (for the eventual and dubious pleasure of freewheeling the whole stony way down again) and strike out for Lough Cunnel, where something might be happening. The lake is tucked into a fold of bog, invisible until the final, grudging revelation of water. Also, in December, the mountain keeps a dark finger on Cunnel until noon. From one step to the next, the tawny glow of moor-grass is extinguished, and the regular squelch of my boots becomes a crunching over white-frosted hummocks of sphagnum, a crackling through puddles cellophaned with ice. These noises are suddenly shocking, as if the shadow has added an echo to them. Pausing, I intercept other echoes which seem, however, impeccably in context: the shouts of a farmer to his dog. He is climbing up from the far valley, from Doolough Pass, and eventually appears at the rim, an angular figure with a dark thread of a stick, perfectly drawn in Indian ink against the far, sunlit scarp of the Sheeffrys. The dog ripples up the side of Mweelrea to reclaim a pair of ewes. His master and I lift an arm to each other, across half a mile of mountain.

Nothing is happening at the lake, a long, sunken mirror curved like a scimitar (or a banana). You would love to skate on it, up and down all alone, if it were frozen and if you could skate. I have seen it with a heron and a cormorant and, memorably, with an otter tearing into a trout on a flat rock (the sight is oddly sympathetic: one's teeth pick up the vibrations of the quivering fish, the bones singing like wires).

Not far from the rock is a mossy flush, bright green, where I have found the droppings – more cheroots – of Greenland white-fronted geese. The lake was always a safe roost, except when hunters like Ethna's father climbed up beside the water-falls of the Glencullin river and waited with their heads down in the dusk. Séamus has gone, and so have most of the geese whose high, quick gabble used to be a night-sound for the Gavins at their thatched farm under the mountain (that was a Gavin, with the stick).

Séamus McManus, originally of Cavan, later of Westport (he was manager of the dole office), was once a great walker of mountains. The heathery hulk of Cuilcagh presided over Ethna's childhood in the 1940s as Mweelrea stands over us now. Its presence was part of the very food on her plate. 'Grouse again!' she protested (or so she insists) as Séamus came down from the mountain with sooty shotgun and bulging game-bag. She remembers gate pillars draped with feathery corpses and birds being parcelled up for relatives in towns.

If not grouse, then trout, for he was also a formidable angler: literally one of the best. Over the wood-stove in our living room hangs a heavy bronze shield, his trophy from the Tostal world trout competition. Séamus lived for the first rise on Lough Mask; indeed, it cost him his wife and family. The department offered him promotion to a desk job in Dublin, but he knew where he was happy: in a punt on the lake, drifting among islands, and afterwards in the pub, smoking his pipe with the same few friends; a large, hospitable man. His wife Mai, shut out from all such rituals and driven by ambitions of her own, departed for New York with the three youngest. She ended up working in the First National Bank, near the ferry for Staten Island. Ethna remained in Westport, to be there when her father came home, lilting an unvarying refrain that rose and fell gently, like waves in reeds.

The mountain is stacked above me, light trickling down its dark ledges. I choose, for the novelty of it, an ascent by a long gully running up the left-hand profile (at sunset I often sit by the stove with binoculars, browsing on the detail of buttress and scree). 'Ascent' is too grand a word. Mweelrea can be climbed straightforwardly by trudging up it in zigzags from the seaward side: a friend in her seventies, taking her time, managed it comfortably in the dry summer of '95. This northern gully is steeper and more energetic, a staircase of old boulders, some of them sporting in their cracks the neat, pastry-cutter's rosettes of St Patrick's cabbage. This is one wild parent of London pride (the other a saxifrage from the Pyrenees), and thus conjures for me, Proust-wise, the glazed brown rope-moulding that edged the brief front garden path of 29 Arundel Street, Kemp Town, Brighton 7, the diamond pattern of its tiles, the short wall where I leaned my bike, the clotted silver paint of its mudguards. London pride, with its obliging pink panicles, seems to dog the footsteps of minor urban lives. On Inishturk, it is recorded, St Patrick's cabbage has joined English stonecrop as the first plants to colonise the walls of ruined cottages, while lady fern creeps in to claim the floors.

Above the boulders and steep grassy ledges comes a long slope of scree to the ridge. I hated the scree in Germania Land: it was raw, sharp-edged and hadn't finished sliding, was waiting for the next cliff-fall to push it on down. Mweelrea's sandstone scree has long reached accommodation, one stone's edge with another; a mosaic of lichens creeps across the violet rock as if to weld it all together. Still, it gives beneath my boots and kicks loose. I scurry, slowly, upwards.

Mweelrea was a nunatak (an Inuit word): that is, when glaciers covered Ireland, its peak was one of many in the West left sticking up as islands in the ice. This is where the high scree comes from, and the layer of frost-shattered rock that carpets the broad ridges and summits. Deer sedge and woolly hair-moss soften one's footfalls across these great deserted stages in the sky.

The way to the summit follows, at a respectful distance, the edge of the eastern corrie: a cliff falling two thousand feet, almost vertically, to two little lakes below. The lip of the cliff is worn with fluted shapes where wind, trapped and focused by the horseshoe of rock, has scooped out the gravel. On the summit itself, even on a calm day, there can come a sudden sound such as a very big dragonfly ought to make, a scaly, shimmering sound. It is a whirlwind that touches nothing, then dies away.

Once, climbing to the cairn through racing veils of cloud, I saw a figure already in possession, a silhouette fading and darkening in the silvery shifts of light. It was a young woman, with a stick and a rolled-up blanket under her arm. She was German and a Green, neither of which surprised me, and a craft-guild cabinet-maker, which did. She preferred to work slowly, she said, without power tools or adhesives, taking time to make furniture perfectly. She had just spent two months on the opposite side of the Killary, watching a Connemara man build a currach. He had rowed her across to climb the mountain, 2,688 feet straight up from the shore. She was not even mildly out of breath. We talked for a while, and forgave each other for being there, and took our separate ways down.

I was thinking about the act of choice in how to live. How the great mass of people are denied it, or scarcely discern what it is. How so many drift on, not knowing what they want, or wanting everything.

Our young goat-herding friend beyond the Sheeffrys has sold his flock and gone to be a company lawyer: one of the few, perhaps, to take to it as another life, a real desire. Once, bringing us a piece of his new blue cheese to taste, he confided his next winter's project: weaving on a twenty-four-inch loom beside the fire. His enthusiasm filled me with self-reproach: that was the sort of thing I should be at. I could hear the patient clack of the loom and the swell of the symphony on radio; see the glow of the window across the bog.

I sit at my word processor now, feet resting on a small rag rug, thick and warm in stripes of red and purple. I wove it in our first December here, from strips of cloth cut from old clothes. Each strip was looped with a crochet hook through the weave of a hessian sack, a slow craft. A close look will show where I stopped, in mid-row, deciding that half a rug would have to be better than none.

We have other friends, quite elderly, who live up a stony track at the edge of the Blue Stack Mountains, in Donegal. Their old cottage was thatched until recently, and I still have to duck my head at the door. A little windmill powers a battery for a radio-telephone, but otherwise Judith and Jerry have managed without electricity for many years. They are cultivated, professional people, and I suppose you would call them New Age, into positive energy-lines and shiatsu. Judith is a healer, with a busy practice in herbal medicine; Jerry paints very good landscapes. They exude serenity in a business-like sort of way; beside them we seem very restless.

'Simplicity, simplicity, simplicity!' enjoined Henry Thoreau, from his cabin in the woods. At twenty-eight, he was trying to rid himself of 'all that was not life'. And then, after two years, he left the woods 'for as good a reason as I went there. Perhaps it seemed to me that I had several more lives to live, and could not spare any more time for that one.' He had learned what he felt was his greatest skill – 'to want but little'.

What we have had was never a Walden-style simplicity. Goats, ducks, hens, beehives, a pony, fishing the spillet and sowing twenty sorts of vegetable to stock two freezers became really quite complicated. After the car rusted apart and we learned to manage most things with a bicycle and trailer, there was, if you like, a certain austere equilibrium for a few years, our lives quite contained between the acre and the shore. Then, as old abilities drew us back into film-making, a car reappeared and other comforts followed: a warm house chief among them. Driving off through the mountains to edit video on a digital computer in Connemara is probably near the best of both worlds. But I wish I did not *want* both worlds. I wish I had finished my rug.

The road to Connemara loops around the mountain, then around the head of Killary harbour. On a winter morning the sheep are slow to rise from the tarmacadam and have to be hooted to their feet. In the fiord's inner reaches, where winter calms weave the mountain's reflections together, the sheep graze the bladderwrack at low tide, white dots on the wide black selvedge of weed.

The road joins the fiord at Bundorragha, where the salmon start climbing their pools to Delphi. This is also the start of the 'wild' shore, running back to the sea below Mweelrea. Here, in December, the mussels under the bladderwrack are plumply full of meat. An hour or two in the right place, at the bottom of the tide, provides as heavy a bag of them as I want to carry on my shoulder, teetering and sliding over the rocks.

My fingers get sore from twisting the mussels from their moorings and from the sharp-edged barnacles that stud the biggest of them. Out in deep water, farmed mussels grow smooth and clean as grapes, bunched on the ropes beneath rafts and barrel-lines. They are too young to have barnacles and too high in the water for starfish to reach and pull open. I like the simplicity of farming mussels here. In early summer the water of the inner fiord, much freshened from the rivers, is positively gauzy with natural mussel-spat the size of a mouse's fingernails. It drifts in underwater showers and settles on any convenient surface: notably the dangling ropes moored there for the purpose. Then the farmer cleans his ropes of spat by pulling them through his hands: the spat left in the ropes' crevices are quite enough to rear. The barrel-line is towed nearer the sea and left in fathoms rich in plankton. In the January of the second winter, if no storm has wrecked the gear and if the market is holding up, the *moules* are ready for Paris.

My own harvesting is taken note of by the heron, who knows what it is to stoop over glittering, seaweedy shallows for rather longer than one wants to. In Africa there is a black heron that lifts and curves its wings to make a canopy over its head, thus cutting out all the glare from the water. The grey heron of Ireland just stands there, peering over at an angle that cuts out reflections, the ripples glinting in its golden eyes and lighting up its undersides.

The heron is December's bird, if only for these companionable stances at the fiord. But the month is not all ripples and mirrors. There are days when, battling down to the strand with head bowed against the wind, I surprise a heron hunched in the waves of the estuary. It lifts its wings like Otto Klemperer at the rostrum and lets itself be snatched aloft. A heron in a high wind ought to be an aerodynamic disaster: five feet of wings and only four pounds of body: how can it possibly mould those turbulent armfuls of air? But then, just as it seems likely to be blown inside out, like an umbrella, its wings find their arc, the neck is tucked in, and the legs trail out as a rudder. Away it goes, out above the bay to Connemara, a flying weather vane with its own, elected south.

A blurred anvil of cloud comes trailing hail across the islands, then draws aside from a window in the northern sky, an aperture of polar greeny blue. A different green in the waves, cold and glassy; their splashes would cut you. Long, scuffed trails of hoof-prints reach out from the dunes to the litter of sea rods at the tideline – banners thrown down by a retreating army. Can a heifer, dangling a rod from the corner of its mouth, tell the sweeter stems of *Laminaria saccharina* from the tougher shanks of *Laminaria digitata*?

As punctual as any leaf-fall on land, the casting up of kelp begins in the weeks before Christmas. In the course of a few quiet tides a whole beach may be heaped waist-deep with a slithery mass of toffee-coloured stems and fronds. They are winnowed from a forest that starts below the bladderwracks and stretches out into deeper water until, at around a hundred feet, the light becomes too weak for it to grow. Only when the spring tides retreat to their uttermost is the upper fringe of the forest revealed, its fronds writhing like eels in the surge of slack water. These belong to *L. digitata*, its stems anchored to the rocks with the gnarled fist called the 'holdfast'. Further down the underwater slope grows *L. hyperborea*, so little used to being uncovered that its stems refuse to lie flat. They are furry with accretions of other life – red seaweeds, sponges, sea mats – and grazed by the rasping teeth of sea urchins. Once a year, the kelp casts these passengers adrift and starts anew.

Deepest of all grows *L. saccharina*, its undivided, frilly ribbon floating out in the calmer deeps for as much as twenty feet. Its sweetness is due to a sugar called mannitol and is a secret once

shared between the children of coastal crofters, Scottish and
Irish. In *Morning Tide*, his novel set in Caithness of the 1930s,
Neil Gunn describes 'young Hugh' searching among sea rods
at the tideline and cutting off a slim young stem. Then:

> Scraping the transparent skin off its end with white, even teeth,
> he bit on it exactly as a dog bites on a bone. Saliva flowed into
> his mouth, and with wet, red lips and sharp teeth he sucked and
> gnawed, moving the tangle-end this way and that until his
> stretched mouth ached . . . Once you had started gnawing,
> you could not stop.

There is still a ritual, almost leisurely, collection of rods in
December by a few men and boys living beside the shore, who
dry them for the alginates industry. It is a faint echo of the kelp
harvesting and burning that dominated this coast in winter from
the eighteenth century to the middle of the twentieth, the seaweed's tarry residue a source first of soda, then iodine. Between
the First and Second World Wars, there were kelp kilns all along
the shore from Thallabawn to the corner of Clew Bay and the
dense smoke wafted the smell of iodine far into the hills. A local
friend of my own age, now a successful builder in San Francisco,
was reared near the shore at Emlagh Point, a reef of savage black
rocks jutting out between the strands. He remembers, as a child
of seven or so, being rousted out of bed at 3.00 a.m. on moonlit
nights of spring tides in November and December. As he and his
brothers and sisters pulled on their clothes, the curtains were kept
tight so that no chink of light from the lamp should alert the
neighbours. Ten families competed along the one shore, wading
into bitter waves to lay hands on the stems as they drifted in.
By Christmas, a family might amass forty wet tons, worth one
hundred and sixty pounds, a fortune. That was late in the 1930s,
the final decade of iodine; the wounds of the Second World
War were rinsed with more agreeable and industrially profitable
antiseptics.

Drifts of neglected sea rods send me slithering and stumbling in
my mortuary patrol south from Roonagh, a tape measure in

one pocket and in the other a field-guide to whales and dolphins, now somewhat marked by oily fingers. Whales I am usually told about; dolphins are reported only when fairly fresh, their smiles still in place. But many arrive not looking or smelling their best, colours faded, skin missing. I judge size and build; then, to be sure, pull apart the rubbery jaws, counting little white teeth. Some species have rows like a zip fastener, forty to fifty each side, top and bottom, so that I have to tap with a pencil-point to keep count. It is all data for somebody's computer. If it is worth offering whales and dolphins safe passage in Irish waters, then we should know more about their lives, migrations, mortalities.

Winter also brings a natural toll of sea birds that I would rarely get to meet otherwise, their corpses set ashore with hardly a feather out of place. Puffins, in particular, seem to arrive immaculately dressed for dinner, the brilliant medal-ribbon colours of their bills only a little dulled since summer. I stoop over guillemots, fulmars, kittiwakes, a rare little auk, sometimes a sprawling white goose of a gannet, bill like a dagger, eyes aimed from a mask darkened against sea-dazzle.

Once, in a storm of early winter, I was brought a young gannet which had literally dropped out of the sky at the feet of beachcombing friends. First-year birds, at six or seven months old, can find migration difficult in gales: they are too busy flying to catch enough fish, and exhaustion finally brings them down. At this age, a gannet is black all over – rather, black flecked with white, an elegant, polka-dotted silk. The eyes are a beautiful sapphire-blue, not at all the strange, adult silver that Ronald Lockley likens to the eye of a squid.

My waif weighed so little for her size (the choice of sex occasioned by solicitude); she was clearly starving. I thawed a mackerel from the freezer and donned gauntlets to push big chunks of it down her gullet. Two days and four mackerel later she was bursting out of her box to leave white splashes all over the room. In a lull in the gales I folded her down into the box, tied it on the back of my bicycle and, reaching the strand at first light, waded into the surf to launch her like a big toy yacht.

She ducked her head a few times, shook water over her feathers, and turned to face the breakers. As the foam broke over her, she put down her head, kicked with great webbed paddles and was through. For the next ten minutes she swam steadily out to sea, climbing each wave and plunging through its crest. A flotilla of shags moved aside for her. They could dive from the surface to catch food, but a gannet plunges from the air. I watched her, a dwindling black dot, willing her to try the updraft from a wave, but she was not ready. I turned away at last, wishing her luck towards Capricorn.

The lapwing flocks of winter draw themselves a line on the sky above a lake or a marsh and form up along it, their white bellies flashing in the sun. They float there for a while in a long rippling column and then *whoosh* down to feed again at the edge of the water. The sky parade is beautiful and uplifting and gives me a chance, when in census-taking mode, of counting along the line in tens or twenties or whatever I feel I have time for. Then (this is at Roonagh Lough, north along the shore towards Emlagh), I count the cruising rafts of mallard, wigeon, teal, and discover, on the machair beyond them, a little flock of silvery geese: barnacles, no less – thirty-five of them strung out across the grass.

My inventory is just about complete when a figure creeps into one corner of my binoculars. It wears a soft hat and waders and carries a gun. It advances into a channel of water, finds it too deep in the middle, retreats and crouches on a spit of grass. Then the gun goes up and, disconnected by distance, the shot drifts across to me. He misses, it seems; and again, and a third time. Then his son comes along with a giddy black spaniel and it is his turn to miss a few times. I don't know why I suppose that a man with a gun is always good at using it, especially if he is wearing the right sort of hat. The sky above the lake is now full of duck, whizzing at every angle, out of range, and the geese are heading back to their windy island offshore. There is nothing for the spaniel to swim for.

This is the scene I must now fix in my mind for the days in December when a sound, as of corks popping, floats up from the saltmarsh below us. Too easily I become possessed by a sullen sort of anguish. It is not a few gun club locals after mallard that I see in my mind's eye, but a gang of tweed-jacketed Italians, imported by some unscrupulous hotelier, ringing the little snipe marsh to bang away at every bird to rise. We all have our stereotypes, our paranoias. To many shooters, any talk of 'animal rights' hints at a conspiracy being nurtured among romantic city-dwellers, to end by dispossessing even anglers of their fish and pet-lovers of their dogs.

The passion and politics on either side of the conflict at once stirs and sickens me, so that I swing about, saying, 'Yes, but –' to both. I have lost all wish to shoot anything myself, but can see perfectly well how shooting works to preserve woods and moors and marshes that might otherwise be lost to wildlife. I recoil from the macho male bonding of shooting, but enjoy the company of men who shoot, who often know more about nature than I do, who love, in almost a totemistic way, even the quarry they kill. The culture of field sports, for all its excesses, has been richly integrative of people with the natural world, and with each other. Most of the time, hunters and anglers are merely cadging from the natural surplus of species, and substituting one kind of death for another. As for cruelty, this is a torment we have invented for ourselves, a matter internal to humankind. It is important to ecology only for what it says about attitudes to nature.

Where the divide now lies, in weighing up human responsibility to wild nature, is between keeping man as some sort of wise, superior 'steward' of the planet, conserving its resources primarily for human benefit, and the acknowledgement that other species – animals, plants, fish, even whole landscapes – have an intrinsic value, an independent right to exist. I find myself in harmony with the so-called 'deep ecology' of philosophers like Arne Naess of Norway. This holds that human life is privileged only to the extent of satisfying vital needs, and that the maintenance of richness and diversity of life demands a huge reduction in the numbers of our own species.

To be convinced of all this, it helps to have a personal relationship with nature which is intuitively satisfying, even shamanistic. 'Thinking like a mountain' has been one, not very helpful, metaphor. 'Thinking like a cabbage' may be my version of it, given the rapt reward I feel in conspiring in the mystery of growth. Atheistical, not quite scientific, I seem to be flirting all the time with some spontaneous, irrational insight that could tuck me, too, up a hill-track without electricity. What seems to hold the balance between science and shamanism is keeping myself open to the poetic vision – whatever that might be.

On a fine winter's day, with the sun rolling low along the Connemara hills, I sometimes walk long stretches of the strand with my eyes shut. This is at once more comfortable, replacing the glare and glitter with a warm, vermilion glow, and an interesting psychic experience: to boldly go, as it were, across the Earth's surface in an altered perceptual state. Navigation is by the angle of the sun behind its rosy awning, and by the sound of the breakers tumbling into foam a few yards to my right. The challenge is to walk two or three hundred yards (any more, and I panic and insist on taking fixes) without wandering too much to either side.

It is all very childish, but also a conscious celebration of Lebensraum and solitude. What I hear as I walk (Meg loyally at heel) seems to become more elaborate at every step. First, of course, the waves, dragging on sand, then the far cascades along the curl of the breakers; next, the twitter of sanderling, back and forth at the edge of the foam; oystercatchers shrilling on the rocks; whoopers on the lake; ravens on the mountain. Sometimes, looking back along my splay-footed course, I find it interwoven with a fox-track on the same bearing, or crossing the swift prints of otters on their way up to the dune pools.

Sound carries clearest on hard, frosty days, but these are always infrequent on this coast and likely, it seems, to grow

rarer. I prize the clear dawns that silver every leaf in the shadow
of the mountain, and love those few minutes when the sun
reaches out from Killary to touch the white rim of the dunes.
The strand is frozen and glittering right to the edge of the tide
and my walk becomes a march, as on a road. Once, watching a
flock of oystercatchers, I saw six which seemed to have only one
leg; then the monoplegic birds put down the foot they had been
warming and ran off along the wave-edge with the rest. On that
excursion, too, I found the little lake at Dooaghtry gleaming
like an opal in the reeds. Its resident swans were two mounds of
gilded feathers at the centre, seemingly trapped in the ice. But I
was not to be had a second time, and moved in until they rose
and retreated, carefully, on broad black feet.

   The sun's point of setting has been moving southwards island
by island. In midsummer we looked north-west to Clare Island
for the glow that seemed to last all night. Then it was Inishturk
that cradled it for a week or two, first in this black notch, now
that. September brought the children's storybook sunsets, with
Mister Sun sliding into the bare sea in a perfect scarlet sphere:
three, two, one, gone! Those were nights I hoped for a conse-
quent 'green flash', an optical phenomenon special to the desert
in Egypt and some smokeless oceans; perhaps I blinked and
missed it. By November, the sun is setting behind Gustin and
Clodagh's house on Inishbofin, but almost always into cloud
on the horizon, leaving a skyscape elaborately gilded, a sea
turned to moonstone.

   At the winter solstice, the fire goes out behind Tully Mountain across the bay. Its smouldering afterglow is reflected in the
channel as a strip of crimson neon in the cold black sand, and
even before it has faded the stars are glittering behind me, over
Mweelrea. The silhouette of the mountain cuts off the world to
the east, enhancing the private prospect of infinity. Around me
in the garden, blackbirds are squealing in the shadows, and a
wren, feeling the cold, whirs past in a blur of stubby wings.
Yet what I am thinking about, and making a point of it, is
O'Connell Street in Dublin, where the wagtails are drifting

down to roost above the coloured lights in the plane trees. It is the only time of the year when I feel the least care for the city, such is the potency of Christmas Past.